WORLD TRAVEL

ALSO BY ANTHONY BOURDAIN

Nonfiction

Kitchen Confidential:
Adventures in the Culinary Underbelly

A Cook's Tour: In Search of the Perfect Meal

Typhoid Mary: An Urban Historical

Anthony Bourdain's Les Halles Cookbook:
Strategies, Recipes, and Techniques of
Classic Bistro Cooking

The Nasty Bits: Collected Varietal Cuts,
Usable Trim, Scraps, and Bones

No Reservations: Around the World on
an Empty Stomach

Medium Raw: A Bloody Valentine to the World
of Food and the People Who Cook

Appetites: A Cookbook
(co-authored with Laurie Woolever)

Fiction

Bone in the Throat

Gone Bamboo

The Bobby Gold Stories

Get Jiro! (co-authored with Joel Rose)

Get Jiro: Blood and Sushi
(co-authored with Joel Rose)

Hungry Ghosts
(co-authored with Joel Rose)

WORLD TRAVEL

---

an irreverent guide

ANTHONY BOURDAIN

and Laurie Woolever

ILLUSTRATIONS BY WESLEY ALLSBROOK

ecco

An Imprint of HarperCollinsPublishers

CONTENTS

1 | INTRODUCTION |

7 | ARGENTINA | BUENOS AIRES 7 |

13 | AUSTRALIA | MELBOURNE 13 | SYDNEY 16 |

23 | AUSTRIA | VIENNA 23 |

29 | BHUTAN |

35 | BRAZIL | SALVADOR 35 |

39 | CAMBODIA | ANGKOR WAT 43 | KAMPOT AND KEP 43 |

45 | CANADA | MONTRÉAL & QUÉBEC 45 | TORONTO 50 | VANCOUVER 58 |

63 | CHINA | HONG KONG 63 | SHANGHAI 68 | SICHUAN PROVINCE 73 |

79 | CROATIA |

85 | CUBA |

93 | FINLAND |

97 | FRANCE | CHAMONIX (FRENCH ALPS) 97 | LYON 100 | MARSEILLE 108 | PARIS 110 |

121 | GHANA | ACCRA 121 |

125 | INDIA | MUMBAI: EATING ON THE STREET 125 | PUNJAB 128 | RAJASTHAN 132 |

137 | IRELAND | DUBLIN 137 |

141 | ISRAEL | JERUSALEM 141 |

145 | ITALY | NAPLES 145 | ROME 149 | SARDINIA 157 |

163 | JAPAN | OSAKA: CITY OF EXCESS 163 | TOKYO 167 |

175 | KENYA |

181 | LAOS |

187 | LEBANON |

191 | MACAU |

197 | MALAYSIA | BORNEO ADVENTURE: KUALA LUMPUR, KUCHING, IBAN LONGHOUSE ON THE SKRANG RIVER 197 | PENANG 202 |

205 | MEXICO | MEXICO CITY 206 | OAXACA 211 |

215 │ MOROCCO │ TANGIER 215 │

221 │ MOZAMBIQUE │

227 │ MYANMAR │

233 │ NIGERIA │ LAGOS 233 │

239 │ OMAN │

247 │ PERU │ LIMA 247 │ CUSCO AND MACHU PICCHU 250 │

253 │ PHILIPPINES │ MANILA 253 │

259 │ PORTUGAL │ LISBON 260 │ PORTO 261 │

265 │ SINGAPORE │

275 │ SOUTH KOREA │ SEOUL 275 │

283 │ SPAIN │ BARCELONA 283 │ SAN SEBASTIÁN 286 │

291 │ SRI LANKA │

299 │ TAIWAN │

305 │ TANZANIA │

311 │ TRINIDAD AND TOBAGO │

317 │ UNITED KINGDOM │ LONDON, ENGLAND 317 │ EDINBURGH, SCOTLAND (PRONOUNCED "EDINBURRAH," PLEASE) 322 │ GLASGOW, SCOTLAND 324

327 │ UNITED STATES OF AMERICA │ LOS ANGELES, CALIFORNIA 327 │ MIAMI, FLORIDA 335 │ ATLANTA, GEORGIA 338 │ CHICAGO, ILLINOIS 344 │ NEW ORLEANS, LOUISIANA 354 │ PROVINCETOWN, MASSACHUSETTS 359 │ DETROIT, MICHIGAN 362 │ LIVINGSTON, MONTANA 367 │ NEW JERSEY 371 │ NEW YORK CITY 378 │ PORTLAND, OREGON 394 │ PHILADELPHIA, PENNSYLVANIA 398 │ PITTSBURGH, PENNSYLVANIA 402 │ CHARLESTON, SOUTH CAROLINA 405 │ AUSTIN, TEXAS 410 │ SEATTLE, WASHINGTON 413 │ WEST VIRGINIA 418 │

423 │ URUGUAY │ MONTEVIDEO 425 │ GARZÓN 426 │

435 │ VIETNAM │ CENTRAL VIETNAM: HOI AN AND HUE 435 │ HANOI 438 │ SAIGON/HO CHI MINH CITY 441 │

Appendix: Film References **447** │ Acknowledgments **451** │ Cited Quotes **453**

WORLD TRAVEL

INTRODUCTION

It was never my intention to be a reporter, a critic, an advocate.
It was also never my intention to provide audiences with
"everything" they needed to know about a place—or even a
balanced or comprehensive overview. I am a storyteller. I go
places, I come back. I tell you how the places made me feel.
Through the use of powerful tools like great photography, skillful
editing, sound mixing, color correction, music (which is often
composed specifically for the purpose) and brilliant producers,
I can—in the very best cases—make you feel a little bit like I did at
the time. At least I hope so. It's a manipulative process. It's also a
deeply satisfying one.

—ANTHONY BOURDAIN, 2012

Did the world need another travel guide, and did we need to write
it? In March 2017, when Tony and I began to discuss the idea for this
book—an atlas of the world as seen through his eyes (and the lens
of television)—I wasn't entirely sure. He was ever busier and more
prolific, with a publishing imprint, an interest in a travel website, and
several film and writing passion projects atop his demanding TV career. With so much content out there and in the works, I sometimes
felt that we were careening toward "Peak Bourdain."

I had, however, thoroughly enjoyed the process of writing a
cookbook (*Appetites*, published in 2016) with Tony. We met in 2002,
when I was hired to edit and test recipes for *Anthony Bourdain's Les
Halles Cookbook*, his first entry in that category. I started working as

his assistant (or, as he liked to say, "lieutenant") in 2009, and over the years I'd become involved with various editing and writing projects in addition to the more ground-level tasks of an assistant; I wasn't about to say no when he asked if I'd like to work on another book with him.

We worked well together. I'd spent enough time in daily correspondence with Tony to have a good sense of the way he'd choose his words and set his rhythm. He wrote nearly impeccable prose, but on the occasion when it needed a bit of tidying or fleshing out, I was able to do that, I think, without detection.

The publishing business being what it is, and Tony's impossible schedule being what it was, it was nearly a year from that initial conversation to when our work on this book began in earnest. Our first order of business was to sit down and brainstorm what would go into it—the places, people, food, sights, markets, hotels, and more that had stuck with him, without aid of notes or videos, throughout nearly twenty years of traveling the world in the service of making television.

One spring afternoon in 2018, I sat across from Tony at his dining table, in the Manhattan high-rise apartment he had lovingly styled into a reasonable facsimile of a suite at his favorite Los Angeles hotel, the Chateau Marmont (see page 329). He'd picked up smoking again, a number of years after quitting; he'd been talking earnestly about a plan to stop, but in the meantime, in response to complaints from his neighbors, he'd recently installed an industrial-strength smoke-eater machine, of the kind and caliber normally seen only in casinos and bars.

I'd chosen my seat, under the ceiling-mounted contraption, rather poorly: while Tony chain-smoked and free-associated for over an hour, recalling best-loved dishes and hotels and people, the machine's powerful vacuum sucked the smoke across my face and into its maw. I left the apartment smelling like a late-1990s bar crawl through hell, but in possession of an hourlong audio recording in which we'd laid out a blueprint for the book, a window into what had shaped his understanding and appreciation for some of the world's most interesting places, as he tirelessly explored and documented them.

After this conversation, Tony went back out to keep exploring the world for his television show *Parts Unknown*—Kenya, Texas, Manhattan's Lower East Side, Indonesia—while I started to track down old episodes, began to painstakingly transcribe the relevant bits, and wrote lists of questions. My plan was to get a few chapter outlines completed and hand them to Tony, to make sure we were on the same page, and to get him started on filling in the juice, the essential Tonyness. Only, I never got a chance.

If I'd known that that single meeting would be the only one we'd have about the book, I would have pushed him for more specifics in those places where he'd said, "Let's come back to it," or "See what you can pull up." It is a hard and lonely thing to coauthor a book about the wonders of world travel when your writing partner, that very traveler, is no longer traveling that world. And, to be honest, in the difficult days and weeks after his death, I once again found myself asking, "Does the world need this book?"

Of great comfort in the immediate aftermath of Tony's departure, and even now, more than two years later, is the steady chorus of admiration for what he accomplished while he was here, and the expressions of deep sorrow over the loss of him, from many corners of the world. The sheer magnitude of his cultural impact became clear to me only after he died.

Maybe the world *could* use another travel guide, full of Tony's acid wit and thoughtful observations and a few sly revelations of the mysterious contours of his battered heart, stitched together from all the brilliant and hilarious things he'd said and written about the world as he saw it.

We had initially planned for Tony to write a number of essays about specific topics that moved him—his abiding love of France; the countries in which he was no longer welcome, by decree of one irritated government or another; the eccentricities of various European palates; a specific *onsen* outside Kyoto that was so hushed, luxurious, and polished that it remained his favorite, even after many return trips to Japan.

He was gone before having the chance to write those essays, so I have recruited a number of Tony's friends, family members, and colleagues to contribute their own collected thoughts and memories about places they experienced with Tony. You'll find recollections of visits to France, Uruguay, and the New Jersey shore from Tony's brother, Christopher Bourdain; a story from Tony's producer and director Nari Kye of coming to terms with her Korean roots while shooting in Seoul; the producer and musician Steve Albini on the places he wishes he could share a meal with Tony in Chicago, and more.

You'll notice that, while this book does include basic information on topics like transportation and hotels, this is far from a comprehensive guide to any one location. Prices, exchange rates, travel routes, geopolitical stability, and the business of making and selling food and beverages are all flexible, changing things; for the most up-to-date and detailed information about how to take a train between Ho Chi Minh City and Hanoi, say, or exactly which buses will get you from Midtown Manhattan to the Bronx, you will want to supplement this volume with a fat, full-color guidebook dedicated to one city or country, or, you know, the internet.

Please note, too, that in certain cases, some of Tony's quotes have been slightly edited or condensed for clarity; these quotes have been pulled from a variety of sources, chief among them the written transcripts of his television shows *No Reservations*, *The Layover*, and *Parts Unknown*, along with the various essays Tony wrote in support of certain episodes, and, on occasion, remarks he made to various publications about a specific person or place.

I have tried, as much as possible, to stick to the plan for this book as Tony laid it out. In some cases, a beloved restaurant or bar has permanently closed, or had a change of ownership and with it a change in product, ambience, or attitude. And in some cases, a business has succumbed to the "Bourdain effect," which is to say, once a low-key restaurant or bar or sausage kiosk was featured on the show, its number of customers often skyrocketed, with Bourdain-inspired pilgrims showing up in droves to try the thing that Tony had on camera. In theory, this was a good thing, a coveted thing for businesses, but it could also utterly disrupt a beloved local institution, turning it into a sideshow or, depending on how the business handled it, a shitshow. Tony and his crew were aware of this possibility, and sensitive to it, though of course it was ultimately a decision each business owner made.

There are risks, and there are rewards, of being exposed to the entire world's hunger to eat, travel, and live like Tony.

"**Who gets to tell the stories?**" asked Tony on the Kenya episode of *Parts Unknown*, which he made with his CNN colleague W. Kamau Bell. It was the last episode for which he recorded narration, and the winner, in 2019, of an Emmy Award for television writing.

"**This is a question asked often. The answer, in this case, for better or for worse, is, 'I do.' At least this time out. I do my best. I look. I listen. But in the end, I know: it's my story, not Kamau's, not Kenya's, or Kenyans'. Those stories are yet to be heard.**"

ARGENTINA

BUENOS AIRES

"Buenos Aires: capital of Argentina, second-largest country in South America. It's got a quirky, unique character all its own. It looks like no other place, and it feels unlike any other." Tony visited Argentina for *No Reservations* in 2007, and he returned nine years later with *Parts Unknown* for a more focused look at the city, in a hot and semi-deserted summertime.

"It's got sort of a mournful, sad, sweet quality that I like. Fits with the architecture. January and February are the hottest months here, middle of summer, and most Porteños who can afford it get out of town, to cooler climes.

"Argentina has the distinction of being home to more head-shrinkers per capita than anywhere else in the world. Now, it's a proud country. I mean, one of the stereotypes is that Argentines are too proud, that they're full of themselves. Vain. If this is so, why is psychotherapy so huge in this country? I mean, this is the kingdom of doubt. It's an extraordinary thing, because in many cultures, to confess that you need to even confide in someone is seen as a sign of weakness. Here, everybody does it, and in no way frowns upon it."

Tony submitted to an on-camera therapy session with a psychologist, footage of which was woven throughout the episode; in it, he disclosed a recurring nightmare of being trapped in a luxury hotel, and the depressive spiral that a bad airport hamburger could bring on.

"I feel like Quasimodo, the Hunchback of Notre Dame—if he stayed in nice hotel suites with high-thread-count sheets. I feel kind of like a freak, and . . . very isolated."

ARRIVAL IN BUENOS AIRES, AND GETTING AROUND

Buenos Aires has two airports, the larger of which is Ministro Pistarini International, also known as **Ezeiza International** (**EZE**), which is fourteen miles from the center of Buenos Aires. It handles 85 percent of the country's international traffic, and it's a hub for Aerolineas Argentinas. EZE services flights from all over South America, select North American cities, and a handful of European and Middle Eastern cities. Taxis queue outside the arrivals hall; the trip from EZE to the center of the city takes about thirty-five minutes and will cost about 1,750 Argentine pesos, or about US$30. Taxi drivers do not expect a standard percentage of the fare as a tip, but rounding up or asking the driver to keep the change is always appreciated, especially if he or she has handled your luggage. There are also bus lines from EZE, and car rentals are available.

Buenos Aires's smaller airport, handling exclusively domestic traffic (with the exception of a single Montevideo, Uruguay, flight), is **Jorge Newbury Airfield**. It's just a mile and a half from Buenos Aires's downtown area, with bus lines, metered taxis, and rental cars available.

Travelers already in Uruguay may choose to cross the River Plate (actually an estuary) on a ferry from Montevideo to Buenos Aires, a journey of just over two to just over four hours, and costing between 2,900 and 8,700 pesos, or US$50–$150 each way, depending on time of day and whether your journey is by boat only or includes

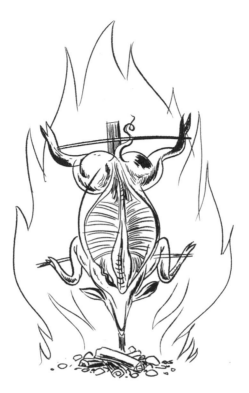

a bus transfer. Bear in mind that as this is an international crossing, you will pass through security, passport control, and customs, just as if you were flying. The two major carriers are Buquebus and Colonia Express.

In town, Buenos Aires is well served by bus routes, along with a seven-line underground metro system known as Subte, which links the downtown to the outer reaches of the city. Both bus and metro fares are paid via a rechargeable SUBE card, available in metro stations, at official Tourist Assistance Centers, and at various *kioskos*, or corner tobacco and candy shops, throughout the city. For detailed city transit information, visit www.argentina.gob.ar/sube.

IN THE MOOD FOR MEAT

Tony enjoyed **Bodegón Don Carlos**, **"an unassuming, family-run joint across from [La Bombonera] soccer stadium,"** owned and run since 1970 by Juan Carlos Zinola, who goes by Carlitos, his wife, Marta Venturini, and their daughter, Gaby Zinola. It's in the La Boca neighborhood, which, despite its reputation as a slightly seedy area, is a lively tourist destination by day, for soccer fans, the contemporary art crowd drawn to Fundación Proa, and the masses seeking cheap amusement at the artists' haven turned schlocky permanent street fair, Caminito.

Historically, there hasn't been a menu at Bodegón Don Carlos; diners are greeted and asked how hungry they are, and what they like to eat, and then dishes are delivered accordingly—meatballs, Spanish *tortilla patata*, tomato salads, empanadas, blood sausage, steaks, pastas, and more. Word on the street suggests that the number of foreign visitors has grown since Tony's visit, and that menus, with prices, are available on request, though still it's worth it to surrender and put oneself in Carlitos's capable hands.

BODEGÓN DON CARLOS: Brandsen 699 La Boca, Buenos Aires C1161AAM, Tel +54 11 4362 2433 (full meal with beverage about 3,500 pesos/US$60 per person)

"On the outskirts of town, in the roaring summer heat, the fires still burn hot. A tempting miasma of meat fills the midafternoon air."

Tony met his on-camera therapist, Marina, at **Los Talas del Entrerriano** for a traditional *parrilla* lunch: plate after plate of ribs, steaks, sausages, and, at Marina's insistence, *achuras*, or, as Tony might have called them, "the nasty bits": intestines, kidneys, blood sausage, and more. **"On the parrilla,"** Tony observed, **"many parts of once living things sizzle and char for the pleasure of those Porteños who remain** in town. Meat is king in fire, and we shall go hard in honoring the flame."

Los Talas is a cavernous, casual place, with tables that seat up to ten people; smaller groups are seated together to fill a table. The portions are enormous, the sides and drinks are afterthoughts, the flames are hot, and the mood is lively.

LOS TALAS DEL ENTRERRIANO: Avenida Brigadier Juan Manuel de Rosas 1391, Jose Leon Suarez, Buenos Aires, Tel +54 11 4729 8527 (about 1,750 pesos/US$30 per person)

AUSTRALIA

MELBOURNE

"Australia: a new world at the other end of the world, a rapidly deepening and expanding culture of food and chefs, extraordinary wines, a few important melting pots with a whole lotta space in between. The Crocodile Dundee image—the whole 'shrimp on the barbie,' beer-swilling 'matey' nonsense was an unfortunate misstep.

"I've been here many times, and the Australia I love is a very different one than the folksy, outdoorsy wild kingdom, with the Foster's silliness of films and commercials."

Considering the distance from his New York City home, Tony spent a fair amount of time in Australia, between television shoots, book promotion (the Aussies are voracious consumers of his writing) and speaking gigs, most recently at the twentieth anniversary of the legendary Melbourne Food & Wine Festival. He was frank in his love of the city:

"Melbourne has been described, superbly, as 'like San Francisco without the fog,' a fantastically mixed culture of Chinese, Vietnamese, Greek, Lebanese. I've always felt particularly connected to the Melbourne chef mafia, a lovable bunch of home teamers and visiting Brits who, for some time, have been making magic out on the edge. Sydney's fine dining is great, but it's Melbourne I keep coming back to. Maybe it's friends, maybe it's the ingredients; I expect it's the uniquely Melbournian attitude. Everybody has to have a favorite place, and in Australia, Melbourne is mine."

ARRIVAL AND GETTING AROUND

Melbourne Airport (MEL), locally known as Tullamarine, is Australia's second-busiest airport after Sydney's. Served by all the big carriers of the Pacific Rim—Qantas, Singapore, Cathay Pacific, Air China, Virgin Australia, and more—it's about fourteen miles from the city's central business district.

A taxi, hailed from a rank outside the arrivals hall, from the airport to downtown Melbourne will take about thirty minutes, depending on traffic, and will run about $60 Australian/US$40; tips are appreciated but not expected.

There's also a SkyBus shuttle that runs frequently between the airport and the city, which is A$19/US$13 one way or A$36/US$25 round trip (www.skybus.com.au).

Once in the city, you can avail yourself of Melbourne's extensive public transportation system, composed of trains, buses, and trams, all under the umbrella of Public Transport Victoria (www.ptv.vic.gov.au). The city also has a bike-share program, and taxis can be hailed on the street or engaged from dozens of ranks around the city.

MARKETING AND CHOWING DOWN IN MELBOURNE

"Queen Vic Market is a sprawling, busy indoor area where it seems everyone comes for their vegetables, fish, dairy, and meat, avocados, monkfish, excellent slabs of meat—for not too much money."

Established in 1878, the Queen Victoria Market does attract tourists and serve local chefs, but in fact it's also the place where supermarket-eschewing locals shop and eat. Over six hundred vendors operate in a space that covers two city blocks.

"A bratwurst, incongruously enough, is the typical lunch for your market-going Melbournian. This is probably Melbourne's most famous street food. You come to Melbourne, you go to the Vic Market, you have a bratwurst. This is something that everyone, everyone does," Tony observed, while visiting with chef Paul Wilson in 2009, for *No Reservations*. The pair sought out his beloved "meat in tube form" at Bratwurst Shop, a "sensible fucking breakfast," which he found to be "chunky, spicy . . . beautiful, man."

QUEEN VICTORIA MARKET: Corner of Elizabeth and Victoria Streets, Melbourne 3000, Tel +03 9320 5822, www.qvm.com.au

BRATWURST SHOP & CO.: Queen Victoria Market, Shop 99–100, Dairy Produce Hall, Melbourne 3000, Tel +03 9328 2076, www.bratwurstshop.com (basic bratwurst about A$8/US$5.50)

Tony was wild about the pleasure and pain brought on by good Sichuan cooking, and **Dainty Sichuan**, helmed by the husband-and-wife team of Ye Shao and Ting Lee, left its mark.

"Sichuan is one of my favorite regional Chinese styles, and it's surprisingly hard to find the real thing, even in Manhattan, where most cooks in Sichuan restaurants are, in fact, from Hong Kong or Fuzhou. Best known for its intense heat, Sichuan [cuisine] is actually a wonderfully sadomasochistic interplay between pleasure and pain, between the scorching, searing bite of the dried red Sichuan pepper and the cooling, more floral relief, the tingling, numbing component of the tiny black Sichuan flower pepper."

Upon arrival at Dainty Sichuan, he noted, "You could smell it right away, walking in the door: The peppers of Sichuan cooking. There's a reason the legends persist, of Sichuanese cooks spiking their dishes with opium. Nothing else explains the powerful addiction one develops to something that just hurts so bad." You can get your fix with servings of "mouth-watering" chicken, pork heart and tongue, fatty pork belly and cumin-flavored pork.

"What do you do to top that, now that my palate's been blown out by the flavor equivalent of a weekend at Caligula's house? It—it's surreal. This is really surreal. It's wacky, in a good way. You actually forget you're in the bustling urban center of Melbourne. You're somewhere else, riding wave after wave of flavor into another dimension."

DAINTY SICHUAN: 176 Toorak Road, South Yarra, Melbourne 3141, Tel +61 3 9078 1686, www.daintysichuanfood.com (typical meal about A$60/US$40 per person)

Tony abdicated all dinner-related decision making to his gang of Melbourne chef friends, which is how he frequently found himself eating congee, suckling pig, hot pot, and steamed whole fish to sop up the booze at **Supper Inn**, a modest Chinatown Cantonese joint that's been consistently serving a late-night crowd (it stays open till 2:30 a.m.) for over four decades. Ascend a timber-paneled staircase to a fluorescent-lit dining room that, in the later hours, will invariably be crammed with employees of Melbourne's hardworking service industry. As Tony recalled clearly, in planning this chapter, **"That place is good."**

SUPPER INN: 15 Celestial Avenue, Melbourne 3000, Tel +61 3 9663 4759 (about A$30/US$20 per person)

SYDNEY

"Sydney, Australia: famous for its temperate, sunny climate; warm and inviting beaches; turquoise blue water."

But for the extremely long flight to get there from New York, Tony's visits to Sydney were what he would call **"low impact"**: agreeable weather, first-world accommodations, lots of great food and wine, and no language barrier. Australia was a place where he could relax and take it all in.

In 2012, during the final season of *No Reservations*, he noted, **"For the first time, actually, I'm starting to experience real estate lust.**

"Nobody bitches about Sydney. . . . Daytime drinking is really underrated. This is one of the great things about this country. You drink in the street. A good time to be eating in Australia, and it's only getting better. People do well in this town."

ARRIVAL AND GETTING AROUND

Sydney Kingsford Smith International Airport (SYD) is Australia's largest and busiest airport, located about five miles from the city center. It is the main hub for Qantas, and is served by all the major Pacific carriers, and many domestic airlines.

To get from the airport to the city, you can take a taxi from the queue outside arrivals halls, an approximately twenty-five-minute ride for about A$50/US$34. Tips are appreciated but not expected.

There are also various shuttle options, which can be arranged at Redy2Go desks in the terminals.

Sydney's Airport Link train departs every 10 minutes, and is part of the city's multi-line metro and train network. Purchase an Opal card on the platform or in selected newsstands in the airport terminal. The one-way fare is about $A20/US$13.50 for adults and $A16 / US$11.50 for children (www.airportlink.com.au).

BUENOS AIRES BY WAY OF SYDNEY, LIVING SEAFOOD, CLASSIC STREET PIES, AND "THE TEMPLE OF ALL THINGS MEAT"

In Sydney, Tony spent time in the company of Ben Milgate and Elvis Abrahanowicz, chef-owners of **"the wonderful, absurdly delicious, crazy-ass Argentinean-themed Porteño—a restaurant that takes the new-to-Australia craze for fatty hunks of meat to, well, *extreme* lengths. The animals rotate slowly, slowly on the track on wheels, right in the middle of the dining room. Nearby, the wood-burning *parrilla*. It's hot on the meat station, hot enough to melt those tattoos right off, but these are some dedicated motherfuckers."**

Since Tony's 2012 visit, the restaurant has relocated (and taken its open-fire equipment with it). In keeping with plant-forward dietary trends, some of the grill's real estate has been given over to vegetables, though the beloved whole pigs, sides of beef, blood sausages, and sweetbreads remain. Gone, alas, is Gardel's, the bar upstairs from the original location, where first-come, first-served guests waited patiently with a drink; fortunately, however, Porteño now accepts reservations.

PORTEÑO: 50 Holt Street, Surry Hills, Sydney, Tel +61 2 8399 1440, www.porteno.com.au (average meal about $A120/US$82 per person)

Golden Century is "where all the chefs—and I mean all the chefs—go sooner or later. Mostly later, like late at night when drunk, after service." Wherever there's a thriving urban restaurant culture, there are these chef havens, for late-night camaraderie. "When you're in the restaurant business, you really feel, especially after a shift, you can't talk to normal people. You need to see people who understand what kind of a strange and terrible world you live in, you know?"

At Golden Century, which Linda and Eric Wong have owned and operated for over thirty years, restaurant lifers and civilians alike choose their supper from "tank after tank of the fruits of the sea, right to your plate, after a brief interval in the wok, served with a cold beer or three." Or a bottle of wine: the list is impressively broad and deep, especially given the simplicity of the room and the no-frills service. Early in the day, classic dim sum service is also available.

Try the mud crabs, wok fried with ginger and shallots. Or, if you're feeling bold, order the whole raw and cooked lobster dish: "Cut, remove brains, extract tail meat, then dice. Pair with raw salmon and oysters. It emerges from a thick cloud of dry ice like Zeppelin at the Garden, 1975. And the rest of Mr. Lobster, salt-and-pepper style, batter fried with Sichuan peppercorns. If there's an Aussie national dish, this might well be it."

GOLDEN CENTURY: 393–399 Sussex Street, Sydney 2000, Tel +61 2 9212 3901, www.goldencentury.com/au (about $A80/ US$55 per person)

"Curried beef, a heaping scoop of mashed potatoes, a volcano crater full of mushy peas, and an eruption of brown gravy. Come on, you know you want that. Look at that: a volcano of love. This is one of those things you just kinda gotta do in Sydney."

Grab a plastic fork and a beer and you're ready for the Curried Tiger Pie, the signature dish at **Harry's Café de Wheels**, a once mobile cart, now a permanently affixed kiosk, vending meat-filled pastries in the eastern suburb of Woolloomooloo since 1938 (with a brief respite during World War II, so that its founder, Harry "Tiger" Edwards, could enlist in the Second Australian Imperial Force).

"It may not be the best meat pie in the world, or even in Sydney, but it is certainly the most famous, it is certainly the most traditional, even inevitable. And it's just damned good. You've only got to ask yourself, of any town, 'What do they do better in this town than anyplace else?' And the meat pies are pretty fucking good here." In addition to the flagship, there are now multiple Harry's locations around Sydney and its suburbs, as well as outposts near Melbourne, Newcastle, and Shenzhen, China.

HARRY'S CAFÉ DE WHEELS: Corner of Cowper Wharf Roadway and Dowling Street, Woolloomooloo, NSW 2011, Tel +02 9357 3074, www.harryscafedewheels.com.au (pies and hot dogs from about $A6 to $10/US$4–$7)

"This is the most magnificent butcher shop, the temple of all things meat on the planet. Victor Churchill's was the oldest butcher shop in Sydney, dating back to 1876, but now, after an enormously expensive renovation, it is the realization of a dream, a gift from Anthony Puharich to his father, Victor Puharich, a third-generation butcher who emigrated here from Croatia, and busted his ass to send his son to school and take care of his family."

Victor has since become one of the largest wholesale meat cutters in the country, and his retail shop is indeed exquisite, more like a fine clothing or jewelry shop than a meat-cutting room.

"This is not business: this is love. The antique slicer, the glass-encased cutting rooms, the old wood boards. Refrigerated shelves show off a dizzying array of classic French pâtés, terrines, and charcuterie."

In addition to cuts of raw and dry-aged meat, all of it raised domestically, Victor Churchill proffers a wide range of charcuterie, pâtés, terrines, and sausages with French, Spanish, and Italian roots, as well as chickens cooked on an antique rotisserie. A sampling of *jamón*, prosciutto, chorizo, salami, duck rillettes, and ballotine of rabbit will convince you: **"The place is magic."**

VICTOR CHURCHILL: 132 Queen Street, Woollahra, 2025 NSW, Tel +02 9328 0402, www.victorchurchill.com (prices vary)

AUSTRIA

VIENNA

"Any country where they speak German, I'm already kind of ambivalent about."

Tony's Christmastime visit to Vienna, for *No Reservations*, is a great example of a trip in which his initial reluctance to enjoy a place was slowly, and to his surprise, replaced by enchantment.

"Vienna: capital city of Austria, once the seat of the gigantic Austro-Hungarian Empire and now a city of 1.3 million people. I've always been hesitant to come here, for no good reasons, really; unreasonable prejudice and the aftermath of childhood trauma.

"When I was a kid, I had an Austrian barber named Helmut who invariably butchered me into looking like one of the Little Rascals as I sat under a mural of an Alpine vista. Then there was *The Sound of Music*, which was set in Salzburg, not Vienna, but which I hated and always associated with anywhere in the neighborhood. And then there's all those amazing traditional pastries and sweets for which Austria has always been justifiably famous. I don't really like sweets. That's why I stayed away."

Although Vienna is such a culturally rich city, having seen centuries of empires rise and fall, an important breeding ground for musicians (the elder and younger Johann Strauss, Johannes Brahms, Anton Bruckner, Gustav Mahler); artists (Gustav Klimt, Egon Schiele);

architects (Otto Wagner, Adolf Loos); as well as the father of modern psychoanalysis, Sigmund Freud—despite all this, Tony was immune to its charms. Or rather, he *was* immune, until he discovered an Austrian antitradition that appealed to his dark sensibilities.

"Krampus Day: a day where people dress up in furs and demon outfits to honor Saint Nick's evil counterpart, Krampus. He's sort of like Santa's enforcer. You're not on Santa's nice list, but on his naughty list? Krampus comes over and fucks you all up." He would later try to work an animated Krampus segment into one of the legendarily twisted *No Reservations* holiday specials, but it was, ultimately, too dark for the network.

"I just had a lotta mixed emotions about the place, which is maybe why I've put off coming here for so long, but I have to say, I find it charming here. I've found chefs pushing the boundaries of taste and, frankly, decency, with really good, simple food and a place that understands the power of pork. This city has turned me around, the ghost of Christmas present has shown me something new. I feel vaguely Christmasy. Yeah, I feel like Scrooge, you know, at the end when he gets all happy and wants to buy gifts and stuff. Merry fucking Christmas, everybody."

ARRIVAL AND GETTING AROUND

Vienna International Airport (**VIE**) is the country's largest, handling hundreds of flights within Europe each day, along with several to and from Africa, Asia, and North America. VIE is the headquarters and hub for Austrian Airlines.

VIE is about eleven miles from the city center; a metered taxi, widely available in ranks outside the terminals, will take twenty to thirty minutes, depending on traffic, and will cost about 35 euros/

US$39, plus the expected 10 percent tip. The City Airport Train (CAT) is another option, taking passengers from the airport to Wien Mitte train station, in the city center, in just sixteen minutes, for 12 euros/US$13.25 one way, or 21 euros/US$23 round trip; children up to fourteen years old travel for free. Those departing the city for the airport can also check luggage and obtain passes for upcoming flights upon boarding the CAT at the train station. See www.cityairporttrain.com for details.

Once in town, the Viennese public transport system, **Wiener Linien**, composed of subways, local trains, buses, and trams, is comprehensive, excellent, and easy to use. Single rides cost just over 2 euros, with various volume discount passes available. All modes of transport operate on an honor system, meaning there are no formal ticket checks or turnstiles, just plainclothes agents who will occasionally check all tickets and issue steep fines for those who have not paid a fare.

FERRIS WHEEL

Inside one of Vienna's largest public parks, the Prater, is an amusement park, the Wurstelprater, and inside of that is the world's oldest operating Ferris wheel, originally built in 1897, and rebuilt, after a fire, in 1945. Climb into one of its boxy, windowed wooden cabins for a true thrill ride, 212 feet in the air.

"One of the more famous scenes from film history happened here: the Riesenrad Ferris wheel at the Prater. Orson Welles and Joseph Cotton; film, *The Third Man*. Orson Welles, playing Harry Lime, has agreed to meet his old friend Holly Martins at the Prater, and take the Ferris wheel up. And up top, in rather menacing fashion, he slides the door open, which, shockingly, you're not allowed to do. He

looks down and he's at the famous speech [which Tony more or less approximated from memory; Harry's dialogue, from the screenplay by Graham Greene, is as follows]:

'Don't be melodramatic. Look down there. Would you feel any pity if one of those dots stopped moving forever? If I offered you twenty thousand pounds for every dot that stopped, would you really, old man, tell me to keep my money?'"

The Riesenrad may be old, but it is scrupulously maintained, having been refurbished several times in the postwar years, with a backup generator in case the power is cut, and manual operation capacity should all else fail.

RIESENRAD FERRIS WHEEL: Riesenradplatz 1, 1020 Vienna, Tel +43 1 7295430, www.wienerriesenrad.com (adults, 12 euros/ US$13.25; children 3–14, 5 euros/US$5.50; children under 3 free)

SERIOUS PORK AT THE NASCHMARKT

"Since I've been so rude and dismissive of all things Austrian, I don't have any friends here. Fortunately, my driver turns out to also be an erudite young man of many facets: Clemens, a DJ, gourmand, professional driver, enabler, and good fucking guy. And he knows what I like."

It's hard not to like the **Naschmarkt,** Vienna's largest outdoor market, with about 120 stalls of produce, meats, fish, poultry, cheeses, baked goods, imports from the Middle East, Asia, and India, and a Saturday flea market, plus a number of bars, cafés, and restaurants.

"Clemens guided me through the Naschmarkt for its meat-centric central destination, **Urbanek.** Urbanek is magnificent; my kind of wonderland; a justifiably famous center of man-on-pork love. . . . Rarely have I seen so much good stuff in one tiny, tiny little place. Great cheese, most of which I'm unfamiliar with. Hams and cured pork products that would give even Hef an unassisted stiffy. A family business, of course, run by Gerhard [Urbanek] and his sons, Thomas and Daniel."

Sample a bit of everything, then take away a package of ham, smoked pork, and cheese, to be made into a cordon bleu: wrapped in a pounded pork loin, breaded, and deep-fried in pork fat, in a little kitchen at the back of butcher Huerta Gruber's shop. Alas, Gruber died in 2013, and her shop has closed, but there are other purveyors of cordon bleu in Vienna; inquire of the Urbanek family, or a trusted Austrian guide.

NASCHMARKT: Linke & Rechte Wienzeile, Vienna,
Tel +43 1 40005430, www.wien.gv.at

URBANEK: Naschmarkt, stall 46, Vienna, Tel +43 1 1 5872080 (wine, ham, bread, and cheese for two people, about 50 euros/US$55)

BHUTAN

"Bhutan: a remote, relatively rarely visited kingdom of myth and legend, high in the Himalayas, known as 'land of the thunder dragon.' [Bhutan] has existed contentedly, in a state of self-imposed isolation, for centuries.

"Located between India and Tibet, Bhutan, about the size of Switzerland, is caught between the old world and the new. Tourism was only allowed starting in the 1970s. The number of foreign visitors each year is strictly limited, to protect Bhutan's culture and environment. There are no Starbucks, no KFCs, no king or clown. Basically, they don't want you to come here, at least not en masse.

"Until about fifteen years ago, the East-West Highway was the only road in Bhutan. Bisecting the country, it twists through some pretty gnarly mountain passes, with, at times, a crumbly cliff face on one side and harrowing freaking drop-offs on the other. The road is undergoing a major expansion, with plans to have it fully paved by, well . . . soon.

"Respect for the natural world is fundamental to Bhutan's spiritual identity. More than half the country is off-limits to development or timbering. A whopping 50 percent of Bhutan's GDP comes from hydropower."

ARRIVAL

"One of the reasons [Bhutan's] not on the tourist trail is it's hard to get to. Flying in, you hang on to your seat as the plane negotiates some alarming maneuvers through narrow mountain passes, before dropping into the country's only international airport [Paro], said by some to be the most dangerous in the world."

There are three airlines that fly into that airport, **Paro (PBH)**, from Bangkok, Singapore, Kathmandu, and a handful of Indian and Bhutanese cities. These are Bhutan Airlines, Drukair, and Buddha Air. Pilots must be specifically certified to land at Paro, because of its geographic challenges, and landings are limited to daylight hours.

Taxis are available for hire, though you may want to arrange one in advance, through a reputable travel company, to avoid the scrum of drivers competing for your business upon arrival, and also to avoid the typical tourist overcharge. Indian rupees are widely accepted as currency, as is the Bhutanese ngultrum, whose value is pegged to the rupee. The fare from Paro to the capital, Thimphu, about a thirty-mile drive, should cost about 1,100 rupees/ngultrum, or $15–$20 USD, for a four-passenger car.

Tips haven't traditionally been part of the culture, but they are becoming more widely accepted and expected as the tourist industry expands in the country. Ten to 20 percent is a good tip for a taxi driver; in restaurants and hotels, the same applies, but do examine your check to see if a service charge has already been added.

AT HOME IN AMAN

Tony was taken with the various luxury Aman resorts he called home while traversing Bhutan. Designed by the esteemed late Australian architect Kerry Hill, with an exquisite sensitivity to the surroundings, using the raw materials of the region whenever possible, the Aman properties are supremely quiet and restful, as befits a little-discovered Himalayan kingdom.

In Thimphu, Tony stayed at the Amankora hotel, the flagship Aman property in Bhutan, located on a forested hillside and styled after a Bhutanese *dzong*, or fortress. In Punakha, Bumthang, and Paro, he stayed in Amankora lodges. At all four properties, the spacious wood-and-metal-clad open-plan bedrooms feature woodstoves (lit by hotel staff), king-size beds, huge bathtubs, and all-inclusive dining room and room service options.

The Punakha Lodge, located in a fertile subtropical valley that is the winter home of Bhutanese royalty, is distinguished by the prayer flag–covered suspension bridge that must be crossed to gain access to the lodge. The Paro property, located close to the airport, is a good

option for starting or ending one's visit to Bhutan. And the Bumthang Lodge is situated in an area with dozens of temples and monasteries.

Of course, all this comfortable, quiet luxury does not come cheap. As of this writing, suites start at about 60,000 rupees/ngultrum / US$850 in the low season, 90,000 rupees/ngultrum/US$1,250 in the high season.

AMANKORA: +975 2 331 333, www.aman.com/resorts/amankora (prices above)

MOMOS IN THIMPHU

Tony may have slept in luxury, but on a 2017 trip to Bhutan with the film director Darren Aronofsky, the adventures were found closer to the street.

Aronofsky, fresh from the release of his film *Mother!*, a dark allegory about man's destruction of the environment, was driven by his curiosity about a country that has, for now, been spared the worst effects of unchecked development.

"Morning in Thimphu, Bhutan's capital and largest city. It has a rapidly growing population of 100,000, as Bhutanese have begun the inevitable move away from a rural, agrarian lifestyle.

"Our first meal [at Menzu Shiri] becomes our go-to favorite for the rest of the trip. If I'm not on camera, chances are I'm somewhere eating these bad boys: momos. Plump, flavorful, often quite spicy dumplings, filled with meat, cheese, or veg. Did I mention Darren is a vegetarian?"

MENZU SHIRI: just off Norzin Lam Road, Thimphu. No phone, no website. Plate of 5 momos about 72 rupees/ngultrum (US$1).

IN SEARCH OF THE DIVINE MADMAN

"It's a two-and-a-half-hour drive from the capital to the picturesque mountain village of Punakha. This is a must-see destination, and one-time home to Bhutan's revered and beloved Drukpa Kunley—known as the Divine Madman."

Around **Chimi L'Hakhang**, also known as the Temple of Fertility—which was built to honor Drukpa Kunley—you will find a profusion of penis paintings, drawings, and sculptures on display.

"For centuries, Bhutan has celebrated the—um—phallus. All this is the legacy of Drukpa Kunley—a lama and holy man who lived five hundred years ago, and spread the tenets of Buddhism, along with a healthy skepticism for the institutions of power. He reveled unapologetically in casual sex, the copious use of spirits—and seduction. Smiting demons—and making frequent friends—with what is referred to as his 'flaming thunderbolt of wisdom,' a term you and I are unlikely to get away with."

BRAZIL

SALVADOR

"I think that Salvador in particular is a place where, no matter what, people should come. Even people who are afraid to travel, who said, 'Oh, well, but I hear . . .' No! You know what? Live your life, man. You should not miss a place like this, cause there aren't a lot of places in the world that even come close to this. You find yourself in the heart of the heart of Brazil—where the magic comes from. If you wanna get there, just follow the sound of the drums. Things seem to just sway and move constantly. It's a place where everybody is sexy. I don't know if it's the booze, or the music, or the tropical heat, but after a while bouncing from place to place, wandering down old cobblestone streets, different music issuing from everywhere, a different party, people flowing out of buildings, one gathering commingling with another, the music mixing, it really does seem that everybody is moving to some mysterious, unknowable pulse."

There is, of course, beauty in Salvador, a city of three million people in the northeastern section of coastal Brazil. There is great food, music, art, that tangible sensuality—but there is also a troubling history.

Salvador is the capital of the state of Bahia. It was the nation's capital from 1549 to 1763, and the colonial section known as Pelourinho was, in 1558, the first place where slave ships landed from West Africa and established trading operations in the New World.

"It is useful to know that of over twelve million Africans dragged, ripped, and kidnapped from their homelands, nearly five million ended up in Brazil; 1.5 million of them in Bahia alone. Pelourinho became the locus of a vast infrastructure of plantations and the slave trade that powered them—making this city the most opulent in the New World. Pelourinho, the colonial center of the city, is now a UNESCO heritage site, its brightly colored colonial buildings and cobblestone streets a reminder of the way the modern world was built."

GETTING THERE, GETTING AROUND

Salvador International Airport (SSA) is also known as Luis Eduardo Magalhaes Airport. There are direct flights to Salvador from Miami, Lisbon, and, seasonally, Paris, as well as several connections from cities across Brazil and select South American cities. The airport is twelve miles from the city center, which can be accessed by various bus routes, or by taxi, for about 160 reals/about US$40. Tipping drivers isn't expected in Brazil, but rounding up by a handful of reals would be appreciated.

Salvador has metered taxis, a two-line subway system, and an extensive bus system, along with a funicular and an Elevador Lacerda, a large public elevator that connects the lower and upper levels of the city.

CAIPIRINHAS, *QUEIJO COALHO*, *ACARAJÉ*, AND *DENDÊ*

Across Brazil, morning and night, you'll find plenty of opportunities to indulge in caipirinhas, which are widely available in bars, in restaurants, and made fresh at modest pushcarts on the beach.

"The caipirinha, man, this indispensable icon of Brazilian beach culture, is known to start with fresh lime. Muddle and mash with more lime juice, sugar, ice, the magic ingredient, cachaça—that's basically the distilled liquor of the sugarcane. Shaken, not stirred, and you've got yourself one of the world's truly great cocktails. The utility beverage, good for any time of day, or any social occasion."

Also popular on the beach are the *queijo coalho* vendors, who will gently toast the cheese over a portable rig, often just a metal bucket of coals and embers, until it resembles a golden-brown campfire marshmallow.

For another ubiquitous Bahian snack, join the dozens, if not hundreds, of hungry Salvadorans outside **Acarajé da Dinha**.

"What is *acarajé*? Behold: a paste, a batter, a falafel-like wad of smushed-up black-eyed peas, seasoned with ground dried shrimp and onions, deep-fried till crispy and golden, in some chili-spiked *dendê* oil. On the top you got your *vatapá*, which is, sort of, a shrimp curry paste, and your tomato salad, your fried shrimp, your *camarão frito*. A must." It's a lively, crowded scene, with tables and chairs in the nearby plaza at a premium, so be prepared to stand and eat.

ACARAJÉ DA DINHA: Largo de Santana, Salvador Bahia, Tel +71 3334 1703 (about 16 Brazilian reals, or US$4)

A note about *dendê* oil: *Dendê* is a bright red oil, used extensively for frying and seasoning cooked foods in Brazil, especially Bahia, made from the fruit of the African oil palm tree, which is native to Angola and Gambia, and also widely planted in Brazil. *Dendê* oil has a rich, nutty flavor, a true marker of Bahian cooking, especially when mixed with coconut milk, chili peppers, and cilantro.

First time in Brazil? One note of caution: "I love the *dendê* oil. You know, it takes some getting used to. The first time I was here, you eat it, you shit like a mink for hours afterwards. But now, no problems! Lovin' it."

CAMBODIA

Cambodia—beautiful, wild, with an extraordinarily painful recent history of unimaginably horrific genocide—is a place about which Tony expressed both awe and rage. He was passionate and well read about the US government's disastrous involvement in Southeast Asian politics of the Cold War era, both the overt Vietnam War and the covert bombing campaigns in Laos and Cambodia. Tony first visited Cambodia in 2000, for *A Cook's Tour*, and then a decade later with *No Reservations*.

"Since my last visit to Cambodia, I've been to nearly every corner of the globe, and I'm not going to say—as much as I'd like to believe it—that I've gotten any smarter. After a while, even the most beautiful scenery threatens to become moving wallpaper—background—but other times, it all seems to come together: the work, the play, all the places I've been, where I am now, a happy, stupid, wonderful confluence of events. Rice paddies whipping by, the music in our skull just right. If something profound ain't happening, at least it feels like it is.

"On April 17, 1975, the Khmer Rouge rolled their tanks into Phnom Penh. It was a day that brought an end to years of bloody civil war. It was also a day that ushered in a period of terror, madness, and mayhem on an unimaginable scale."

Over 1.7 million were killed, Tony noted, "led by French-educated Pol Pot, who referred to himself as Brother Number One. They set out to create an ultra-Marxist agrarian wonderland, but first, the

past would have to be erased. Two thousand years of Cambodian culture and history came to an immediate end. It was declared year zero
and everything that came before it was to be erased from existence.
Literally overnight, entire cities were emptied. There were inhabitants marched off to the countryside, slave laborers forced to farm
the land as a means of realizing Pol Pot's agrarian utopia. Money
was abolished. Books were burned. Families purposely broken apart.
Teachers, merchants, doctors, and almost the entire intellectual
elite of the country were murdered. The scale of killing was so im-
mense that whole areas, later known as 'killing fields' in and around
Phnom Penh, were used to dispose of the bodies.

"When in 1979 the neighboring Vietnamese overthrew the
Khmer Rouge, sending Pol Pot and his buddies into the jungle, it
may have saved the country, but the troubles hardly ended. Simply
put, some of the same bastards from the old days are in positions of
power today.

"These streets weren't paved last time I was here," he observed
in 2010. "In 2000, it was wilder and far more dangerous, a place still
reeling from the days when this city was reduced from a population of two million to just a few Khmer Rouge officials. Clerks, office workers, taxi drivers, cooks were marched into the country and
forced to farm. Anyone unfortunate enough to be a doctor, a lawyer,
a professional, multilingual, even if they only wore glasses, they were
killed.

"Once you've been to Cambodia, you'll never stop wanting to
beat Henry Kissinger to death with your bare hands," Tony wrote
in 2001 in *A Cook's Tour*, the companion book to his TV series of the
same name. "You will never again be able to open a newspaper and
read about that treacherous, prevaricating, murderous scumbag . . .
without choking. Witness what Henry did in Cambodia—the fruits
of his genius for statesmanship—and you will never understand why
he's not sitting in the dock at The Hague next to Milošević."

GETTING TO AND AROUND CAMBODIA

There are no direct flights between the United States and Cambodia; you'll connect via China, Japan, or Korea into one of the country's two major international airports, in Phnom Penh (**PNH**) or Siem Reap (**REP**). From either airport, take a taxi or *remorque/tuk-tuk* (a small trailer with covered seating, pulled by a motorcycle) to your hotel for about 40,000 Cambodian riel/US$10 for a taxi or 33,000 riel/ US$8 for a *tuk-tuk*. Drivers do not expect tips, but they are always appreciated.

COLONIAL LUXURY

Tony made no secret of his love for the luxurious, well-preserved (or well-renovated) colonial hotels of Southeast Asia, and when in Phnom Penh, he stayed at **Raffles Hotel Le Royale**. Opened as Le Royale in 1929 as an oasis for well-heeled travelers, it was the home base for journalists covering Cambodia's 1970–75 civil war, before being closed in the wake of the Khmer Rouge victory and the atrocities that followed. The Raffles group presided over a painstaking renovation, reopening the hotel in 1997; of particular note is the Kaf-Kaf gin and tonic on offer in the hotel's Elephant Bar.

RAFFLES HOTEL LE ROYALE: Sangkat Wat Phnom, 92 Rukhak Vithei Daun Penh, Phnom Penh, Tel +855 23 981 888, www.raffles .com/phnom-penh/ (rooms start at about 814,000 riel/US$200 per night)

Tony also used the **Raffles Grand Hotel d'Angkor**, built in 1932 and restored in 1997, as his home base for exploring nearby Angkor Wat (see the following section), and it remains a fine luxury choice. Since his last visit, Siem Reap has welcomed some new luxury hotel options, including the boutique **Jaya House Riverpark**, whose impeccable 1960s Modernist design sense is matched by its excellent food, peerless support of environmental and social causes, and commitment to hiring locals and promoting the work of local artisans.

RAFFLES GRAND HOTEL D'ANGKOR: 1 Vithei Charles de Gaulle, Siem Reap, Tel +855 63 963 888, www.raffles.com/siem-reap (rooms start at about 814,000 riel/US$200 per night)

JAYA HOUSE RIVERPARK: River Road, Siem Reap, Tel +55 63 962 555, www.jayahouseriverparksiemreap.com (rooms start at about 1,020,000 riel/US$250 per night)

EATING IN PHNOM PENH

"I've also said it over and over again: if you're going to a country, particularly in Southeast Asia, [where] you've never been before, it's a very good idea to go to the market first, see what they're selling, get an idea of what they're good at, what the people are buying." In Phnom Penh, that would be the **Central Market**. Ramshackle in the extreme in 2000, but cleaned up considerably by 2010, it nonetheless retained, for Tony, its olfactory and gustatory signatures:

"This is more of the way I remember Cambodia—the smell of jackfruit, woodsmoke, dried fish, raw chicken, and breakfast. *Ka tieu*, a pho-like noodle soup with chicken, pork meatballs, and greens in a vibrant-looking and tasty broth, is always the expressway to my heart."

CENTRAL MARKET: Calmette St. (53), Phnom Penh, Tel +855 98 288 066. No website (prices vary on *ka tieu* and other soups, noodle dishes, and sweets, 2,000–12,000 riel/US$0.50–$3)

ANGKOR WAT

"At Angkor Wat, the centuries-old seat of power of the Khmer empire, I gave up taking photographs of my travels. How could any lens capture the scale, the grandeur of a kingdom that once ruled this part of the world and then inexplicably crumbled into the jungle?"

Use a Siem Reap hotel as your jumping-off point, and give yourself at least one full day to explore Angkor Wat, the vast sandstone temple complex built in the twelfth century and still a symbol of the genius, devotion, and ingenuity of the Khmer civilization. There are plentiful food stalls across from the temple entrance, and you may choose to rent bicycles or hire motorbike drivers to facilitate your explorations.

KAMPOT AND KEP

"Originally settled and heavily developed by Chinese traders, Kampot was once Cambodia's main port city. The Chinese merchant class, of course, seen as foreign by the Khmer Rouge, were very nearly wiped out. . . . Today, the area's Chinese population is a shadow of what it once was, but its influence is still visible in the architecture, the people, and the food. This area was also known for peppercorns, and its once thriving pepper plantations."

In nearby **Kep-sur-Mer**, once a seaside resort for French elites and, later, Cambodian high society, there are the husks of once grand Modernist villas to be explored, and the Crab Market. Be sure to order its signature dish, Kampot pepper crab. "With ingredients this fresh, simple preparation is all that's needed—garlic, fresh greens, sautéed peppercorns, and fresh river crab." There are a number of casual restaurants vending the dish; follow the crowd.

CRAB MARKET: Street 33A, Krong Kaeb, Tel +855 10 833 168. No website. Prices vary.

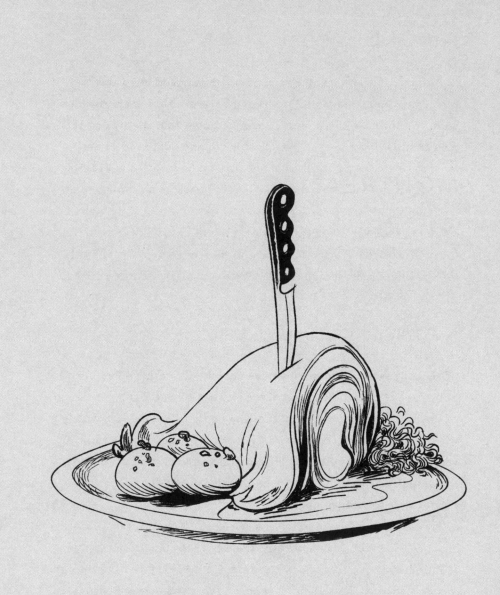

CANADA

MONTRÉAL & QUÉBEC

Montréal and the province of Québec held a special appeal for Tony, and he made episodes of *No Reservations*, *The Layover*, and *Parts Unknown* there, variations on themes of excess, and the ways in which Québec is neither Canada nor France, but something all its own.

"I will confess my partisanship up front: I love Montréal. It is my favorite place in Canada. The people who live there are tough, crazy bastards, and I admire them for it. Toronto, Vancouver, I love you. But not like Montréal. Why? I shall explain. All will be revealed.

"What should you know about Montréal? Well, that it's not little Paris, north of the border. You don't really have to speak French to come here. And you don't come here to eat French food, though there's plenty of it should you want. Food is, however, a major, major reason to come here."

ARRIVAL AND GETTING AROUND

You can drive to Montréal from any point in the continental US or Canada (with a passport), or take an Amtrak train from New York or VIA Rail Canada from various points, or you can fly.

"Montréal is close [by air]—about an hour and change from New York City. If you care, its exact location is on an island at the confluence of the Saint Lawrence and Ottawa Rivers. That's not so important to know. Montréal is located in southwest Québec, however. That is important to know. If you're flying, chances are you'll arrive at Trudeau International Airport (YUL), about twenty miles from the city center."

From the airport, a taxi to the city will take about thirty minutes and cost a flat fare of CA$40/US$30 plus tip. Société de Transport de Montréal operates a shuttle bus between the airport and the main bus terminal, Gare d'autocars de Montréal–Berri-UQAM métro station, that takes forty-five to sixty minutes and costs about CA$10 / US$7.50. For more information, visit www.stm.info/en.

Once you're in town, turn to the metro whenever you don't feel like walking or taking a metered taxi. **"The Montréal metro system is modeled, they say, on the Paris Métro. And it ain't bad. It runs about three dollars for a trip, or eight bucks for a twenty-four-hour pass. If you're driving, cool, just know that here, French would come in handy. The street signs are only in French. Directions can be tricky, too. And it's worth knowing as well that the speed limits are in kilometers per hour, not miles. So be aware of that little detail as well, okay?"**

TIME TO EAT

"I don't really know what Montréal is like for normal people. What I can tell you is that, for chefs, it's notoriously a very dangerous place." A small gang of Montréal chef-owners have been known to ply visiting chefs with impossibly rich foods and large quantities of wine and spirits. Among these quasidiabolical caretakers were chefs **Normand Laprise** of **Toqué!** and **Brasserie T!**, **Martin Picard** of **Au Pied du Cochon** and **Cabane à Sucre**, and **David McMillan** and **Frédéric Morin** of **Joe Beef**, **Liverpool House**, and **Le Vin Papillon**. Recently, however, McMillan and Morin have both quit drinking alcohol, substantially dialed back their excesses on all levels, and begun to publicly address substance abuse and other problems that have been historically inherent to the hospitality business.

Begin a day's eating in Montréal's Sud-Ouest neighborhood, specifically at **Brasserie Capri**. What is it?

"A pub, a Canadian pub—a Québecois pub, more accurately—and exactly, exactly what I like. Big hunks of freaking pork knuckle—this, you don't see much of elsewhere. This is a dying art: marinated and boiled pork knuckle, served with boiled potatoes."

Capri is unfussy, and presents more like a sports bar than a restaurant, with televised games, video poker machines, and plenty of patrons there strictly for the booze, but there's breakfast, lunch, and dinner available for those who seek it. (Note that the pub has changed locations since Tony shot there in 2012.)

BRASSERIE CAPRI: 2687 Wellington St, Montréal, QC H3K 1X8, Tel 514 935 0228 (pork knuckle entrée about CA$16/US$12; sandwiches about CA$13/US$10)

"Montréal is a chef town. It's a stay-up-late-and-have-a-good-time town. Food and drink, that's something they do well, and often to excess here, yet always with panache. Montréal's Little Burgundy neighborhood: once a divey, neglected part of town, but then came this, the magnificent Joe Beef—flagship restaurant of these two characters, Fred and Dave. The place's namesake was a quartermaster for the British during the Crimean War. His (some say) supernatural ability to scrounge meat for his men, even when the chips were down, made him a legend. His legendarily bawdy, shall we say, tavern, in Montréal, made him a larger-than-life figure in the history of Montréal's drinking class. It was only right, then, that these two continued the proud tradition while boldly forging some of their own. The menu is wonderful and unapologetically over the top at times. And it changes daily."

JOE BEEF: 2941 Notre-Dame West, Montréal QC H3J 1N6,
Tel 514 935 6504, www.joebeef.ca (appetizers about CA$15/US$12;
entrées about CA$40/US$30)

"Smoked meat. You can't not do this when you come to Montreal.
There's no way out. Gotta do it. And Schwartz's here, opened in
like, 1928, is not just Canada's oldest, but arguably the best at this
pastrami-like magical substance. So good that it's well worth pushing
yourself through the crowd, sitting down cheek by jowl with strangers, and eating one of these gloriously messy mountains of meat."

Some advice for travelers: "About to get on a plane? Eat something good before you go to the airport, something big and good
that's going to knock you on your ass."

With that tip in mind, in Schwartz's single white-tiled room, packed
with crowds, polish off a steaming smoked brisket sandwich with a
pickle on the side, washed down with a cherry soda. "I'll be uncon-
scious by takeoff. I can leave Montréal with a clean conscience now."

SCHWARTZ'S MONTRÉAL DELI: 3895 Boulevard Saint-Laurent,
Montréal, QC H2W 1X9, Tel 514 842 4813, www.schwartzsdeli.com
(smoked meat sandwich about CA$10.50/US$8)

"Once every few decades, maybe every century, a nation will
produce a hero—an Escoffier, a Muhammad Ali, a Dalai Lama, a Joey
Ramone—someone who changes everything about his chosen field,
who changes the whole landscape. Life after them is never the same.
Martin Picard is such a man. A heretofore unencountered hybrid of
rugged outdoorsman, veteran chef with many years of fine dining
experience, renegade, innovator. He is one of the most influential
chefs in North America. He is also a proud Québécois. And perhaps
he, more than anyone else, has defined, for a new generation of
Americans and Canadians, what that means.

"The tradition of the *cabane à sucre*, or sugar shack, is as old as maple syrup here in Québec, where 70 percent of the world's supply comes from. Deeply embedded in the maple syrup–outdoor lumberjack lifestyle is the cabin in the woods, where maple sap is collected and boiled down to syrup. Over time, many of these cabins became informal eating houses; dining halls for workers and a few guests. And Martin Picard has taken this tradition to what is somehow both its logical conclusion and insane extreme, creating his own Cabane à Sucre, serving food stemming directly from those humble-yet-hardy roots."

Guests lucky enough to secure a reservation, which tend to sell out very quickly each December, will enjoy a meal that can run to a dozen courses. "Let the madness begin: A whole lobe of foie gras with baked beans, on a pancake, cooked in duck fat, of course, cottage cheese, and an egg, cooked in maple syrup. Sautéed duck hearts, gizzards, and pig's ear, topped with a heaping pile of fried pork rinds.

Oh, and a calf brain and maple bacon omelet . . . panko-encrusted duck drumsticks with shrimp and salmon mousse, and maple barbecue sauce. Tourtiere du shack: a whole Laracam cheese, foie gras, calf brain, sweetbreads, bacon, and arugula. And now the main course: a homegrown, smoked-right-out-front, local ham, with pineapple and green beans almondine. And [a] practically prehistoric old-school Canadian classic: maple syrup is heated, then poured on snow, becoming a kind of taffy."

Cabane à Sucre was previously open only during maple syrup harvest season (late winter to early spring); it now also receives customers during apple harvest season (mid-August to mid November), and the new Cabane d'à Côté, which, as the name suggests, is "next door," feeds guests year-round.

AU PIED DU COCHON CABANE À SUCRE: 11382 Rang de
la Fresnière, St-Benoît de Mirabel J7N 2R9, Tel 514 281 1114,
www.aupieducochon.ca (12-course meal about CA$70/US$54)

TORONTO

"Toronto: largest city in Canada, fifth-largest in North America. 'Never been.' 'Just passed through.' 'Didn't make much of an impression.' Yeah, that's pretty much its reputation.

"It's not a good-looking city. Not a good-looking town. I mean, they sorta got the rest of the architectural fads of the twentieth century. Cryptofascist Bauhaus. Every public school in America. Every third-tier city library. Soviet chic. But Toronto's steel-box exterior conceals, in fact, a uniquely wonderful and weird interior."

ARRIVAL AND GETTING AROUND

The main international airport is **Lester B. Pearson International**, also known as **Toronto Pearson Airport** (**YYZ**). Its two terminals are served by dozens of major international and domestic airlines, chief among them Air Canada, and are connected by the 24/7 Link train.

As the airport is about fifteen miles northwest of Toronto's downtown, a metered taxi will take thirty to sixty minutes, depending on traffic, and will cost CA$50 to CA$75/US$40–$65 plus 15 percent tip, depending on your destination. There's a public bus to the city for CA$3.25/US$2.50 as of this writing, which takes over an hour, as well as Union Pearson Express, an airport-to-city train that's about CA$13/US$10 each way. Find all the ground transport info you need at www.torontopearson.com.

Toronto also has a small airport, **Billy Bishop Toronto City Airport** (**YTZ**), located on Centre Island, just south of downtown Toronto, and accessible by car or ferry. Porter Airlines provides the majority of the service in and out of YTZ, with flights to Newark; Boston; Washington, DC; Chicago; Myrtle Beach; Orlando; and a number of Canadian destinations.

Once you're in town, you can walk, take taxis, or avail yourself of Toronto's subway system. Schedules, routes and fares are at www.ttc.ca.

STAY IN HIGH STYLE

Though the Drake remains the center of cool boutique hotel culture in Toronto, there are also options to go way upscale. **"If you're traveling for work and want to stick your accounting department with unpaid bills for your swank accommodation, you should probably**

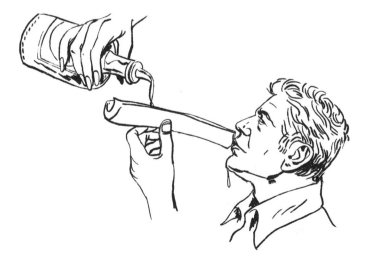

On the Origins of the Bone Luge

BY JEN AGG

Most people don't tell the truth. They mean to. They may even think they generally do, most of the time, but they don't. I mean, what even *is* the truth? A subjective notion about the correct way to live isn't the same as, say, hard science, like the earth's gravitational pull dictating that when things go up, they must, in fact, fall down.

As someone who unblinkingly believes in her ideas as being the *most correct*, I appreciate other truth tellers—even if we don't always agree—who will perhaps varnish some harsh truths, but who will always try to be honest.

Which is why I was bouncing off the walls in 2012, literally vibrating with excitement, when I heard that Anthony Bourdain would be shooting a segment for the Toronto episode of *The Layover* in my then-four-year-old restaurant, the Black Hoof. The Hoof was a special restaurant, deserving of the international attention it would soon receive, thanks in no small part to the Bourdain Effect, or, as I like to call it, "getting Tony'd."

Tony was famously a truth teller, and there is perhaps no greater truth about Toronto than how ugly the city is. It's really, really ugly, and he noticed. ("It's not a good-looking city.") I'm so glad he did; it always feels strange to me when well-traveled people don't mention its hideousness, as though if we all ignore the problem it will cease to be one, which is generally a terrible idea.

Aside from its one big con, Toronto has many pros. It's a city of neighborhoods; a city of many cultures (although we are not nearly as integrated as we like to pretend we are, especially to our American pals); a city that had to push so hard against its WASPy instincts that it had no choice but to grow into something much cooler than it ought to be. That's the city I grew up in; that's the pull of home for me: a city of possibilities where I've made many dreams come true.

I wanted to show Tony, through my restaurant, that Toronto wasn't New York, but maybe it was just as cool. I mean, we served *horse meat*. Name me a New York City restaurant that would dare.

The production crew came by a day ahead, to sort out the details and plan the hours-long shoot. They struck me as people who were not only good at their jobs, but also a smart, fun bunch—I liked them immediately. The director, Tom Vitale, had the final say on whatever intricacies were being worked through. He was very charming and polite, but he had one request I wasn't sure I could deal with.

Good documentary television exists in the tension between the creative mastermind with the singular vision, and the people behind the scenes making sure that the vision is executed into something eminently watchable. Sometimes you have to create story arcs, and make sure the viewer is invested in real-life events that are going to unfold as they're going to unfold. On one end of the spectrum are shows like *The Bachelor* or any of the Real Housewives series, and *The Layover* obviously had a fuck ton more integrity than those franchises, while being extremely watchable. However:

The camera operators planned their angles and shots for the next day, while Tom and I made small talk, into which he slipped, oh-so-casually, "I heard you guys do bone luges here." I had no idea what that was, so he clarified: After scraping and sopping up the last of the glistening marrow out of halved and roasted veal bones, you pick something like sherry or bourbon, and hold the narrow end of the bone to your mouth, as you would with a beer funnel, while a game pal pours the shot down through the wider end, and into your mouth.

I was skeptical, very skeptical. I feared appearing on a show I loved as, essentially, a shooter girl—a fear that turned out to be entirely warranted. I also worried that if we did this whole bone luge thing on the show, we'd be doing it for guests, forever and ever, in an *Edge of Tomorrow*–style loop. I wasn't wrong about that, either.

So I expressed a fair and reasonable amount of doubt. We'd never served anyone a bone luge before, I said. It wasn't, like, *our thing*. At *all*. But Tom was adamant, and so, on shoot day, I played along, if a bit unhappily, pouring bourbon down a still-warm marrow bone into Anthony Bourdain's mouth. I was incredibly uncomfortable, which is very rare for me. But I did it.

And then, once the episode aired, I had to do it again, and again, and again. I'd avoid it as much as possible, but people would often request me specifically, which did nothing to ease the feeling of being a shooter girl. (Not that there's anything wrong with being a shooter girl! I just didn't *personally* want to do that.) Sometimes

stay at the excellent Ritz-Carlton—comfortable beds and a good steak on-premises."** Add to that an in-house spa and saltwater pool, Frette bed linens, marble bathrooms, deep soaking tubs, and the kind of warm, attentive and polished service one would expect at such a joint.

RITZ-CARLTON TORONTO: 181 Wellington Street West, Toronto, ON M5V 3G7, Tel 416 585 2500, www.ritzcarlton.com (standard rooms start at about CA$725/US$550 per night)

DRINKS, PORKS & KNIVES

The cocktail hour is a civilized convention, befitting a civilized city like Toronto. **"Cocktail Bar in Little Italy [is] a perfect place for a predinner Negroni."** A stylish place, Cocktail Bar is owned by the repeople even requested the exact table that Tony used in the scene, which I didn't even try to accommodate, unless they were willing to wait a long time for it. And, people are funny; sometimes they would.

I watched the episode once, when it originally aired in 2012, and only recently watched it again. I was happy to be reminded that the only thing I said on camera was, "I feel like a shooter girl, and it's actually just a little humiliating." With the perspective of time, though, I have to agree with Tom's instinct to insert this bit of bone luge weirdness. It crystalized the segment, was such a huge hit, and, to be completely honest, we made a lot of money off supplemental bone luges. Tony never knew that it was a manufactured bit, and, frankly, it became such a part of Hoof lore that it doesn't matter. Time really is a flat circle.

nowned restaurateur and author Jen Agg, who chose to close her flagship restaurant, **Black Hoof**, on a high note, after a decade of indelible influence on the Toronto restaurant scene (see Agg's essay, "On the Origins of the Bone Luge," page 52). Fortunately, Cocktail Bar remains very much in business (along with her restaurants **Grey Gardens** and **Le Swan French Diner**, and the bars **Rhum Corner** and **Bar Vendetta**, which occupies the old Black Hoof space), purveying thoughtfully conceived and executed drinks like the Whiskey Business (bourbon, rye, Irish whiskey, scotch, fig liqueur, and bitters) and the Absinthe Whip, flavored with orange, pistachio, and coconut. "We also have a nice wine and beer list," Agg advises via the website, "but you should probably have a cocktail."

COCKTAIL BAR: 923 Dundas Street West, Toronto, ON M6J 1W3, Tel 416 792-7511, www.hoofcocktailbar.com (cocktails average CA$14/US$10.50)

And then, for after-dinner drinking, there's **Cold Tea**. **"Cold Tea is an excellent example of a refined and wonderful bar, discreetly tucked away from the herd. Enter through an unmarked door, pass by the ladies selling authentic dim sum, continue on your way to fine beverages."** Tucked into the Kensington Mall, with a welcoming patio and a rotating roster of local chefs creating snack-food pop-ups to sate hungry drinkers, Cold Tea takes its name from the clandestine practice—said to have originated in Toronto's Chinese restaurants—of serving beer in a teapot to late-night guests whose thirst extends beyond last call (currently 2:00 a.m.).

COLD TEA: 60 Kensington Avenue, Toronto, ON M5T 2K2, Tel 416 546 4536, www.instagram.com/coldteabar (draft beers CA$9/US$6.75; cocktails average CA$14/US$10.50; snacks average CA$10/US$7.50)

Tony accompanied the Toronto food and business writer David Sax to the historic Saint Lawrence Market, where some two hundred vendors sell produce, meats, seafood, baked goods, dry goods, and more. The pair were in single-minded pursuit of **"the original old-school Torontonian sandwich—the classic peameal bacon sandwich at the Carousel Bakery. Accept no substitutes."** In a time before widespread refrigeration, Toronto hog butchers would wet-cure lean boneless pork loin to make back bacon, then coat it in ground yellow peas (which at some point were traded in for the cornmeal of today). Griddled and served on a kaiser bun, with horseradish and maple-spiked mustard, it's **"tasty and crispy."** Chase it with a Canadian classic dessert, the butter tart. **"It's like a pecan pie without the pecan."**

CAROUSEL BAKERY: Saint Lawrence Market, 93 Front Street East, Toronto, ON M5E 1C3, Tel 416 363 4247, www.stlawrencemarket.com (peameal bacon sandwich CA$6.50/US$5; tarts CA$1.50/US$1.15)

Another day, another pork sandwich. At **Porchetta & Co.**, in Little Italy, the signature sandwich was for a time the only item on offer (the company has since expanded its menu to include fried chicken, a pastrami banh mi, arancini, and a range of sides, including poutine).

"It's not a traditional porchetta in the sense of [being made from] a whole pig," the restaurant's owner, Nick Auf Der Mauer, told Tony. "It's a marinated pork shoulder butt that's wrapped in prosciutto . . . we wrap that in cured pork belly with the skin on." The cracklings are then removed and roasted to maximum crispiness, then piled atop the main event, on a toasted roll. The end result is **"juicy and delicious"**—in other words, **"kinda genius."**

PORCHETTA & CO.: 545 King Street West, Toronto, ON M5V 1M1, Tel 647 351 8844, www.porchettaco.com (sandwiches about CA$10/US$7.50)

Tosho Knife Arts is, according to Tony, **"an awesome shop, unlike any other; the kind of Toronto hidden gem that's there for the taking, if you know where to look. Owners Ivan Fonseca and Olivia Go know everything there is to know about knives."** The shop is stocked mainly with super high-quality cooking, utility, and tactical knives from Japan, each with its own purpose. The staff can point you to different knives for octopus, noodles, breaking down a chicken, cutting through a lobster shell, and a knife with a blood drain hole, to avoid a suction delay when removing one's blade from a victim. They also offer sharpening accessories, services, and classes.

TOSHO KNIFE ARTS: 934 Bathurst Street, Toronto ON M5R 3G5, Tel 647 722 6329, www.toshoknifearts.com (knives range from CA$100 to many thousands)

VANCOUVER

"What makes one city better than another? What makes a city . . . cool? Size? Location? Infrastructure? Natural resources?

"I came here first on book tour, and liked it immediately.

"Sure, it rains all the time. And there's no shortage of vegetarians. And they have a public beach filled with albino nudists. Yet it recently ranked the most livable city in the world. It's a restaurant town. It's a foodie town. It's a chef town. It's a multicultural city. A proverbial melting pot . . . So, how about this cool thing? Where do we track that down?"

ARRIVAL, AND GETTING AROUND TOWN

Vancouver International Airport (YVR) receives flights from all over British Columbia and the rest of Canada, the United States, and Mexico, along with a handful of cities in Europe and Asia. To get from the airport to the city, visitors can take the Canada Line Skytrain, originally built to handle the onslaught of visitors to the 2010 Winter Olympics, to downtown Vancouver, for CA$7.75 to $9/US$6–$7, de-

pending on your final destination and time of day. It's a twenty-five-minute ride; purchase tickets from the machines on the platform.

The airport is a nine-mile drive from downtown Vancouver, which can take anywhere from twenty to forty-five minutes in a taxi, hotel shuttle, or rented car, depending on traffic. Taxis charge a flat rate depending on your destination; expect to pay about CA$40/about US$30.50, including tip.

Pacific Central Station is Vancouver's train and bus terminal, servicing Canadian VIA Rail and Amtrak passengers, along with Greyhound and a host of other bus companies. The Rocky Mountaineer is a private tourist train line with its own eponymous station, and connections to Seattle and Canadian points north and east.

Get around town on foot, on a bike, via car or taxi, or use Vancouver's extensive public transit system, composed of three SkyTrain lines connecting the city to the suburbs, buses, commuter trains, and ferries. All the public transit info you need is at www.translink.ca.

EATING IN "CHEF TOWN"

"It probably helped that the first three people I met were three chefs: Pino [Posteraro], [Hidekazu] Tojo, and Vikram [Vij]. Three completely different chefs, making completely different food, but all three typical of the kind of diversity emblematic of Vancouver.

"Pino is the chef of Cioppino's Mediterranean Grill, which serves, unsurprisingly, modern Italian food with largely local ingredients. Pino was a pioneer in this neighborhood [Yaletown]. And he did it through grit, determination, and liberal use of child labor, apparently." (Pino's son, an adolescent at the time of Tony's last visit, could often be spotted working in the kitchen.) More than a decade on, Pino and his team continue to deliver an excellent experience.

CIOPPINO'S MEDITERRANEAN GRILL AND ENOTECA:

1133 Hamilton Street, Vancouver BC V6P 5P6, Tel 604 688 7466, www.cioppinosyaletown.com (appetizers CA$16–24/US$12–$18; pastas CA$30–$40/US$23–$31; entrées CA$38–$48/US$29–$37)

Like Pino, Tojo has also been an unusually steady presence in the dynamic Vancouver restaurant scene; his eponymous restaurant celebrated its thirtieth anniversary in 2018. Tojo is credited with introducing *omakase*-style Japanese dining to Vancouver, and local legend maintains that it was he who invented the now-ubiquitous California roll, as a gateway drug to his earliest Western guests, some of whom were uncomfortable with raw seafood wrapped in seaweed.

"Tojo, unlike a lot of transplanted Japanese chefs, relies heavily on what is available locally, rather than getting everything flown in from Tokyo. He celebrates Vancouver's rather extraordinary bounty of fresh seafood, and adapts his daily menu possibilities to that. More traditionally, he gets to know his customers personally, remembering their likes and dislikes, and building their meals around that knowledge."

Treat yourself to fatty bluefin tuna, uni, a tempura-fried zucchini blossom stuffed with a fresh scallop, and a Dungeness crab salad with mustard-miso dressing.

TOJO'S: 1133 West Broadway, Vancouver BC V6H 1G1, Tel 604 872 8050, www.tojos.com (entrées CA$28–$45/US$21–$35; *omakase* menus start at CA$80/US$61 per person for six courses)

And, rounding out the trio, **Vikram Vij** is also a Vancouver pioneer and mainstay, having been creating phenomenal Indian dishes with his business partner and ex-wife, Meeru Dhalwala, since 1994. **"Vikram is a strange and wonderful mix of idealistic hippie and smart businessman, and [Vij's is] the best, most modern and creative Indian restaurant in town."** In recent years, Vij has moved his eponymous flagship to a new location, expanded his second spot, Rangoli, into the former Vij's space, scaled up his line of frozen foods to national-grocer-freezer-case levels, written a memoir, and opened two new restaurants, My Shanti and Vij's Sutra.

VIJ'S: 3106 Cambie Street, Vancouver, BC V5Z 2W2, Tel 604 736 6664, www.vijs.ca (appetizers about CA$16/US$12; entrées about CA$30/US$23)

"But what about Vancouver's street food? An indigenous, mutant form of wiener, perhaps? Japadog is one such place. Seaweed sprinkles, daikon radish, and wasabi mayonnaise—the reason for Japadog's name is crudely obvious, yet gratifying.

"If life has taught us anything, [it's that] mystery meat in a tube form—mark of quality. Locals stacked up to eat it. Recognize these signs. Japadog is increasingly where the elite meet to eat."

What was once limited to a single outdoor hot dog stand is now a veritable minichain, with six metro Vancouver locations, a roving truck, and two stands in Los Angeles, vending dogs with about two dozen combinations of Japanese condiments and seasonings (such as the Terimayo, a beef frank with teriyaki sauce, fried onions, and Kewpie mayonnaise; the Negimiso dog, a turkey frank topped with miso sauce and shredded cabbage; and the Yakisoba, an arabiki sausage topped with griddled noodles). Some locations also offer french fries, seasoned with the likes of Japanese pickled plum (*ume*), butter, soy sauce, and dried ground seaweed.

JAPADOG (original location): 899 Burrard Street, Vancouver BC V6Z 2K7, Tel 604 322 6465, www.japadog.com (hot dogs CA$6–$9/US$4.50–$7)

CHINA

HONG KONG

"China, but not China, a thing all its own. Basically, if you can't enjoy Hong Kong for a few hours or days, there's no hope for you."

Tony visited Hong Kong three times: first, as a relative travel novice, for *No Reservations*: he cheered on the horses at Happy Valley Racecourse, witnessed the dying art of bamboo noodle making, and was rendered airborne and nimble in the hands (and extensive riggings) of Jackie Chan's personal stunt team. A few years later, he returned, cranky and sweaty, for *The Layover*, using his forty-eight hours to have a custom suit made, ride the Star Ferry, buy a cleaver, and eat roast goose and dim sum. And on his third visit, for *Parts Unknown*, he fulfilled a dream of spending long shooting days and nights with a personal hero of cinematography:

"All of us, when we travel, look at the places we go, the things we see, through different eyes. And how we see them is shaped by our previous lives, the books we've read, the films we've seen, the baggage we carry.

"Years ago, when I first watched the stunningly beautiful films of director Wong Kar-wai, it shaped forever the way I see Hong Kong. From that point on, my hopes, my expectations of this city, would be seen through that lens, a lens that was, in nearly every case, pointed by, focused by, this man: Christopher Doyle, longtime resident of Hong Kong, known by his Mandarin name, 'Du Ke Feng.' His

earlier works with Wong Kar-wai were distinguished by unspeakably gorgeous images of beautiful people moving through spaces both unfamiliar and yet painfully intimate; alternately jagged, frenzied, innovative, languid, composed, chaotic. I obsessed over his work. Fetishized it. Longed to see Hong Kong like the characters in so many of his films longed for each other. And I feared, like those characters, I would be denied. I was wrong."

ARRIVAL AND GETTING AROUND

Hong Kong International Airport (HKG), on Chek Lap Kok Island, is, as Tony said in *The Layover*, "the front porch to mainland China and the rest of Asia . . . a major stopover, a frequent layover." One of the world's busiest airports by volume of passengers, it is the home base of Cathay Pacific. British Airways, Virgin Atlantic, Singapore Airlines, Korean Air, and dozens more major carriers also land flights there every day.

To get to the city from the airport, you can take a taxi, or a shuttle or van prearranged by your hotel. For an approximately US$200 fee, the Peninsula Hotel will send a driver meet guests at their gate with a motorized cart, escort them through baggage and customs into the special limousine parking area, and drive them to the hotel in a Rolls-Royce Ghost equipped with Wi-Fi, bottled water, and a cool towel for your face. You can also take the Hong Kong Airport Express, a train that will get you to Central Hong Kong in about twenty-five minutes, for about HK$115/US$15.

Hong Kong's Mass Transit Railway (MTR) has ten lines that reliably shuttle you around and across the city, comfortably and safely, with directions and announcements in English, Cantonese, and Mandarin.

"The way they talk about their subway system around here, you'd think they were getting paid every time they mentioned it. It is

clean, easy to navigate, and gets you to over sixty destinations easily and comfortably." Buy tickets and consult maps in the stations.

Taxis are also readily available in Hong Kong, though traffic can be intense (and fares expensive). Uber operates in both Kowloon and Central, and to get between them, a ride across the harbor on the Star Ferry is romantic, efficient, and cheap—about HK$3/US$0.40 in either direction.

As of this writing, Hong Kong is experiencing political upheaval and sustained protests that have occasionally disrupted airport service and mass transit; keep an eye on news reports and consult your country's embassy before planning travel.

ROAST MEAT, NOODLES, DRUNKEN CHICKEN, ELBOWS, FISH TRIPE, SPICY CRAB, AND THE NEW OLD WAY: HONG KONG

"I'm constantly asked, 'What's the greatest food city in the world?' And I always say that no one can say you're wrong if you say Hong Kong."

Once you touch down in Hong Kong, make a beeline to the tiny, packed **Joy Hing's Roasted Meat,** a Cantonese *char siu* (barbecue) joint that's more than a century old. Or, for another *char siu* option, have lunch at **Kam's Roast Goose,** which has a reputation for perfect goose and pork, and is the holder of a Michelin star to boot.

"Yeah, I like pork, and I know I talk about it a lot and how it's wonderful and how it's, like, the best thing ever. But in fact, in fact, the best thing ever is actually goose."

JOY HING'S ROASTED MEAT: Chong Hing Building, 265–267 Hennessy Road, Chai Hu, Hong Kong, Tel +852 2519 6639, www.joyhing.com (typical goose or pork portion over rice about HK$47/US$6)

KAM'S ROAST GOOSE: 226 Hennessy Road, Wan Chai, Hong Kong, Tel +852 2520 1110, www.krg.com.hk (roast goose over rice about HK$53/US$7)

"The love of money and shiny new things is slowly but surely erasing the past. So, before it's gone, this is a reminder. This is the way Hong Kong used to eat: at *dai pai dong*s. Cheap, delicious food served from open-air stalls. Pull up a plastic stool, crack a beer, fire up the wok."

As chef Gazza Cheng explained to Tony on *Parts Unknown*, the name *dai pai dong* means "big license place." And, as the aforementioned love of shiny new things continues apace, there were, in 2018, only twenty-eight remaining licensed *dai pai dong*s in the whole of the city, one of them being Gazza Cheng's own **Keung Kee**. Try the drunken chicken: "hacked-up birds, cooked in hot pot with medicinal roots and herbs that will no doubt make me strong." Follow that with fish tripe in egg custard, topped with *youtiao*, a kind of crisp fried Chinese breadstick.

At another *dai pai dong*, called **Sing Heung Yuen**, the menu is heavy with a specific type of comfort food: elbow macaroni in tomato soup, topped with fried eggs and spam; thick white toast, buttered and drizzled with honey; and a milky caffeinated beverage known as Hong Kong milk tea or, locally, "silk stocking tea," so named for the look of the elongated filter used in its making, and for the color of the drink itself.

KEUNG KEE: Shop 4, Yiu Tung Street, Sham Shui Po, Hong Kong, Tel +852 2776 2712 (typical meal HK$20–$40/US$2.50–$5)

SING HEUNG YUEN: 2 Mee Lun Street, Central, Hong Kong, Tel +852 2544 8368 (typical meal HK$20–$40/US$2.50–$5)

"At first, Hong Kong is an utterly foreign world, a shock to the system. Am I lost? Not exactly. I find myself wandering Temple

Street, known for its night markets and street food, grit and gristle. It's an instinctive move."

The Temple Street Night Market is the last of its kind in the city, a collection of clothing and souvenir vendors, street entertainers and, on Woo Sung Street and Temple Street, north of the temple complex for which it is named, plenty of vendors serving noodles, seafood, soups, roasted and grilled meats, cold beer, and sweets to patrons crowded around small plastic tables on stools and folding chairs.

TEMPLE STREET NIGHT MARKET: Temple Street, Jordan, Hong Kong, www.temple-street-night-market.hk (prices vary)

Atop the Java Road wet market, in the North Point neighborhood, you'll find **Tung Po**, a raucous, sprawling Cantonese seafood joint.

"It is awesomeness itself, I tell you from personal experience. Eat everything, but do not miss the black squid ink pasta—amazing. And do make a reservation. This place is busy, and busy for a reason."

TUNG PO SEAFOOD AT JAVA ROAD MARKET: 2nd floor, Java Road Municipal Services Building, 99 Java Road, North Point, Hong Kong, Tel +852 2880 5224 (dishes HK$88–$233/US$11–$33)

"Lau Sum Kee is run by the third generation of a family who still prepare their wontons from scratch, and make their bamboo noodles the painfully labor-intensive, time-consuming old-school way. Lau Sum Kee is one of the last operations in Hong Kong to do this. It commands respect, and believe me, it results in the perfect noodle."

Lau Sum Kee's *jook sing* noodles are made of wheat flour, duck and chicken eggs, and oil. The proprietor, Lau Fat-cheong, who runs the business with his brothers, mixes the dough and kneads it by sitting on one end of a large bamboo pole, applying just the right amount of pressure so that the noodles and wonton wrappers are compact and springy, a physically difficult, at times even punishing process. At the shop, the wontons are stuffed with pork and a whole shrimp, and the noodles are tossed with shrimp roe.

LAU SUM KEE: 48 Kweilin Street, Sham Shui Po, Hong Kong, Tel +852 2386 3533 (noodles and wontons HK$30–$50/US$3.50–$6.50)

"Chef-owner May Chow is the creative force behind Happy Paradise, a restaurant and bar serving traditional Cantonese dishes made with modern cooking techniques. Sautéed prawns with pan-roasted pumpkin, dried shrimp roe, and prawn oil; tea-smoked pigeon, served medium rare, sea salt on the side; Hakka-style chicken, poached in Shaoxing wine with oyster mushroom fried rice and shiitake broth; pig brain with burnt pear vinaigrette—all of it truly, stunningly delicious."

On *Parts Unknown*, Chow sat down with Tony in **Happy Paradise**'s hypermodern, neon-accented dining room. "How do I be modern, but not lose the soul of it?" she asked. "Those are dishes that I feel even Hong Kong people don't do so much anymore, because it's such an old-fashioned dish, so we want to make it cool again."

HAPPY PARADISE: 52–56 Staunton Street, Central, Hong Kong, Tel +852 2816 2118, www.happyparadise.hk (dishes HK$78–$220/US$10–$28)

SHANGHAI

Tony made two trips to Shanghai: in 2007 for *No Reservations*, and again in 2015 for *Parts Unknown*. He was astonished by the pace of change that had manifested between those two visits.

"Shanghai: an exploding economic superpower, where buildings go up as old ones go under, where the history gives way to what appears to be an inevitable future as capital of the world.

"If you live in Manhattan, as I do, and you think you live in the center of the world, Shanghai will confront you with a very different reality. Turn down a side street—it's an ancient culture. The centuries-old mix of culinary traditions, smells, flavors. A block away, this: an ultramodern, ever-clanging cash register, levels of wealth, of luxury, the sheer volume of things and services unimagined by the greediest, most bourgeois of capitalist imperialists."

Shanghai is a city of twenty-five million people, cleaved into two sections, old and new, by the Huangpu River, itself a tributary of the Yangtze. The old section, west of the river, includes the Bund, whose dozens of historic buildings along the waterfront once housed Western-owned banks, trading houses, publishing concerns, and consulates, along with Chinese banks and government headquarters. The eastern side includes the newer, built-up and most populous section, Pudong, which means "East Bank," and is home to Shanghai's World Financial Center and a number of skyscrapers that make up the city's iconic waterfront skyline.

ARRIVAL AND GETTING AROUND

Shanghai has two major airports: **Pudong (PVG)**, which mostly serves international flights, and **Hongqiao (SHA)**, with a few international flights and a number of regional and domestic routes.

PVG, a hub for China Eastern Airlines, is the busiest international airport in China. To make the nineteen-mile journey from PVG to the center of Shanghai, you can take the Shanghai Metro, one of several bus routes, a high-speed train, or a metered taxi, which should take about forty minutes and cost 170–240 Chinese yuan/US$24–$34, depending on your destination. Taxi drivers do not expect tips, but rounding up the fare to avoid asking for change is appreciated. For ground transportation details, see www.shanghai-airport.com.

Essential Shanghai Dishes, According to "China Matt"

For his visits to mainland China, Hong Kong, and other selected parts of Asia, Tony was accompanied and guided by **Matt Walsh**, an American journalist who has been living in Hong Kong for two decades, and whom Tony and his crew called, affectionately, "China Matt."

"It's worth noting that many Shanghai restaurants have several dishes that are Sichuanese in origin," said Walsh. "Shanghai is at the other end of the Yangtze from Sichuan, and several classic dishes came down the river, were adopted by the local cuisine, and toned down for local tastes. *Ma po dou fu, gan bian si ji dou* (dry fried string beans), and *kou shui ji*' 'mouthwatering chicken'—are among such dishes."

Walsh shared what he calls "an incomplete short list of other important Shanghai dishes":

SHIZI TOU: "Lion's head meatballs," made of pork and seasoned with ginger, scallions, sesame, soy, and sugar.

XUE CAI MAO DOU BAI YE: Tofu "leaves" (actually sheets), with young green soybeans and "snow vegetable," or finely chopped pickled mustard greens.

XUN YU: The name translates as "smoked fish," but it's actually deep-fried and served glazed, at room temperature, as an appetizer.

SHENGJIAN BAO: Panfried yeast dough dumplings filled with seasoned pork, lightly seared in a pan and then steamed to finish cooking.

DONGPO ROU: Pork belly braised in soy sauce, rice wine, and stock, with sugar, ginger, garlic, scallions, and star anise; it's a dish that is more closely associated with nearby Hangzhou.

LONGJING XIAREN: River shrimp, stir-fried with longjing tea leaves. This is also a Hangzhou dish, but it's prepared broadly within the region.

HAIRY CRAB: Also known as Chinese mitten crab, for the brown fur on its claws, hairy crab is a burrowing river crab that emerges (and is hunted by hungry humans) in the ninth and tenth months of the lunar year, typically between September and November. It's prized for its sweet flesh and golden roe, and is traditionally served steamed with a simple sauce of vinegar and ginger.

The most famous source of "the best" hairy crabs is Yangcheng Lake, outside Shanghai. Yangcheng Lake hairy crabs are highly regulated to prevent counterfeiting; however, if crabs raised elsewhere are plopped into Yangcheng Lake for a short dip, they can then legally be called "authentic" in origin. Go figure.

XIAO LONG BAO: The little soup dumplings, of course. I recall Tony referring to them as "the world's most perfect food."

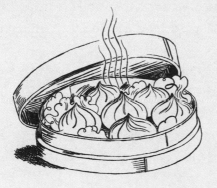

If you're arriving in Shanghai from another part of China, you may be routed to **Hongqiao,** also a China Eastern hub. It's located about eight miles from the city center, which you can reach via metro, bus, or metered taxi, the later of which takes about thirty minutes, with an average fare about 100 yuan/US$15. See www.shanghai-hongqiao -airport.com for ground transportation details.

The city itself has excellent and extensive public transportation, including over a thousand bus lines operated by a number of compa-nies, a thirteen-line subway system (with more lines in development), and metered taxis. The official website of the city's transit system is www.service.shmetro.com, but from the United States, you'll have better luck loading a commercial site like www.chinatravelguide.com.

EATING IN SHANGHAI

"What is classic Shanghainese food? What's distinctive about it? It's often black, or dark, and heavily inflected with oil, soy, and sugar. Shanghai is, and has been for some time, a city of immigrants. And the food reflects that genealogy: a combination of people from neighboring Zhejiang Province, known for their liberal use of sugar, soy, and vinegar; and from Jiangsu Province, known for fresh ingre-dients and attention to preserving the aliveness of its dishes. It's the best of both worlds: great sauces, great ingredients."

For soup dumplings, or *xiao long bao*, it's hard to do better than **Fu Chun Xiaolong**.

"*Xiao long bao*: literally, 'small steaming basket buns,' but I translate them in my head as 'pillows of happiness that will scald your tongue and throat if you don't know what you're doing.' Look, there are a lot of reasons to come to China, and to Shanghai in par-ticular, but these babies, done right? These things alone are worth the trip.

"The wonder that is the soup dumpling requires an unearthly, or at least physically unlikely, suspension of boiling-hot broth and savory meat in a near paper-thin, immaculately crafted envelope of dough.

"How is it done? Basically, a gelatin-rich broth is made with pork stock. It's chilled into a solid, and worked in with the filling. Upon steaming, it melts into a delightfully mouth-searing ambrosia. Dangerous, impossible, and unspeakably delicious."

FU CHUN XIAOLONG: 650 Yuyuan Road, Jing'an District, Shanghai Shi, 200000, Tel +86 21 6252 5117 (6 pork *xiao long bao*, 12 yuan/ about US$1.70; full meal 85–110 yuan/US$12–$15)

"Maybe the number one thing that the seriously food-crazed traveler coming back from Shanghai will tell you to eat, other than the soup dumplings of course, is *zi ran pai gu*, or simply, cumin ribs." The place to go is **Di Shui Dong.**

"It takes two cooks working at once to make this dish. One deep-fries the ribs in hot oil until just right; another toasts the ginger, cumin, and other spices in a wok, and then in go the ribs. And if you're a devotee of what's called *wok hei*, you sit as close to the kitchen as possible to capture that elusive, fast-dissipating breath, the flavor of the wok itself."

DI SHUI DONG: 56 Maoming South Road, 2nd floor, Huaihai Road District, Shanghai, Tel +86 21 6253 2689 (cumin ribs about 60 yuan/ US$8.25)

SICHUAN PROVINCE

"You know what I like? I like Sichuan Province, located in the southwest of China, over a thousand miles from Beijing. A region so fertile and lush that it's been referred to as China's breadbasket.

"It's the spicy, sensualist heartland of all the things I love about China. Man, I love the food here. The collision between very, very old and very new. An exploding middle class. A lot of history. And food that can burn you down to a charred, smoking little stump."

About once a year, Tony brought his friend Eric Ripert, chef of New York's three-Michelin-star-holding Le Bernardin, along on a TV shoot. Somewhere along the line, an aspect of playful torture became baked in to the dynamic of these episodes, which was never more apparent than when the duo ate their way around the region, in 2016, for *Parts Unknown*.

"I figured if I'm going back to Sichuan, I should bring a friend. Someone unused to the—how shall I say—level of heat commonly found in the food here. Someone who's never been to China before, and is unused to its ways. I'm talking, of course, about Eric."

In preparing Ripert for the days to come, Tony cautioned his increasingly concerned friend, "Drinking culture is very important here, and if we go to a formal meal, your ability to drink leads to a number of assumptions about you. You know? Your general manliness. Penis size. Your worth as a human being."

ARRIVAL

Shuangliu International Airport (CTU) services Chengdu, Sichuan Province's capital city. CTU is a hub for Air China and Sichuan and Chengdu Airlines, and has direct flights from many cities in China and throughout Asia, as well as direct flights from Chicago, Los Angeles, New York, San Francisco, and Vancouver, a handful of major European cities, and various cities in Australia. It's about ten miles from the airport to the center of Chengdu; upon arrival, you'll have the option to take a metered taxi for 60–80 Chinese yuan/US$9–$11, one of three city buses, or a high-speed train that each cost about 11 yuan/US$1.50 per one-way trip. Train and subway information can be found at www.chengdurail.com, and the easiest way to access bus information is at www.chinatravelguide.com.

EATING IN CHENGDU

"Here's something they talk about a lot in Sichuan when discussing food: two elements of flavor, personified by two ingredients that are integral to so much of the cooking around here. The Sichuan peppercorn, known for its flowery, aromatic flavor and its tingly, mind-arranging, mouth-numbing effects. A phenomenon called *ma*. And the spicy chili peppers like *erjingtiao*, or the even hotter Facing Heaven Chili, provide the *la*, pure heat. So, if you imagine, like, Ilsa, She-Wolf of the SS, tormenting you with nipple clamps as the *la*, the *ma*, provided by the pleasantly deranging peppercorns, would be like the naughty nurse with the ice cubes.

"Noodles, that's where you should start around here. Chengdu is famous for little spots like this—**Xiao Ming Tang Dan Dan Tian Shui Mian**, named after a much-beloved Chengdu noodle snack."

Acclimate your palate with a visit to one outpost of this Chengdu minichain, where you can sample the signature *dan dan mian*, wheat noodles tossed by the diner in a complex blend of chili oil, seasoned ground pork, and a savory sauce that balances sweetness, acidity, bitterness, saltiness, and spice.

XIAO MING TANG DAN DAN TIAN SHUI MIAN: 1 Jiangjun Street, Luo MaShi, Quingyang Qu, Chengdu Shi (no phone, no website) (*dan dan* noodles about 10 yuan/US$1.40)

At **Tian Tian Fan Dian**, give yourself the chance to warm up to the chewy goodness of spicy pickled chicken feet. **"*Lao zhi chi* literally means 'spicy chicken,' but the dish, in practical terms, is a game of finding the bits of chicken in the mountain of ass-burning goodness. C'mon, it's fun for the whole family! 'Is that a tiny nubbin of hacked chicken? Or a nuclear cluster of chili seeds?'**

"For me, the apex of Sichuan food, my absolute favorite, improbably enough, is a tofu dish. The legendary *mapo dofu*, or, 'pockmark granny tofu': ground pork or beef, cubes of bean curd, in a rich, deeply nuanced, fiery but intensely satisfying sauce of chili oil, bean paste, garlic shoots, ground Sichuan peppercorns, and MSG. This dish, done right, has got it all. Oh, that's so good. It's a perfect balance of stuff going on in here. I just love, love, love this dish."

TIAN TIAN FAN DIAN: Yu E Street, Wuhou Qu, Chengdu Shi, Tel +86 28 8557 4180 (typical plates 12–40 yuan/US$2.50–$5.75)

In the Sichuan region, one dish is almost universally enjoyed, a lunch or dinner that a family or group of friends might gather around once a week or more: Sichuan hot pot.

"Look deep. Deep into the murky depths of that most glorious and iconic of Sichuan dishes. It burns. It burns you down to your soul.

"The way it works is, you order a whole bunch of ingredients— meat, vegetables, noodles, fish—whatever you like, a lot of different ingredients, and you feed them into the pot. The inner ring is a more neutral broth. The outer ring, though, is the good stuff. The hard stuff.

"Common ingredients like tofu and seaweed, various meats and fishes, are stirred in, along with ingredients that are, shall we say, less familiar to the Western palate. As it cooks down it gets stronger and stronger, and the heat more intense—a delicious yet unpredictable silt of spice gathering at the bottom of this river of hot lava."

CHONGQING LIANGLUKOU HUO GUO: Gao Xin Qu Zizhu Bei Jie 2 Hao, Chengdu Shi, Tel +86 2885561337, www.cdliangkuo.com (hot pot about 80 yuan/US$12 per person)

CROATIA

Tony was an avid reader, often consuming the history and literature of a place before visiting, so as to better understand the people he was about to meet, and to put in context the things he'd see and hear. For the Croatia episode of *No Reservations*, he read Rebecca West's *Black Lamb and Grey Falcon*, a two-volume book that details her six-week expedition, undertaken in 1937, through the Balkan states, published on the eve of Germany's invasion of Yugoslavia.

The rest he'd gleaned from **"twenty-four-hour cable news, [about] a war that took place nearly two decades ago,"** referring to the Balkan or Yugoslav wars that broke up the former Yugoslav state and resulted in the deaths of at least 100,000 people between 1990 and 2001.

"I didn't have any idea what Croatian cuisine was, zero. I had no picture in my mind. I knew vaguely that it had been part of Rome or part of the Venetian empire way back; that it was pretty. But that was about it.

"You know, I'll tell you honestly: if you like food and you haven't come here to eat, you're really missing the fucking boat. This is world-class food; this is world-class wine; this is world-class cheese. The next big thing is Croatia. If you haven't been here, you're a fucking idiot. I'm an idiot."

Though the Dalmatian coast, in the southern part of the country, is justifiably a magnet for those seeking a Mediterranean dream vacation away from the hordes in more well-traveled areas of Europe, Tony's visit focused on the northern and central coastal areas and islands, areas even more luxuriously underpopulated.

ARRIVAL AND GETTING AROUND

Zagreb's **Franjo Tudman Airport (ZAG)** is the country's largest and busiest airport, located in the north central region of the country, and about a three-hour drive from Rovinj, where Tony began exploring various Croatian coastal locations for *No Reservations*. It is primarily served by Croatia Airlines, along with flights to and from European and Middle Eastern cities on British Airways, Qatar Airways, Air Serbia, KLM Royal Dutch Airlines, Air France, and others.

From the airport, a metered taxi to Zagreb city center is about 150 kuna, or about US$25, for a fifteen- to twenty-five-minute drive. Tips are not customary, but wages are low throughout the country, and a small tip of 5–10 percent would be appreciated. There is a shuttle bus between the airport to the Zagreb bus station, for 30 kuna/ about US$4.50; see www.plesoprijevoz.hr/en for details.

If you're planning to spend time in the city of Zagreb, a beautiful, historic, and easily navigable city, you can traverse it on foot, or take advantage of the bus and tram system (see www.zet.hr/en for routes, schedules, and fares, which range from 4 to 15 kuna/US$0.60–$2.25, depending on time of day and duration of ride.

Rijeka is considered the gateway to the country's islands. Though you can get there from Zagreb via Croatian Railways, a trip that will take about four hours and cost about 111 kuna/US$17, if you want to explore the coast, you're going to need to rent a car once you get there.

Note that Croatia is not part of the European Union; some hotels and restaurants may accept euros, but they are not legally compelled to do so.

COASTAL LOOKOUT

On the hilly, rocky, and forested coastal island of Pag, situated in the Adriatic Sea, you'll find a hotel that's a perfect microcosm of Croatian hospitality. **"This place, Hotel Boskinac, tucked away on a hill looking out over all this, well, it's an amazing, crazy-ass spot, [with] one of the best restaurants in the country."**

It's an intimate place, with just eleven rooms and suites. There's a winery on site, and olive groves and cheese-making facilities nearby. Chef and winemaker Boris Suljic serves dishes such as octopus stewed in a clay pot with tomatoes, garlic, potatoes, and white wine; lamb tripe, **"simmered with shallots, pancetta, and carrot until mellow and tender,"** hand-rolled pasta with braised lamb, a frittata made with dried octopus, and local cheeses.

"You know, if you like Italian food, you are already 90 percent of the way toward really digging the food here. And by the time we get this selection of Pag cheeses, all made from the milk of these happy sheep, who've been grazing on uniquely-salty-from-the-sea herbs and grasses, we are pretty goddamn happy. This is world-class food; this is world-class wine; this is world-class cheese. It was fucking awesome, from the second we sat down, until now."

HOTEL BOSKINAC: Skopaljska Ulica 220, 53291 Novalja–Pag Island, Tel +385 53 663500, www.boskinac.com (rooms start at about 1,500 kuna/US$223 per night)

Croatian chef and restaurateur David Skoko personally catches the fish that's cooked at his family's restaurant, **Konoba Batelina**. Skoko makes a mission of seeking out the underrated and undervalued seafood that others might overlook.

"The money catch around here is sea bass, but that's not what we're going for. We're looking for trash, what comes up with the nets, the stuff that fishing folk have learned to work with after the so-called good stuff is sold and gone. The family restaurant is a place suddenly, on the strength of a recent *MasterChef* appearance, very popular for what they've been doing all along. David and his mother, Alda, make magic with what, until recently, nobody wanted.

"Lightly dressed raw lobster, so fresh it's still moving. Bastard's still looking at you while you eat its lower half. Yeah, lobster's not exactly trash fish, but live a little, right? Shark liver, on the other hand—not a lot of call for that. But there should be. It's real good. And monkfish tripe? That sounds about as appetizing as getting into an elevator after the Situation hotboxed it. But you know what? It's awesome. It's the first time I've ever had that anywhere on earth."

The restaurant interior is low-key and homey. It's cash only, they do not accept walk-ins, and the menu varies depending on that day's catch.

KONOBA BATELINA: Cimulje 25, 52100 Banjole, Tel +385 52 573 767 (average meal about 250 kuna/US$37 per person)

"The village of Plastovo sits high above Skradin, a quiet fishing hamlet. But, significantly, it shares the same latitude as Tuscany across the Adriatic. It's here at the Bibich family winery that it all comes home for me, the food, the wine, the whole thing."

Alen and Vesna Bibic are the owner-operators, presiding over a business that's been in the family for a very long time. "My family has been here for centuries, and we have been making the wine for at least five centuries," Alen explained to Tony. "It's Mediterranean, true Mediterranean, with lots of sun. You have lots of sugar in your grape. We are 220 meters above the sea. And the mountains are behind, so we get this fresh, cold breeze every night, in summertime, and we keep acidity and aromas in the wines."

Centuries of existence in the Balkans also means centuries of witness to conflict and change, and indeed Bibic occupies land that has been variously identified as Italian, Hungarian, Serbian, and now, Croatian. Alen and Vesna consider themselves Dalmatian, an ancient tribal identity that transcends geopolitics. The recent Balkan wars were hard on the Bibich property, which was situated on the front lines of the conflict, and became studded with land mines. Much was destroyed, and much had to be rebuilt and replanted in the aftermath.

These days, however, visitors can enjoy **"a little not-so-impromptu twelve-course meal of epic quality, accompanied by equally epic wines."** Bibic's chefs offer dishes like local oysters with Worcestershire foam, lemon dust, trout roe, and cucumber sorbet and smoked savory yogurt with garlic foam.

If you're lucky, you'll encounter their supermeaty Skradin risotto:

"If you know me at all, you know that it's all about this: slow, slow, slowly simmering ragù of veal, along with several other cuts that will remain secret. This has been going on all day, since before sunrise, carefully tended, and stirred constantly. Then the rice: more gentle, careful stirring, cooked to just right, a sprinkling of cheese from the island of Pag, of course, and the scent coming off this thing fills the yard, driving anything, man and beast alike, mad with desire. This is the single best mouthful of food I've had in this country."

BIBICH WINERY: Zapadna Ulica 63, Plastovo, 22222 Skradin, Tel +385 91 323 5729, www.bibich.co (lunch tasting menu plus paired wines, 1,120 kuna/US$170; dinner tasting menu plus paired wines, 2,240 kuna/US$335)

CUBA

"This is the Cuba I grew up with: The missile crisis. 'Duck and cover. Hide under your desks, kids. Cover yourselves with wet newspaper, 'cause we're all going to die.' We were two nations in a never-ending state of war."

For over a half century, relations between the United States and Cuba were frozen by an economic and travel embargo; diplomatic relations were practically nonexistent.

In late 2014, though, the tides began to shift. President Barack Obama, in a speech from the White House Cabinet Room, declared, "Today, the United States of America is changing its relationship with the people of Cuba. In the most significant changes in our policy in more than fifty years, we will end an outdated approach that, for decades, has failed to advance our interests, and instead we will begin to normalize relations between our two countries. Through these changes, we intend to create more opportunities for the American and Cuban people, and begin a new chapter among the nations of the Americas. . . . To the Cuban people, America extends a hand of friendship." A sense of the unknown future was palpable.

Since then, the shining hope of open travel, free communication, and a warm, friendly relationship between the two countries has been complicated by the subsequent Republican administration's policy changes and rollbacks. There were mysterious sonic attacks with serious health effects on employees and their families of the US embassy in Havana. After a brief window of opportunity, as of this writing, US citizens are once again forbidden from travel to Cuba under the "people to people" rule, and strict caps on the amount of money that Cuban Americans can send to family members on the island have been renewed. There is talk, in State Department circles, of returning Cuba to a list of state sponsors of terrorism.

That being said, US citizens may still visit Cuba under one of twelve approved categories of travel, and all the major carriers have regular flights to Havana and some of Cuba's other airports. It is still possible—and was, in Tony's view, advisable, to go.

"However you feel about the government, however you feel about the last fifty-five years, there aren't any places in the world that look like this. I mean, it's utterly enchanting. Yes, the future is here. But the past, too, is everywhere. The buildings, the cars, the gears of the whole system, are still largely stuck in time.

"I've been to a lot of places, but I can't think of another place that's been less fucked-up by time than Havana. Say what you will about everything else: it's beautiful, heartbreakingly beautiful. The Cuban people [are] openhearted, friendly, relentlessly curious, sophisticated about nearly everything. If you can, you should come here with your eyes open and see. See everything you can, both the good and the bad. Look at it, because it's beautiful, and it's still here."

ARRIVAL AND GETTING AROUND

José Martí International Airport (HAV) is Havana's airport, nine miles southwest of the city, in Boyeros. It is the country's largest and busiest airport, where the majority of flights from overseas arrive. There are, however, ten airports in total on the island, many of which are located in specific resort areas, and all handle international as well as intraisland flights.

From HAV, if you are not part of a tour with an organized shuttle bus to your hotel, you can take a taxi to your destination, which should cost $20–$25 Cuban convertible pesos (CUC), the equivalent of US$20–$25, plus a customary tip of about CUC$3 per trip. Agree on a fare with your driver before you depart the airport, as meters are rarely in use in most taxis.

There is also a local bus from the airport, but it departs only from the domestic terminal, and the fare must be paid in Cuban national pesos (CUP), making this a less-appealing option for most visitors arriving from overseas.

Once in Havana, you can get around town using shared taxis, or colectivos, that run a fixed route and pick up passengers along the way, if they have room to do so. Private taxis and car services are also available, for a rate of CUC/US$30–$40 per hour. There's a seventeen-route city bus system in Havana, and for CUP$1 per ride (the equivalent of a nickel), it's hard to beat the price, although there will be inevitable crowding and lack of air-conditioning. For a great resource for information about Cuban public transport, including Havana's bus system, check out www.cubacasas.net.

All the major cities of Cuba are linked by a rail system, Ferrocariles de Cuba, with a robust number of arteries along the way. Train travel in Cuba has had a bad reputation for frequent breakdowns and a distinct lack of comfort. Recently, however, a new fleet of Chinese-made railcars has been set on the Cuban rails, the first part of a plan to revitalize train travel on the island. The trip from Havana to Santiago de Cuba is currently CUC/US$95 for foreigners, and about CUC/US$10 for Cubans. See the train travel website Seat61.com for more information and updates.

EATING IN HAVANA

The state owns and operates restaurants in Havana, and by and large, they're not very good. *Paladares* are privately owned and operated out of the proprietors' homes, and they tend to have better food and service. Once operating in secret, they have been legal since 1993, but are still heavily regulated by the government, with restrictions on the number of seats and paid employees, and a substantial tax obligation.

Running your own *paladar* is a daily series of challenges, but Elizabeth Espinoza has proved herself up to the task. **"[Elizabeth is] the kind of tough, resolute, hardworking operator you need to be in this country if you're going to navigate the complicated and difficult road to owning and operating your own restaurant.**

"In a bright lime-green building not far away down a corridor and around the corner, tourists and locals alike line up for tables at Elizabeth's restaurant, Paladar los Amigos. The minute it was legal, Elizabeth opened this place. The rules, as in any nightmarish, bureaucracy-heavy system, are always changing. But the rules are increasingly ambiguous. A lot depends on who you know."

The menus at *paladares* must remain flexible, a reflection of variable market forces and occasional shortages. **"Today, it's pork. You aren't likely to ever see a fat T-bone steak for sure. *Masa de cerdo*, marinated, hacked up, and pan fried. *Escalope*, a cutlet pounded, breaded and fried, served with a trinity of yucca, rice, and beans. Locals actually eat here, too, but are able to because we—meaning tourists and foreigners—basically subsidize their meals. Meaning, we pay more, lots more. It's a two-tier pricing scheme—us and them."**

PALADAR LOS AMIGOS: Calle M, #253, La Habana, Tel +53 830 0880 (entrées CUC/USD$8–$12)

"[Once], a meal at a *paladar* would have been rice and beans. Now, sushi; a certain sign of impending apocalypse." See for yourself at **Santy Pescador**, a well-loved seafood operation in a clapboard house on the bank of the Jaimanitas River, on the outskirts of the city. It's busiest for lunch, when the views from the patio are the best; dinnertime is generally a more relaxed affair.

SANTY PESCADOR: Calle 240A #3C (between Calle 23 and the river), Jaimanitas, Havana, Tel +535 286 7039, www.santypescador .com (lunch CUC/US$10, dinner CUC/US$20–$30)

The Malecón is an enchanting five-mile esplanade, seawall, and six-lane avenue along the coast, stretching from La Punta Fortress to the mouth of the Almendares River, with plenty of stately old homes,

hotels, and parks in between. It's a quintessential Cuban experience to walk along the Malecón, hang out with friends, watch the sunset, admire the monuments and the views, and occasionally dodge a robust wave that smashes up against the wall. The last, long tracking shot of the Cuba episode of *Parts Unknown* was Tony's idea, as he explained in an interview for *Prime Cuts*, a kind of series highlight reel:

"The last shot of the Cuba show [was] very deeply satisfying to me, because I was on the way to a scene, and I just looked out the window at all the couples, and people sitting there, looking out, from the sea wall. And I thought, God, that's a great shot . . . I remember watching that finished product and just holding my breath saying, it almost looked staged . . . That was a really perfect end to a show—no dumb sum-up. . . . It showed you something that was true, and meaningful, and in this case very beautiful—I think hopeful—without having me have to tell you how to feel about it.

"It's been a dream of mine to see a Cuban baseball game. To say that the fans here are passionate would be an egregious understatement. They live and breathe this game. Tickets to the games are less than a dollar for general admission. Snack options are limited, to say the least. None of this, however, gets in the way of the game."

At **Estadio Latinoamericano**, the 55,000-seat home of the Havana Industriales, self-organized groups of fans show up with musical instruments to provide pep music, and the trash talk in the stands regularly turns the air blue. In 2016, the Tampa Bay Rays visited and played the Industriales for a crowd that included President Obama and Raúl Castro, prompting a bit of a fix-up to the stadium's typical state of disrepair, though recent reports indicate that broken seats and general decay remain.

On a daily basis, in a section of the city's Parque Central known as *la esquina caliente*, or "the hot corner," a group of extremely knowledgeable and opinionated baseball fans "are given an official license to assemble publicly, and argue. The discussions invariably become quite heated, and that official status helps when authorities confuse a bunch of people arguing over the utility of the sacrifice bunt for a political row."

ESTADIO LATINOAMERICANO: Cerro (schedules and information available at www.baseballdecuba.com)

PARQUE CENTRAL: bounded by El Prado, Zulueta, San José, and Neptuno Streets

FINLAND

At the urging of a Finnish fan who corralled more than 100,000 of his countrymen into begging Tony to shoot in Finland via Facebook, the *No Reservations* crew descended on Helsinki just after the New Year in 2012, at a time of the season with only about four daily hours of light, and the rest an inky blue-black known as *kaamos*, or "eternal night."

"Helsinki, Finland. What I knew about the place wasn't, shall we say, encouraging. I knew the Finns were tough people, tough enough to fight off Nazis and Russians. Tough enough to handle the cold, harsh climate, the long, depressing winters, the short, binge-drinking summers. I knew it was a place not long on easy smiles, or even eye contact, for that matter."

ARRIVAL

Helsinki Airport (HEL) is the main international airport for the city of Helsinki and surroundings, with flights to and from the rest of Finland, the Nordic countries, and major Asian cities. It's the hub for Finnair, with American Airlines and British Airways and a number of European carriers serving flights as well.

To get from the airport to Helsinki city center, there are various bus lines and an airport train; the one-way fares are 4.60 euros/ US$5.15, and complete route and schedule information are available at www.hsl.fn/en.

A metered taxi from airport to city will cost about 50 euros/ US$56 for the thirty-minute, thirteen-mile drive. Tipping drivers is not at all expected in Finland, though you may wish to round up the fare, for convenience.

"DRINK, DRINK, SAUNA, DRINK"

"In my best-case scenario, I want to be somewhere warm, with palm trees, tropical drinks, the sounds of reggae or Don Ho somewhere in the distance. Someplace with warm, gin-clear water, the smell of suntan oil and warm brown skin. Not this place."

When in "this place," though, a visit to the sauna is all but mandatory. Both a Finnish invention and something of a national pastime, the sauna is **"the number one thing people tell you to do around here."** In Cold War times, it was a way to ensure that confidential conversations remained so, since it's impossible to wire a nude politician or secret operative.

The city's second-oldest sauna, a bare-bones "house of pain" called **Arla**, has been continuously operated in the Kallio neighborhood since 1929. Here you'll find separate facilities for men and women, and a rotating exhibit of local art. Guests may bring their own refreshments; Tony came equipped with beer, gin, and grapefruit cocktails, as well as blood sausages, grilled in the embers of the wood fire that, in conjunction with natural gas, provides the sauna's heat.

Massage services are, of course, available, along with a gruesome combination of cupping and bloodletting, meant to draw out up to nearly a half liter of toxic blood. **"So, our disconcertingly cheerful therapist slides on the surgical gloves, puts on the cups and starts getting stabby, sinking her sharp little hockey stick into my flesh repeatedly and without remorse."**

SAUNA ARLA: Kaarlenkatu 15, Helsinki 00530, Tel +3589 7192, www.arlansauna.net (14 euro/US$15.50 entrance fee; includes towel)

"It's that time again. Time for whatever local specialty—meat in tube form, booze mop, mutant dog—whatever it is that locals need around now when feeling, shall we say, worse for wear. Here, the drinkers tend to need something a little more urgently perhaps, and they are, as a result, maybe, just maybe, a little more forgiving of what's on offer.

"Jaskan Grilli is a beloved late-night favorite, a legend in the drinking class, which is to say, a well-known kiosk behind the Finnish Parliament building, presided over by an ancient woman who dispatches various greasy pucks and tubes of sizzling meat products to sop up the alcohol consumed in the previous hours.

"Start with a microwaved, patty-like substance of mystery meat, followed by a generous tug on the condiment udders hanging from the ceiling. Don't skimp, my friend. Then, pile on the toppings. Garlic, pineapple, mayo, relish, and something cheese-like. It puts the self-loathing back into drinking, and God knows we all need that."

JASKAN GRILLI: Dagmarinkatu 2, 00100 Helsinki. No phone, no website (average plate about 5 euros/US$5.50)

FRANCE

CHAMONIX (FRENCH ALPS)

"French Alps: lovely Italians on one side; the terrifying Swiss are just over there. Close, too close for me, a man with a neurotic childhood fear of alpine vistas, yodeling, even cheeses with holes in them."

For comfort, Tony brought chef Eric Ripert along with him to the Alps for this high-altitude *Parts Unknown* shoot, in 2017.

"My friend Eric, he grew up in mountains like this. He's an expert skier. This is like home to him. I have, in recent adventures with him, been unkind. So I thought it was only fair that he get a chance at payback.

"I am not a graceful skier. I am an enthusiastic one. And that's what you come here for in winter and early spring—some of the best slopes on earth. Also cheese: apparently, lots of cheese."

ARRIVAL AND ACCOMMODATIONS

The closest airport to the Alps is **Geneva International Airport**, once known as Cointrin; it's a usage that is still rather common. This airport serves flights from dozens of European cities, and select cities in the Middle East, Africa, Asia, and North and South America. It is, no surprise, the hub of Swiss International Airlines.

The airport is located on the Swiss-French border and thus has both a Swiss and a French "side," differentiated by the codes **GVA** and

GGV, respectively. One may arrive into and depart from either side without passport issues, but car rental rates often vary between the two sides, and it's essential to return a rented car to the proper side at the end of your stay, to avoid a hefty fine.

Chamonix is about an hour's drive from the Geneva airport, and if you're not renting a car, there are numerous shared and private auto transport options, from buses for about 20 euros/US$23 round-trip, to private taxis for up to 500 euros (US$550). It's possible to make the trip to Chamonix from Geneva by train, for 30 to 40 euros/US$33–$45 each way, but the route is indirect, making it an approximately three-hour journey, with one or more line transfers along the way.

Sleep off your cheese sweats and ski slope exertions in style at the **Hôtel Mont-Blanc**, an historic luxury Alpine resort in operation since 1849 at the foot of Europe's tallest peak, and recently given a complete interior redesign to bring it up to twenty-first-century standards. Stunning views, sophisticated furnishings, exquisite service, a heated outdoor pool suitable for wintertime swimming—in short, an extremely low-impact place to retire and work out the gastrointestinal challenges of a cheese-and-meat-intensive trip.

HÔTEL MONT-BLANC: 62 Allée du Majestic, 74400 Chamonix-Mont-Blanc, Tel +33 450 530564, www.hotelmontblancchamonix .com (rooms start at about 320 euros/US$357 per night)

CHEESE

"Where I learned to ski, you're lucky to get chicken fingers and a Bud Light at the lodge. Here"—meaning **La Table de Plan Joran**, a decades-old fine-dining restaurant on a ski slope—"pan-seared foie gras. For the main, a loin of veal, gently seared and pan-roasted, joined by a wild mushroom sauce and a pretty little medley of vegetables. And I'm all over the cheese course like a one-man army: *tomme de chèvre*, *tomme de savoie au Piment, fromage de chèvre frais, et Cremeux des Reines.* That's from, like, a cow."

LA TABLE DE PLAN JORAN: Domaine des Grands-Montets, Argentière, 74400, Tel +33 4 5054 0577, www.planjoran-restaurant .com (40–50 euros/US$45–$55 per person, lunch only)

After a morning of skiing, settle in for lunch at **La Crèmerie du Glacier.** It's the restaurant of a classically Alpine inn, housed in a 1926 chalet, that specializes in the traditional Savoyard cuisine of the area, based, no surprise, on potatoes, cheese, and cured meats.

First course: *croute aux morilles,* or crusty bread with morels in a cream sauce, topped with Comté cheese. But then: *farçon.* **"I think that means 'cannonball of goodness' in French, because it's a big, heavy, albeit thoroughly delicious loaf of potato, bacon, dried fruit, and cream, slowly steamed in a bain-marie. This meal is a foreshadowing of the kind of light spa food that will become a regular feature of our time in the Alps."**

LA CRÈMERIE DU GLACIER: 766 Chemin du Glacier, Chamonix-Mont-Blanc, 74400, Tel +33 04 5054 0752, www.lacremerieduglacier.com (fondue 15–20 euros/ US$17-$22 per person)

Finally, may we suggest—more cheese? **"Hôtel Du Buet has been around for many years; one comes here for the cheese, in this case the iconic raclette and the equally iconic fondue."** The former is a semihard cow's milk cheese, melted in front of a hearth, then scraped onto potatoes or bread; the latter, a combination of local Emmentaler and Gruyère cheeses, white wine, kirsch, and garlic. As its name suggests, Du Buet also welcomes overnight guests in a twenty-four-room chalet that's been in the Chamet family for over 130 years.

After polishing off about a pound of cheese, and downing a dessert course in which fondue dregs are cooked with bread cubes, an egg, sugar, and brandy, prepare yourself for the indelicate matter of cheese-induced constipation. "You're going to have a big cannonball of crap lodged up your butt like a baby head. The size of a freaking baby head. You will understand the agony of delivery."

HÔTEL DU BUET: Le Buet, Vallorcine, 74660, Tel +33 0450 546005, www.hotelbuet.com (fondue about 16 euros/US$18 per person; entrées 15–28 euros/US$17–$31)

LYON

"This is the story of one man, one chef, and a city. . . . It's about a family tree, about the trunk from which many branches grew. And it's about food, lots of food. Great food, some of the greatest food on earth.

"Lyon is situated in the southeast of the country, midway between the Alps in the east and the Mediterranean to the south. Over the past century, the system here churned out a tremendous number of the world's most important chefs: Fernand Point, Alain Chapel, brothers Jean and Pierre Troisgros, Paul Bocuse. And, as important, it influenced nearly all the rest of them.

"In Lyon, a city that believes absolutely in the power of food, one name is everywhere. A name that brought honor, attention, and millions of visitors to the city. Though there have been many chef heroes in the annals of gastronomy, in Lyon, and even across France, one name stands above all others. Murals, bridges, markets, casual brasseries, the name of Monsieur Paul is everywhere."

ARRIVAL AND GETTING AROUND

Lyon's major airport is **Lyon–Saint Exupéry (LYS)**, serving flights to and from all major destinations in France and Europe, and a handful in Africa, the Middle East, and North America (though nothing direct to or from the States).

The Rhônexpress tram moves passengers between the airport and the centrally located Lyon Part-Dieu train station, with two intermediate stops, a journey that takes about thirty minutes and costs about 16 euros (US$18) one way, 28 euros (US$31) round trip, with children twelve and under riding for free. Routes, schedules, and online tickets are available at www.rhonexpress.fr/en.

The Gare TGV Lyon-Saint Exupéry train station is a five-minute walk from the airport, and offers connections to the city center, as well as dozens of destinations within France.

There are also metered taxis, which take about forty-five minutes to travel the twenty-mile distance to the city center, and will cost 50–100 euros/US$56–$100, depending on traffic and time of day. Taxis can be hailed on the street in Lyon, and you'll find them queued outside the train stations and along a few major thoroughfares. Lyon also has robust metro, bus, and tram systems, as befits the third-largest city in France. Information about routes, fares, and more is at www.tcl.fr.

EATING IN LYON

"Why Lyon? Why here? Look at the fundamentals—the things the Lyonnais think of as birthrights. The right, for instance, to eat delicious cured pork in unimaginably delicious forms: terrine, paté, sausages, rillettes—it's an art that's revered here, and widely enjoyed. And few names garner more respect from aficionados of pig than Reynon."

Pay a visit to Reynon, a charcutier that's been in business since 1937 under the same family ownership, to witness the assembly of rosette, Jesus, cervelas, and sabodet sausages. You will be suitably awed and humbled by the volume, efficiency, and perfection with which the master charcutiers work. And if you get the chance to try your own hand at the craft, you may, as Tony did, cover for your own clumsy and abortive attempts with dick jokes and slugs of wine.

REYNON: 13 Rue des Archers, Lyon 69003, Tel +04 7837 3908, www.reynonlyon.com (prices vary)

"For a dope fiend, feeding the monkey means finding and sticking with heroin. For one poor guy, it's this: French food. In particular, Lyonnais food. The cautionary tale of Bill Buford. Writer, editor, literary lion with a perfectly good job as fiction editor at the prestigious *New Yorker* magazine. At the undignified age of fifty-three, he pretty much pulled up stakes, put his whole past life on hold, and defected to France to learn how to cook." (See Bill's essay about Lyon and Tony on page 104.)

Tony had a meal with Buford at **Le Café Comptoir Abel**, which is a *bouchon*. The *bouchon* is "a uniquely Lyonnais institution: a casual, laid-back kind of pub-slash-bistro with a limited, usually old-school menu and always, always, an unpretentious vibe. People come here to unwind, to relax, and to eat with abandon."

The menu is stocked with absolute classics like *saucisson chaud* with lentils, chicken with morels and cream, and steak frites, prepared under the supervision of chef Alain Vigneron. Try the *quenelles de brochet*, "a-not-particularly-fabulous river fish, pike, folded into a light dough, like pâte à choux, until fluffy and airy but still rich, adrift in a rich, creamy, almost bisque-like Nantua sauce made with crayfish, crème fraîche, white wine, and a splash of brandy."

LE CAFÉ COMPTOIR ABEL: 25 Rue Guynemer, Lyon 69002, Tel +04 7837 4618, www.cafecomptoirabel.com (entrées average 20 euros/US$23)

"Alongside, and some say, above the names of the other culinary giants in and around Lyon, is the name Troisgros. Started by the visionary brothers Jean and Pierre, **Maison Troisgros** received three Michelin stars in 1968, and sparked a dynasty of culinary excellence that continues today with Pierre's son Michel and his son Cesar.

Many have called Maison Troisgros the best restaurant in the world. And in the 1960s, the brothers Pierre and Jean were early, important, and fundamental innovators of what came to be known as 'nouvelle cuisine.'" Go in pursuit of the Troisgroses' signature dish, a fillet of salmon in a sauce of butter, white wine, reduced fish stock, crème fraîche, and tart, lemony sorrel leaves.

"Behold one of their breakout classics: one of the truly game-changing, timeless, most influential dishes in history. It seems now, maybe, a simple thing, but it absolutely turned the world upside-down when it debuted on the Troisgros menu in 1962."

MAISON TROISGROS: 728 Route de Villerest, 42155 Ouches, Tel +33 4 7771 6697, www.troisgros.com (entrées 70–120 euros/ US$190–$225; tasting menus 120–500 euros/US$134–$560)

"In the 1970s, as a young wannabe cook, I managed to lay hands on a French copy of Paul Bocuse's classic cookbook, *La Cuisine du Marché*, and I gaped with wonder at the photos; struggled to translate the descriptions of dishes so fantastic I was quite sure that I'd never ever in my life cook, much less eat."

Tony's chance to eat these dishes finally did arrive, of course—and in the presence of the master Paul Bocuse himself, a few years before his death. Tony recalled:

"Today, I was treated to the greatest hits of a glorious and fabled career. For the first and probably the last time, I sat next to the great man himself, and Daniel [Boulud] and I were served a menu that chefs will look back on in a hundred years, and smile at appreciatively, sentimentally, respectfully." That menu included black truffle soup VGE (named for Valéry Giscard d'Estaing, president of the French Republic from 1974 to 1981), sea bass cooked in a pastry crust with *sauce choron*, pot-au-feu, and, the highlight:

On Lyon

BY BILL BUFORD

Lyon brought out Tony's softness.

Lyon likes to see itself as "the gastronomical capital of the world," and, whether justified or not, there is no question that the city takes its food very seriously. This is what humbled Tony, the city's reverence for the meal.

One especially moving episode was the visit he made to the school canteen where Daniel Boulud ate as a child. These canteens are miracles of food education. (Are they different in Paris? I have no idea. We lived in Lyon five years. We got to Paris three times. Once was to renew a passport. Lyon and Paris exist in a centuries-long relationship of mutual antipathy. In the eyes of Lyonnais: Parisians don't get Lyon. In the eyes of the Parisians: Why would they bother?)

A canteen taught Boulud what a French meal should be. A canteen taught our children as well, twin boys who arrived as three-year old toddlers, instantly installed in the local school.

The meals were performances: always three courses, a vegetable or soup starter, an organic main course (meat or fish and always a vegetarian option), always a sauce, a dairy item at the end, usually a cheese. No one is made to eat. But if you don't finish your first course, you aren't served the second. And if you don't finish it, you don't get dessert.

One Sunday morning, three months after our arrival, I was making omelets. One of my sons, Frederick, came into the kitchen and said, "Dada, I didn't know you could make *une omelette nature*." The things I found packed into this little sentence: that Frederick now called me *Dada*, a French term; that he pronounced the word omelet in the French way, omelette, coming down hard on the '*t*'; and that he liked his without anything inside. French omelets are different from ours. You don't use a whisk. You don't let the egg whites get big or harden. You cook them so that the result is tender to the touch, a little squishy but with bounce. I was then at L'Institut Paul Bocuse and learned how make omelets in a class. The boys learned in their canteen.

La Cuisine Lyonnaise, a classic, published in the 1920s and written by Mathieu Varille, gives historic accounts of what you will find on a Lyonnais plate: quenelles, a fish souffle; the saucisson; chicken in many variations. It also includes rules: that you think about what you're eating; you do not read or listen to music (cell phones weren't around in the 1920s); you don't eat standing up or at any place other than a table; you don't drink water while eating, you drink wine; you eat dessert, always. You appreciate the food that someone has prepared for you.

This is what you learn from age three.

Tony's Lyon episode of *Parts Unknown* is an homage to Paul Bocuse. Bocuse made Tony into a puppy. Tony is not naturally a puppy.

The city's highest culinary expression is in its "grand chefs." The idea is foreign to an American. A grand chef is a nationally recognized designation, a supreme being, the cook as artist, as someone with gifts that inspire awe and pleasure. It is what every young chef with ambition longs to become. There was no chef grander than Paul Bocuse.

Tony's respect for Bocuse seemed to reveal, to me at least, how seriously Tony regarded his early profession. Tony used to downgrade his credentials, dismissing them as those of an adrenaline junkie in a low-level bistro. Secretly, I now believe, he once had longings for greatness. He understood the calling.

Our last night was during the Fête des Lumières, but little of the fête is in the film. It was a mistake to be anywhere near it.

It is a three-night celebration in December that dates from 1852 and that gives thanks to the Virgin Mary. The virgin, evidently, miraculously put an end to an episode of the plague after the city

"As if the chef had been listening to my deepest, darkest secret yearnings: the legendary *lièvre à la royale*, an almost completely disappeared, incredibly difficult preparation of wild hare. The animal is first slowly cooked, then coated by a sauce of its own minced heart, liver, and lungs that has been thickened with its own blood. After more than six hours of preparation, the hare is served, as the chef prefers, whole, on the bone, the rich glorious sauce finished with truffles and chartreuse, napped over and over until it coats like the prayed fervently for her intervention. The residents expressed their gratitude with candles in their windows.

The practice continues, a beautiful, contemplative sight, to find virtually every home illumined thus. But, inspired by "the candle," the practice has expanded into an outlandish light show, a pagan winter rite, a rock show, food everywhere, and very little praying. Hundreds of thousands of people crowd into the city. Almost every plan we had to film during the fête had to be abandoned. A meal was arranged, our last time together, the destination on the other side of Lyon. I couldn't reach it. There were no taxis, because no vehicles were allowed on the streets. There was a two-hour wait to get into the metro. The city has a bike-sharing system, but had no available bikes. I walked a mile, finally found one bike, rode as fast as possible, and arrived, late, in a sweat. It was my last moment in Lyon with Tony, and somehow it seemed apposite, in a city that we all believed we could convey the spirit of, only to keep discovering that it was more complex, more mystical, just outright bigger in every way than any one of us could have known beforehand.

Note: *Buford's book about living and cooking in Lyon,* Dirt, *was published in May 2020.*

richest chocolate. Absolutely the Lost Ark of the Covenant of *cuisine ancienne*.

"**I will never eat like this again in my life.**"

RESTAURANT PAUL BOCUSE: 40 Quai de la Plage, 69660 Collonges au Mont d'Or, Tel +33 4 7242 9090, www.bocuse.fr (entrées 70–125 euros/US$80–$140)

MARSEILLE

"**If you've been to France, chances are, you haven't been here,**" said Tony of the Mediterranean city of Marseille—the second-largest city in France, and its oldest. "**Marseille was once the hub, the rough-and-tumble principal port for France's colonies such as Tunisia, Morocco, and Algeria. As a result, the sights and smells of Africa permeate the city.**

"**The food is famously good—yet it's a victim of bad reputation, bad history. As it turns out, exactly the kind of place I like.**

"**There have been attempts to dissuade me . . . 'Oh, Marseille, you don't want to go there.' And yet . . . it is a beautiful city. It smells good. You smell the different pastries. The tajine, bouillabaisse, and bourride. And it's an extraordinary-looking city, and the people are really interesting looking.**"

ARRIVAL AND GETTING AROUND

Marseille Provence Airport (MRS) is a busy two-terminal airport located about seventeen miles from the city center. There are no direct flights from the United States, but plenty of connections from all over Europe, the Middle East, and Africa.

There are taxi ranks outside the arrivals halls; it's about a thirty-minute drive from airport to city center, and will cost about 55 euros/US$62. Tipping is appreciated but not expected. You may also take a free shuttle bus from the airport to the Vitrolles train station, and from there a Transport express régional train to St.-Charles station, the city's main station. Car rentals are available at the airport, but city traffic and parking will likely make driving a misery.

In the city, the RTM (Régie des transports des métropolitains) administers public transportation, consisting of metro, tram, and bus lines. Buy tickets, which are about 1.70 euro/US$2 per trip, at tram stops, on metro platforms, or upon boarding buses. See www.rtm.fr for details.

Metered taxis can be found at ranks around the city, or hailed on the street.

DECONSTRUCTED BOUILLABAISSE

In a "boat to table" concept scene, Tony and Eric rode along with longline fisherman Eric Fromion, **"one of only a handful of old-style fishermen who work the sea the old-fashioned way. Eric works exclusively for Gérald Passédat, the extremely demanding chef-owner of Le Petit Nice, Marseille's only three-Michelin-star restaurant."**

Passédat's grandfather purchased the property in 1917, and it's been the family business ever since. In addition to the restaurant, there's a luxurious sixteen-room hotel, divided between two villas overlooking the Mediterranean, which share a small pool and a grand patio.

After a not particularly fruitful attempt to fish for the raw materials of their lunch, Tony and Eric were delivered by boat to Le Petit Nice, to experience a remix of a Marseillais classic.

"There is reinvented, deconstructed, and then, usually, there's the thing itself. Passédat's take on bouillabaisse, without a doubt Marseille's most famous dish, is spread out over four courses. First: shellfish carpaccio of raw mussels and clams. Slipper lobster, weaver, angler, and red gurnard, lightly seared, then a touch in the oven. A broth so intense it requires over ten kilos of rock crabs and various bony tasty little fishes to make just one liter of gloriously brown, magical liquid. *Dorade* and *denti*, steamed over seaweed water. Saffron potatoes. And then, finally, comes that magical brown broth.

"And, just when my brain threatens to short-circuit with pleasure, descending as if from heaven itself: cheese. Oh God, the cheese. It's an embarrassment of riches, at least a dozen stinky, gooey, sharp, creamy, sweet, and tangy cheeses to the meal. That is just incredible. *Merci*. Oh yes. Life is good. It is very good in Marseille."

LE PETIT NICE: 17 rue des Braves, 13007 Marseille, Tel +33 4 91 59 25 92, www.petitnice-passedat.com (menus from 120 euros/ US$134 for lunch, and 220 euros/US$245 for dinner; rooms start at 280 euros/US$312 per night)

PARIS

Tony loved Paris. He first visited as a child, as he detailed in *Kitchen Confidential,* and he made the first and 100th episodes of *No Reservations* there, along with an episode of *The Layover.* He was emphatic about converting the skeptical.

"Paris and the French are easy to get wrong. . . . You feel obliged to embrace the stereotype, and of course, to some extent, the stereotypes are true—indulgent, arty, Socialist, what with their free medical care and their long vacations and their un-American propensity for high quality of life. They suffer from the burden of a tradition of fabulously oozing cheeses, rich sauces, historic wines, the kind of thing that tends to pigeonhole a culture, make you think it's all luxury and sodomy. But it ain't all snooty waiters and haute cuisine. . . . People are actually nicer. Good food is cheaper and more casual. . . . You can still get the good old stuff, just a lot of the bullshit seems to have gone the way of the woolly mammoth.

"Paris remains one of the greatest, most beautiful, most magical cities in the world. And like a lot of other really great cities, it's entirely possible to have a bad time. Please don't do that. Just avoid the obvious.

"The absolute worst thing to do when you come to Paris is plan too much. Eiffel Tower, Notre-Dame, Arc de Triomphe, stand in line for hours to experience what everybody says you have to. Me? I like to take it easy in Paris, especially if I'm only in town for a few days.

"Most of us are lucky to see Paris once in a lifetime. Make the most of it by doing as little as possible. Walk a little, get lost a bit, eat, catch a breakfast buzz, have a nap, try and have sex if you can, just not with a mime. Eat again. Lounge around drinking coffee. Maybe read a book. Drink some wine, walk around a bit more, eat, repeat. See? It's easy."

ARRIVAL AND GETTING AROUND

If you fly into **Charles De Gaulle (CDG)**, a major international hub about sixteen miles northeast of the city, take a taxi (50–60 euros/US$55–$67, with 10 percent tip for good service) straight to your hotel, or the Réseau express régional (RER) train to one of several central Paris stops (about 11 euros/US$12.25; all info at www.easycdg.com). There's also a shuttle bus to central Paris (about 18 euros/US$20; see www.lebusdirect.com/en).

If you fly into **Orly (ORY)**, a slightly smaller international hub that's about eight miles south of the city, take a taxi (35–40 euros/

US\$39–\$45, with 10 percent tip for good service) to your hotel, or the OrlyVal train to Antony station, to the RER B train to central Paris, or take the aforementioned shuttle bus.

If you're coming from elsewhere in France or greater Europe by rail, you'll arrive at one of Paris's seven major train stations (the Gares du Nord, de l'Est, d'Austerlitz, de Bercy, de Lyon, Montparnasse, and Saint-Lazare), each of which has a taxi stand and is connected to the vast, efficient Paris Métro (subway) system.

Paris is an extremely pedestrian-friendly city, and observing it at street level one of its great, free pleasures. For longer distances, first consider the **Métro**, about which Tony said, **"even for my lazy ass, it's hard to argue that it's a pretty damn convenient way to get around."** Buy tickets and consult maps in the stations; the Régie autonome des transports parisiens (RATP), which operates the Metro, has created a fantastic free smartphone app with maps, schedules, service alerts and more—in English!—so you really have no excuse.

Taxis are widely available in Paris, lined up at one of 128 taxi stands around the city, or, increasingly, with drivers willing to be hailed if they're fifty meters or more from a stand.

For city cyclists, there's also the Vélib', a self-service bike share system (www.velib-metrople.fr).

CAFÉ CULTURE

Whether or not you have some time to kill before checking in to your hotel, find a nearby café in which to acclimate yourself.

"Ah, Paris, city of light, city of love, city of . . . breakfast? Yes, please. The most important thing to do the instant you arrive in Paris is stop. Find someplace inviting, and slip comfortably into the Parisian pace of life.

It's no accident that the café is so closely associated with the French. And what do we have here? We have a cup of coffee and a

ham sandwich, a row of chairs all pointing in one direction, a little table staring out into the street . . . the simplest of life's pleasures, and yet for many Parisians, this can be an afternoon's entertainment. And I think this gets right to the kernel of what distinguishes the French. Once you allow your senses to guide you, you may begin to find pleasure in many things you would ordinarily overlook. . . . You are now ready to begin to graze through the wondrous, sensual feasts that elude so many of us when we take trips here."

HOTELS: CHECK IN, PASS OUT

"Now, here's the thing about hotels in Paris: you can go the Henry Miller route and wallow romantically in squalor, or live it up big time. For a luxurious, high-end option, there's the elegantly discreet Hôtel Particulier, located in the heart of the historic Montmartre, nestled in a secret alleyway known as the WItch's Rock Passage.

Me, I always stay at L'Hotel in the Saint-Germain-des-Prés. A very discreet joint known for being a love shack to the tragically hip for ages. Even more important, it has the necessary distinction of having had famous people die there. In 1900, the author Oscar Wilde kicked the bucket in room 16. . . . This was his last base of operations for a legendary three-year bender that ended badly."

HÔTEL PARTICULIER MONTMARTRE: 23 Avenue Junot, Pavillon D, 75018 Paris, Tel +33 (0)1 53 41 81 40, www.hotel -particulier-montmartre.com (suites start at about 300 euros/ US$335 per night)

L'HOTEL: 13 Rue des Beaux Arts, 75006 Paris, Tel +33 (0) 1 44 41 99 00, www.l-hotel.com/en-us (rooms start at about 425 euros/ US$475 per night)

EAT AND DRINK IN THE CITY OF LIGHTS

And now, the *real* reason you're here: to eat and drink well.

"In the English-speaking world, there has always been a certain ambivalence about taking pleasure at the table. There has been this notion that if you take too much pleasure in your food, then it might somehow lead to bad character. It might lead to harder stuff, like sex, for instance. I think the French have always understood that, yeah, hell yeah, it does lead to sex, and it should. That residual sense of food being good, food being important, food being worth waiting for, and food being worth spending time with: eating is, and should be, a joyous occasion.

"About the classic French bistro, I am a sentimental fool. To my way of thinking, there is no greater culinary institution in France than the old-school dino-style, unchanged-by-time classic Parisian bistro. And this place, **Bistrot Paul Bert** in the 11th [Arrondissement], is one of the best. However people are cooking one hundred years from now, whoever is cooking, will always, and must always, love and respect this."

BISTROT PAUL BERT: 18 Rue Paul Bert, 75011 Paris, Tel +01 43 72 24 01 (three-course prix-fixe menu about 40 euros/US$45)

"Dark street, no big sign, curtains drawn out in front. Step inside, you're in another world. I mean, this is the way to eat. It's about food. Sometimes you see the uninviting door and just have to go through it. Chefs play this game where they ask each other, 'What would be your last meal on death row?' Almost always, the answer is something simple and hearty that mom made. Well, here [at **Chez Robert et Louise**], they serve what little French boys wanted for dinner: *boudin noir, fromage de tête, côte de boeuf* with a little *sel gris*."

CHEZ ROBERT ET LOUISE: 64 Rue Vieille du Temple, 75003 Paris, Tel +01 42 78 55 89, www.robertetlouise.com (entrées about 18 euros/US$20)

For "one of the great meals in memory," turn to **Le Chateaubriand**. "It looks like a noisy, minimally decorated pub. Not formally trained and personally, along with only a couple of other cooks, manning the ridiculously tiny kitchen, chef Iñaki Aizpitarte has a single prix fixe menu a day. In order to be a true revolutionary, you have to be willing to completely destroy the old. And I don't think any of these guys is interested in doing that. I think they clearly love the old."

LE CHATEAUBRIAND: 129 Avenue Parmentier, 75011 Paris, Tel +01 43 57 55 95, www.lechateaubriand.net (five-course tasting menu 75 euros/US$84)

"The hardest reservation in Paris, they say, is not at some ultra-expensive temple of gastronomy. It's at this place, Le Comptoir, what Eric [Ripert] has called the perfect bistro. He's also very good friends with the elusive chef-owner of Le Comptoir, Yves Camdeborde, [who] used to run a more haute cuisine kitchen, but after twelve years, decided he'd had enough, and wanted to open a more casual place. Right next door, there's L'Avant Comptoir, a tiny,

A Child's View of Paris (1966)

BY CHRISTOPHER BOURDAIN

In 1966, when I was seven and Tony was ten, our French-born grandmother died (in New York City, where she lived most of her life) and left our father the life savings she had squirreled away over four-plus decades working as a high-end custom dressmaker. Our dad had worked a few not particularly lucrative jobs in the classical record business and selling hi-fi equipment at retail; our mom was what we used to call a housewife. Now, with a sudden infusion of cash in hand, they took us on our first really big trip, to France, and *in style*: Tony and I, two kids from New Jersey, got to cross the Atlantic with our mom on one of the great ocean liners, the Cunard ship *Queen Mary*.

Tony and I loved that ship. Our cabin had bunk beds; a round porthole that opened to the sound, smell, and spray of the sea; and a phone booth–size bathroom. For kids, what wasn't to love? We wandered around for hours on our own, occasionally sneaking into the first-class section. There was a gym, equipped with punching bags and rowing machines. A movie theater. A big saltwater pool, somewhere in the lower levels, where the rocking of the ship would randomly transform the shallow end into the deep end. The service was amazing; everywhere on the ship, we were magically attended to by nattily uniformed British staff, called "stewards." One of those professions that's been lost to time, like Pullman porters.

Our itinerary was to include a stay in Paris, and visits with relatives there; a road trip through central France; and a stay with our dad's aunt and uncle, who, in retirement, had moved back to the original small Bourdain family house near Arcachon, in southwest France. (You can see that house, and the areas nearby, in season 1, episode 9, of *A Cook's Tour*.)

We disembarked in Cherbourg, on the coast, and took the train to Paris, where our dad joined us. The luxe experience continued with a stay at Hôtel Le Royal Monceau, near the Arc de Triomphe, then as now one of the poshest hotels in Paris. Tony and I loved the breakfasts there: bottomless baskets of croissants, brioches, *pains au chocolat*, and *pains aux raisin*. And the butter, that amazing French butter.

Other things Tony and I loved in Paris: First, that we got to wander a bit on our own, near the hotel. We loved the subway platforms, almost luxurious, by New York City standards anyway, and the swooshy sounding rubber-tired trains on the Métro Champs-Élysées line. We loved the WHSmith English bookstore on the Champs Élysées, where we loaded up with cool books we'd never seen in the States. At age seven, I loved the oh-so-British Paddington books. And, as Tony wrote in *Kitchen Confidential*, we both became totally enamored of the Tintin books, and the amazing global adventures they contained (almost proto–*Parts Unknown*). I still have every one of them, and I love them still. We bought the five-language *Insult Dictionary*, which provided weeks of laughs and plenty of cross-cultural bonding with French kids.

But most of all, we loved the *food*. I was, for sure, less adventurous than Tony or our parents in 1966, but even so, there was so much wondrous food to be had. What was, in hindsight, a fairly generic and touristy two-story restaurant/café near our hotel called Quick Élysée (not to be confused with a Burger King wannabe chain called Quick, spotted now throughout France and Belgium) was, to me, amazing. Tony and I both loved the steak frites—I found the crosshatched grill marks peculiarly pleasing—and the maître d'hotel parsley-laced butter, melting on the steak. Perfection, as were the french fries—the best we had ever tasted.

Another revelation was the quotidian *jambon beurre*: a few thin slices of fresh, almost sweet, ham, plus that wonderful French butter, on a fresh crusty baguette. It was pure awesomeness in its simplicity, and even better when accompanied by a fresh-made *citron pressé* (fresh-squeezed lemon juice, water, sugar to taste), or perhaps the popular lemon soda whose bottle-opening onomatopoeic name, Pschitt, always made us American kids giggle to hear it.

And then there was the ubiquitous smell, and of course the taste, of the waffles sold out of street carts or small storefronts, seemingly everywhere. We would get our parents to give us a few francs for waffles, and we'd load on the confectioner's sugar, a new pleasure in itself. Why couldn't we get these simple, wonderful things in the United States?

standing-room-only French small plate and wine bar. I jam myself in there with a bunch of other people who are getting loose before they sit down for dinner, or waiting for a table, or just, like, munching on small plates of some tasty, tasty shit. Notice the communal bread and stick of butter. Just squeeze in and grab and smear."

LE COMPTOIR: 9 Carrefour de l'Odéon, 75006 Paris, Tel +01 44 27 07 97, www.hotel-paris-relais-saint-germain.com (five-course tasting menu about 62 euros/US$69)

L'AVANT COMPTOIR: 3 Carrefour de l'Odéon, 75007 Paris, no phone; www.camdebord.com/restaurants (tapas portions 5–15 euros/US$5.50–$17; wine by the glass, between 4 and 17 euros/US$4.50–$19)

"If there's two things you do in Paris, this would be one," said Tony of **Le Dôme**, where he retreated after an unpleasant encounter with a mime in the Jardin du Luxembourg. "It's an old classic, and I mean classic with a capital C, brasserie in the Montparnasse district. After the mime incident, I feel my producer is unlikely to protest when I get a really fucking expensive bottle of wine and the royal deluxe version of the best shellfish tower in Paris: oysters, clams,

Our dad had been to France as a very young child in the 1930s, and again on leave from US Army service in Germany, in the early 1950s, but for Tony and me and our mom, these first trips to France in 1966 and again in 1967 (a less deluxe but still fantastic follow-up trip after our great-uncle died) opened our eyes and changed our lives forever. We all became enamored of, or in love with, or even a bit obsessed with, France, to varying degrees. We got the food bug, the travel bug, and the understanding that you could hang out with people from foreign countries, and learn things, and take pleasure in coming to understand them. This is where it all started.

shrimp, big fucking crabs, and also the classic langoustine, periwinkle, and whelks. You're going to get your hands dirty doing this, by the way, okay? There ain't no way around it. They give you all the tools, but ultimately, you have to dig in, crack, skewer, and suck your way through this thing."

LE DÔME: 108 Boulevard du Montparnasse, 75014 Paris, Tel +01 43 35 25 81, www.restaurant-ledome.com (entrées about 50 euros/US$56; shellfish tower 159 euros/US$177)

"There were some places in Paris that were way ahead of the others—early adopters of young, biodynamic wines, and the sort of my-way-or-the-highway menus that are popular now. Although it's been in business for thirty years, the owners of **Le Baratin** have always been using biodynamic, young wines since the beginning. And chef Raquel Carena's cooking is generally considered to be some of the very best in Paris."

LE BARATIN 3 Rue Jouye-Rouve, 75020 Paris, Tel +01 43 49 39 70, www.lefooding.com/fr/restaurants/restaurant-le-baratin-paris (average two-course meal 40 euros/US$45)

GHANA

ACCRA

"When I came to sub-Saharan Africa for the first time, I felt a mix of anticipation and anxiety. A general feeling that I was in over my head. A more acute awareness of my total lack of knowledge about my destination. I didn't know what to expect. This, I told myself, would be a journey.

"Africa was known for centuries in the West as 'the Dark Continent,' because so little was known about it. And for some of us, like me, it remains a large, mysterious landmass. While some aspects can be clarified with a reference book or a Google search, I'm relying on my senses. To hear the sounds, smell the food: see it, touch it, and of course, taste it.

"Ghana is something special. The first of the sub-Saharan colonies to gain independence, in 1957, Ghana became a living symbol of the idea of Africa for Africans. The nation once known as the Gold Coast is rich in gold and cocoa, but burdened, like so many African nations, with an unbelievably tragic past. It was from here that so many departed to the New World, packed into ships as slaves. And dozens of slave forts still haunt the coast. Most are tourist sites now—but this show is not about the past.

"Modern-day Ghana is an exciting place to see where, hopefully, much of Africa is headed. People here are proud of the fact that this is now a land of democratic elections and rule of law. It has an economy that's still struggling, but is relatively stable and growing.

But it's the food, music, and natural beauty of Ghana that makes this first bite so fascinating."

ARRIVAL AND GETTING AROUND

Kotoka International Airport (ACC) is in Accra, Ghana's capital, situated on the coast. Kotoka is the country's largest airport, serving flights from within Ghana, to and from other West and North African nations; Dubai; Istanbul; London; Brussels; Paris; Amsterdam; Washington, DC; and New York. Africa World Airlines is a Ghanaian company that makes its hub at Kotoka.

To get from the airport to the center of Accra, an approximately five-mile, fifteen- to forty-five-minute drive, depending on traffic (which can be formidable, or worse), take a metered cab, administered by Labour Enterprise Trust Company, at car park 5. A ride should cost about 50 Ghanaian cedis, or about US$10, with an expected 5 to 10 percent tip on the fare. Other cabs are not metered, so you will need to negotiate a fare ahead of time with the driver. Ghana is, in general, a place where bargaining over prices is the norm, so be prepared, and familiarize yourself with the generally accepted value of things before setting out.

THE CHOP BAR: "A UNIQUELY GHANAIAN INSTITUTION"

"I like chops, and I like bars, but what is a chop bar?" asked Tony of his local host en route to **Asanka Local**, a typical chop bar, or casual restaurant where one can get a hearty Ghanaian meal, along with specialties from nearby Côte D'Ivoire, Nigeria, and Togo. The menu is heavy on plantain, beans, peanuts, cassava, rice, tilapia, crab, goat, lamb, beef, yam, and spinach, with plenty of spicy dishes marinated in local peppers, tomatoes, and onions.

"**Your basic meal in Ghana,**" said Tony, having been schooled by his hosts, "**consists of a soup with peanut or spicy palm nut oil, and meat or fish, with a ball of starch, in this case** *omo tuo,* **which is made of pounded rice that you use to pick up the meat and soak up the soup.**" Of his meal of groundnut soup, goat meat, cow tongue, beans, and rice balls, Tony remarked, "**Man, that's so flavorful, so good! It's spicy, but, you know, it's not painful. Just perfect, hearty, powerful flavors.**"

Asanka Local is more than just a restaurant; it's a social occasion, and especially popular on Sundays. "**In Ghana, you also get a chance to sweat after you eat. Having a happening band and dance floor is an important component to any award-winning chop bar like Asanka Local.**"

ASANKA LOCAL: Mowule Street, Accra, Tel +233 50147 8303, www.asankalocalgh.com (typical full meal no more than 55 Ghanaian cedi/US$10)

EATING IN ACCRA AFTER DARK

"**We drove to the Osu area to sample some of the specialties of the famed Osu Night Market. The market exists to serve clubgoers, night workers, and anyone in need of authentic Ghanaian food after the sun goes down. I guess I've eaten at enough street markets now to qualify as some kind of expert, and in my expert opinion, this place earns high marks. Good flavors, strong flavors, you know? Spicy, really interesting combinations of spices. The food smells good, tastes good, and is amazingly fresh.**"

It's an open-sided affair, fluorescent-lit and crammed with fried and grilled seafood, *kenkey* (balls of fermented corn dough), *banku* (fermented corn dough and pounded cassava balls), and an extremely fiery pepper sauce called *shitor.*

For some of the best bites in the market, seek out the pork rib, shank, ear, and belly; the spinach stew; and the slow-roasted bean and rice.

OSU NIGHT MARKET: Basel Street, Accra (prices vary)

INDIA

MUMBAI: EATING ON THE STREET

"I am ready to take on the biggest city in India. Welcome to Mumbai, formerly Bombay. It's a place where the super-rich live in close proximity to the destitute poor—but life here is more complex than that. Everyone knows about Bollywood, the center of the Indian film industry, being located here, but the shipping, financial, and information technology sectors have done a lot more to create and sustain this economy. I kept waiting for streets full of network administrators and accountants to start singing and dancing, but it never happened."

GETTING THERE

Mumbai, known as Bombay until 1995, is served by **Chhatrapati Shivaji International Airport (BOM)**. Terminal 1, once known as Santa Cruz, handles domestic flights, and Terminal 2, once known as Sahar, handles international and some domestic flights. The terminals are located three miles apart, making it essential when arranging transportation for you to know which terminal is relevant to your plans. Each terminal has an interterminal transportation counter in its arrivals hall, where you can arrange for a sedan or SUV to transport you and your luggage between terminals, if necessary, for 215–275 rupees/US$3–$4 for a sedan, or 715–775 rupees/US$10–$11 for an SUV.

A taxi from the airport to the city center will take anywhere from thirty minutes to two hours, depending on traffic. Take a "Cool Cab" if you want to prepay the agreed-on fare (typically 500–600 rupees, or about US$8) and enjoy air conditioning, or take your chances with a black-and-yellow metered taxi, whose drivers have something of a reputation for pulling scams and overcharging visitors, though the rate should be roughly the same as the prepaid cab. For any cab driver, a 10 percent tip for good service is standard.

There are several suburban train stations less than ten miles from either of the two airport terminals, reachable by taxi, but none at the airport proper.

Trains are an essential means of transport around and through Mumbai, with a vast number of stations and routes. The major stations include the stunning Victorian gothic Chhatrapati Shivaji Terminus, formerly known as Victoria Terminus; it's a UNESCO World Heritage site, designed by the British architect F. W. Stevens; and Mumbai Central, formerly called Bombay Central.

BHENDI BAZAAR: "EATING STREET"

"Mumbai is a city rich in culture and history, and I know a lot of people would devote their first trip here to visiting museums, viewing the architecture, and sucking up local color like a vacuum cleaner from hell. I have my own agenda. Tonight, we're on a mission to the Muslim section called Bhendi Bazaar. Specifically, Khau Galli, which translates as 'Eating Street' or 'Food Street.'"

As he wandered Khau Galli in search of lamb brains, Tony was side-tracked by endless temptations, including spiced and grilled kidney and lung kebabs, tandoori chicken, minced lamb skewers, creamy goat brain curry with tomatoes, various freshly baked breads, and "*beida roti*—kind of like an Egg McMuffin, only good: mincemeat and eggs fried up in chapati.

"It may seem to some people that I spend an inordinate amount of time eating guts and brains and lungs, things a lot of people might call 'gross.' I won't deny taking a savage pleasure in shaking people's assumptions about food. But these neglected parts of the animals we eat are more than just nutritious. They're really good. If you're lucky enough to travel to places like India or, for that matter, France, get out of the hotel and try a few local specialties. Finding a new food you like is one of the great things about traveling.

"I don't know if it's because of the prohibition on alcohol or what, but Muslim cooks have some serious desserts and dessert drinks to offer. At the **Taj Mahal Cold Drink House** they call this the *falooda*. The ingredients are fresh coriander seeds, rosewater, noodles—in this case arrowroot, to add a texture somewhat like vermicelli—homemade ice cream in one version, and milk in all versions. . . . I could easily become addicted to this."

Note: Bhendi Bazaar, a market district first established by the colonial government in 1893 as a center for migrant male workers, is now home to over 1,200 shops and some 2,500 increasingly dilapidated residences. Bhendi Bazaar is on the cusp of a massive redevelopment plan, meant in part to shore up unsafe conditions, funded by a community trust. One likely result is that some of the street food vendors Tony visited will have been relocated or closed, so you'd be advised to check with local media and those in the know about where best to find the street foods you're seeking in Mumbai.

BHENDI BAZAAR: Ajmer, Bhuleshwar, Mumbai (prices vary)

PUNJAB

"Amritsar: the Indian Punjab's largest city. Population, about a million. This is a part of India I've never seen, a place I've always been curious about. Punjabis are known for their adventurous spirit; as brave warriors who spread throughout the world bringing great food with them. In fact, much of the good stuff we refer to simply as 'Indian food' comes from here.

"Around here, one of the first things you notice that's different from the rest of India: turbans, the symbol of self-respect, bravery, and spirituality for Sikh men. Amritsar is the home, the spiritual center, of the Sikh faith. The world's fifth-largest and maybe most misunderstood religion. In the heart of Amritsar stands the majestic Golden Temple, the Sikh equivalent of the Vatican. Sikhs are fundamentally against any caste system, believers in religious tolerance.

But they are just as fundamentally warlike when it comes to defending their principles and what they see as their territory.

"The Punjab of the early twentieth century saw some of the most violent resistance to British rule. And when the British finally cashed out in 1947, they carved off a huge piece, what is now Pakistan. And it remains a potential flash point for conflict.

"India and Pakistan were once one country, ripped apart in one of the hastiest, ill-considered partitions imaginable. . . . Drained by the colossal task of fighting two world wars, in 1947, Great Britain decided to end its nearly two-hundred-year rule over India. In an attempt to prevent what the colonials saw as an inevitable civil war among Hindus, Muslims, and Sikhs, the British commissioned Sir Cyril Radcliffe, a lawyer from Wales, to draw up a new border. In one of the largest exchanges of populations in history, many millions of people fled their homes. Almost immediately, religious violence broke out on a mass scale. This is exactly what the partition had been intended to avoid. It is an ongoing struggle, an enduring cause of paranoia, visible all across the region."

ARRIVAL AND GETTING AROUND

Sri Guru Ram Dass Jee International Airport (ATQ) is served by British Airways, Singapore Airlines, Air India, Qatar Airways, and a few regional Indian carriers, with flights to and from the major cities of the Indian subcontinent, Southeast Asia, and a few Middle Eastern destinations. It is located about seven miles from the city center; a taxi will take twenty to thirty minutes, and cost between 300 and 1,000 rupees/US$4–$15, and a *tuk-tuk*, or auto-rickshaw as they're known in Amritsar, will take thirty to forty minutes and cost about 200 rupees/US$2. Taxis and auto-rickshaws are also available for getting around town and to all tourist destinations.

EATING IN THE DHABAS OF PUNJAB

"Punjab is home to some pretty legendary cuisine. In Amritsar, they have a saying: 'The best food isn't cooked in people's homes. You find it on the streets,' often in a dhaba, meaning, 'side-of-the-road food stall.' And there are, like, countless *dhabas* to choose from in this town, but this one is legendary."

Kesar da Dhaba is indeed very well known, having been in operation by four generations of the same family since 1916. The signature dish is *dal makhni*, a combination of black and brown lentils in a ghee-rich gravy seasoned with onions, ginger, and warm spices.

Once meant mainly to serve the population of professional drivers in Punjab but increasingly appealing to the general public, *dhabas* are often situated next to gas stations, and they are frequently open twenty-four hours. Some *dhabas* serve "nonvegetarian" fare; that is, meat and seafood.

"You eat around this part of the world—Punjab in particular—get used to eating a lot of vegetarian. And India is one of the few places on earth where, even for me, that's not a burden. In the Punjab, meat or no meat, you're almost guaranteed a free-for-all of intense colors, flavors, and spices.

"Unlike some of the joyless vegetarian restaurants in my sad experience, vegetables here are actually spicy, all taste different, different textures, and served with extraordinarily good bread. It's multitiered—crispy on the outside, chewy in the middle. If this was what vegetarianism meant in most of the places that practice it in the West, I'd be at least half as much less of a dick about the subject."

KESAR DA DHABA: Anant Seth Wala Church, Passian Shastri Market, Katra Ahluwalia, Amritsar, Punjab 143006, Tel +91 183 255 2103, www.kesardadhaba.com (typical multicourse meal about 60 rupees/less than US$1)

The tandoor, a circular clay oven fueled by charcoal or wood fire, is the defining tool of Punjab cuisine; the geographic layouts and cultural hubs of rural villages often center on a communal tandoor, for the efficient feeding of large groups of people. Skewered meats (typically chicken and mutton) cook over the tandoor's live fire, with their juices dripping onto the coals or wood, creating a pungent smoke, while wheat flour breads, like *kulcha*, are baked alongside the hot interior walls.

"Want something good? Really, really good when in Amritsar? Something local, regional, iconically wonderful? You can't say you've had the Amritsar experience until you've had a little *kulcha* in your life. This is the iconic dish of Punjab. A perfect little flavor bomb of wheat dough, pressed against the side of a very, very hot clay oven, slathered with butter, and served with a spicy *chole*—a chickpea curry—on the side. Did I mention the butter?"

KULCHA MAGBOOL ROAD: Old Octroy, Teja Singh Market Shop No. 1 Amritsar, Punjab 143001, Tel +91 981 567 2729 (typical *kulcha* about 50 rupees/US$0.75)

Of course, there comes a time when even the most open-minded carnivore reverts to his old ways.

"Checking off my list of things to do in the Punjab, I gotta score some animal protein. It's time. I've been going all Morrissey for like two days now, and frankly, that's enough. I need chicken. When we're talking [Punjab] must-haves, tandoori chicken is just that."

While getting your poultry fix at **Beera Chicken**, a *dhaba* known for its ways with nonvegetarian foods, also try the *keema naan*. **"*Keema naan*: mutton ball, dough. Believe me when I tell you—this shit is good. So good that people snap it up the second it comes out of the tandoori oven."**

BEERA CHICKEN: Majitha Road, Sehaj Avenue, Amritsar, Punjab 143001, Tel +91 85669 14747 (typical entrée 400 rupees/US$5)

RAJASTHAN

"Rajasthan [is] one of India's harshest and most desolate regions, located in the northwestern tip of the continent. For centuries, [it was] home to numerous independent feudal kingdoms, and a fierce warrior class who resisted the influence and domination of invaders and neighbors alike. It's one of the most magnificent areas of India, a storybook land of mountaintop castles and forts. [There are] bleak monochrome deserts festooned with flashes of bright color, where even modest homes can be over a thousand years old. There's nowhere else like it on earth. It really doesn't matter where the road takes you here. It doesn't matter where you find yourself when you wake up. Of all the places in the world, it has perhaps the biggest heart and the most beautiful things to see. Whether you wake up in a maharanah's palace or a swank hotel or a cheap hostel or a sand dune in the desert, you're grateful to be alive and still in India."

GETTING THERE

New Delhi's **Indira Gandhi International Airport** (**DEL**), named for the former prime minister, is the closest international airport to Rajasthan. From there, you can take a short flight to Jaipur or Jodhpur, or an approximately six-hour train from one of Delhi's three train stations, to Jaipur Junction, and from there rely on taxis, or rent a car. There are also trains between Delhi and Jodphur, which will take closer to twelve hours. See www.erail.in for schedule, fare, and route information.

WHERE TO STAY

"Dilwara is a charming, picture-book village of old homes and shops, winding streets, and friendly people. One of the most enchanted and enchanting villages I've ever encountered.

"The **Devigarh** is an eighteenth-century fort palace parked in the Aravalli Hills. Let's just say it ain't a Motel 6, 7, or 8. I am just a complete round-heeled pushover for a fine hotel. And this, the Devigarh, come on. This is it, this is the mountaintop. Top of the heap."

The fort, built of locally mined marble, was originally completed in 1760, and opened as a luxury hotel in 1999, after a fifteen-year restoration process. Every room is a suite, ranging from luxurious to outrageous; service is superb, as are the food, the cocktails, and the views.

RAAS DEVIGARH: NH8, near Eklingji Temple Delwara, Udaipur, Rajasthan 313202, Tel +91 291 2636455, www.raasdevigarh.com (suites start at about 17,800 rupees/US$250 per night)

UDAIPUR

"The city of Udaipur dates back to the late sixteenth century, created after the turbulent struggle for control of the region. Today, about 400,000 Rajasthanis call it home. As you'd expect, most of the town's business is done outdoors. Vendors of all kinds line the streets, with vegetables, spices, bread, fruit, and whatever else you need to get through the day.

"**Natraj** is a meatless institution that serves the traditional all-you-cat-eat *thali* meal. I may hate hippies, and while I like vegetables just fine, I usually prefer them served next to a big hunk of pork. But a *thali* meal is a thing of wonder, an all-you-can-eat staple of Rajasthani everyday life that actually makes veg-only fare vibrant, flavorful, and fun. These aren't complicated dishes: there's lentils, okra, potatoes, pickles, curds, beans, and other Rajasthani staples. Natraj is as local a joint as you get. Families, kids, working people, and waiters running around with buckets of more. Look the other way, and your plate is replenished, piled high with food. It just keeps coming."

NATRAJ DINING HALL AND RESTAURANT: 22–24 City Station Road, Udaipur, Rajasthan, Tel +91 94147 57893 (average entrée about 160 rupees/about US$2.25)

ADVENTURE IN ANCIENT JAISALMER

"The main reason to come to Jaisalmer is to visit the enormous fort located in its center, a city within a city. Built in the mid-1100s, the **Jaisalmer Fort**, with its massive sandstone walls, is the world's only living fort. After passing through several towering gates, the visitor encounters a labyrinth of small streets filled with vendors and ancient homes. Thousands of people still live within its walls. And not surprisingly, more than a few cows."

Please note that while this UNESCO World Heritage Site contains functioning hotels within its walls, the use of modern plumbing and the associated wear and tear of live-in tourism have accelerated the decay of this majestic relic; consider staying nearby instead. The website that follows contains links to local accommodations.

JAISALMER FORT: Fort Road, Near Gopa Chowk, Amar Sagar Pol, Jaisalmer, Rajasthan 345001, www.tourism.rajasthan.gov.in/jaisalmer .html

"It's all colors, sounds, movements . . . and guys on camels playing brass instruments? This is one of those scenes where you get the slackjawed and touristy feeling—in a good way. Welcome to the annual **Jaisalmer Desert Festival**, where hundreds of Rajasthanis gather each year to celebrate their culture, streaming in from hundreds of miles away, dressed in traditional costumes."

There are dozens of festivals and fairs year-round in Rajasthan; these events are organized by the regional tourism authority. Exact dates, locations, lodging information, and more can be found at their well-maintained website: www.tourism.rajasthan.gov.in, or, if you have one, from a trusted local travel agency, of which there are many servicing Rajasthan.

IRELAND

DUBLIN

"Ireland: I don't know of another place in the world where the word, both spoken and written, is so celebrated. Where storytelling, through poetry, prose, or in song, is so integral, so influential, so much part of all English-language literature, that we, all of us, regard it almost as a birthright.

"Most of those stories have been sad or angry—celebrating strength over adversity and oppression, bemoaning the bad, commemorating the lost. History, as told through word or song, seems to have happened only, and always, just yesterday."

ARRIVAL AND GETTING AROUND

You'll fly into **Dublin Airport (DUB)**, served by dozens of international and domestic carriers that use two terminals. There are a number of direct and local shuttle bus options for getting into the city from the airport, with fares ranging from 7 to 25 euros/US$8–$28, and all information is available via the airport's official website, www.dublinair port.com. A taxi from the airport to the city center is about 25 euros/US$28. Tipping isn't necessarily expected, but the practice of tipping taxi drivers about 10 percent of the fare is increasingly common and will be appreciated.

In an episode of *The Layover*, Tony explained his preference for a taxi over the bus. "**It's a little more, but not much. And, you get conversation, which is something to be savored in Ireland. If you've got any kind of a heart, a soul, an appreciation for your fellow man, or any kind of appreciation for the written word, or simply a love of a perfectly poured beverage, then there's no way you could avoid loving this city.**"

CODDLED IN PUB CITY

"**What do they do here better than any other place on earth? Answer: Guinness. This delicious, some say magical, probably nutritious, unparalleled beverage. This divine brew is so tasty, creamy, so near chocolatey in its rich, satisfying, buzz-giving qualities, that the difference between the stuff here, and the indifferently poured swill you get where you come from, is like night and day. One is beer, the other, angels sing celestial trombones.**"

One of his favorite places for a Guinness was a bar in the Glasnevin area called **John Kavanagh**. "**Known locally as Gravediggers, due to its proximity to the boneyard next door, the place is gloriously unfucked by time.**" There's no music, no dancing, no television, no Wi-Fi, and they don't book the place out for groups—it's strictly a place to drink in company, often with mourners on their way to or from a burial, as it's been since 1833.

After a few pints, should you want some nourishing bar food, you'll be done right by a bowl of "**coddle, a hearty stew of sausages, bacon, onion, and potatoes, slow-simmered in stock. . . . You hear about it, you want it. And there's more: slow-cooked, simmered-in-cider pigs' feet. You may not think you want it, my friends, but believe me, you do.**"

JOHN KAVANAGH: 1 Prospect Square, Glasnevin, Dublin, D09 CF72, Tel +353 1830 7978 (drink and food prices range from 3 to 11 euros/US$3.25–$12.25)

The Chop House **"is what some used to call a gastropub, an idiotic term coined by those who thought that somehow a properly poured pint couldn't or shouldn't coexist with fine-quality food. I, to tell you the truth, used to be just such an idiot."** Disabused of this notion, Tony declared his visit **"the best fucking meal I've ever eaten in Dublin."**

Chef Kevin Arundel and his wife and business partner, Jillian Mulcahy, have spent more than a decade turning out creative, French-inflected cuisine in a repurposed pub, serving the likes of pan-seared king prawns with lemon, chili, garlic, and smoked paprika butter, porterhouse steaks built for two, and a foie-gras-and-chicken-liver parfait with blood orange jelly.

THE CHOP HOUSE: 2 Shelbourne Road, Ballsbridge, Dublin 4, Tel +353 16602390, www.thechophouse.ie (appetizers about 10 euros/ US$11, entrées about 30 euros/US$33.50)

ISRAEL

JERUSALEM

"First, look around. It's like everybody says. It's pretty. It's awesome. It's urban, sophisticated, hip, like Southern California, only nicer. Then you see the young draftees on the streets and you start to get the idea. This is Jerusalem.

"Israel is bordered by Egypt, Jordan, Syria, and Lebanon. In 1967, after the Six-Day War, Israel took control of the Gaza Strip, the Sinai Peninsula, the West Bank, and the Golan Heights, and annexed East Jerusalem. In 2003, Israel began construction on a wall along the Green Line, representing the Israeli-Palestinian border.

"It's easily the most contentious piece of real estate in the world. And there's no hope—none—of ever talking about it without pissing somebody, if not everybody, off. Maybe that's why it's taken me so long to come here. A place where even the names of ordinary things are ferociously disputed. Where does falafel come from? Who makes the best hummus? Is it a fence, or a wall?

"Just because I was raised outside the faith with no particular attachment or loyalty to Israel doesn't mean that plenty of people on this earth don't hate me in principle. I know that. But the state of Israel: I never really knew what to think.

"I'll be seen by many as a terrorist sympathizer, a Zionist tool, a self-hating Jew, an apologist for American imperialism, an oriental-ist, socialist, fascist, CIA agent, and worse. So, here goes nothing."

ARRIVAL AND GETTING AROUND

Ben Gurion Airport (**TLV**) is Israel's largest international entry point, twelve miles from Tel Aviv and twenty-eight miles from Jerusalem. It serves flights to and from within Israel, and throughout Asia, all of Europe, and a handful of African and North and South American cities.

Car rentals are widely available and, at about 88 Israeli new shekels (US$25) per day, quite affordable. A taxi from the airport to the city center of Jerusalem will take about an hour, and should cost about 265 shekels/US$75. Taxi drivers in Israel do not expect to be tipped.

There is an hourly shuttle bus between TLV terminal 3 and Jerusalem's central bus terminal. It's 15 shekels/US$4.50 each way; purchase tickets in cash upon boarding. See www.bus.co.il for all up-to-date route and fare information.

Visitors can enter Israel from Egypt or Jordan, but be advised that these border crossings can be arduous and slow, with times and rules changing frequently. Check with trusted travel authorities, and be sure to have currency from both countries on hand.

Within Jerusalem, it is easy to hail or order a taxi; a typical five-mile trip should cost about 40 shekels/US$13. There is also a wide-ranging bus system, and a light rail line, that use preloadable Rav-Kav smart cards; get all of the info at www.egged.co.il.

AMERICAN COLONY HOTEL AND MAJDA RESTAURANT: OASES OF CALM

While staying in Jerusalem, Tony's home base was the **American Colony Hotel**, a luxury resort that is the favored lodging of journalists, UN officers, diplomats, and celebrities. It was once a utopian Christian colony founded by a wealthy Chicago couple, Horatio and Anna Spafford, seeking solace in the wake of the shipwreck drowning of their four children. Not given to proselytizing, the Spaffords and their ilk were welcomed by the surrounding community; the colony thrived for about sixty years, surviving a literal plague of locusts and two world wars, but it disbanded in the 1950s due to internal conflicts; the new owners converted the building into the present-day hotel.

The hotel's Old Wing is the former home of a pasha and his four wives; there are four buildings in all, each with its own lush garden. The American Colony is private and quiet, though Tony was entranced by the morning call to prayer.

AMERICAN COLONY HOTEL: 1 Louis Vincent Street, Jerusalem 97200, Tel +972 2 627 9777, www.americancolony.com (rooms start at about 700 shekels/US$200 per night)

"You could almost believe, for a minute or two, that some kind of peace, some kind of reconciliation, meeting of the minds, sanity, is possible, after you visit **Majda**. It's a restaurant in what looks like an idyllic village in the Judean Hills. It feels like an alternate universe for a number of reasons.

"Michal Balanes is Jewish. Jakob Bahrun is Muslim, from a nearby village. They're partners, co-owners of Majda, and also married. Together, they grow and raise much of what's used in their kitchen. Their food reflects both their different backgrounds and their commonalities."

A meal at Majda might include eggs with peppers and tomatoes, or charred okra with onion and mint. "I just had this incredibly delicious meal, completely oblivious to the fact that it's entirely vegetarian. If any of the vegetarian restaurants in New York served food that tasted anywhere near this I would actually . . . go there? I'd consider it."

MAJDA: Ein Rafa, Tel +972 2 579 7108, www.majda.co.il (typical meal about 175 shekels/US$50 per person)

ITALY

NAPLES

Tony embarked on a quest to reconcile his deep attraction to Italian American culture, despite the lack of it in his own DNA, by diving into the classic food of Naples for *No Reservations*.

"Naples, the Naples of our collective imagination. The old country, where one was always led to believe it all started. With a spoonful of nostalgia and even more sauce, we were told the Italian food we ate in America came from here. But to what extent was what we knew of Neapolitan food ever Italian or even from Naples?

"Very little about Naples makes sense in the beginning: not the way they drive, or navigate the roads in Naples's historic central district.

"What you hear from other Italians is that Naples isn't even Italy.

"But that's a very Italian attitude to start with, a not-quite nation of city-states for whom the next village over will always be the worst place on earth. The joke is that the city is filled with thieves, and one does tend to lose things not looked after carefully, including, say, control of the garbage industry, which may be because the Camorra, Naples's powerful brother to Sicily's mafia, have pretty much a hammerlock on everything that goes on here.

"Through history, the area hasn't caught many breaks. Living in the shadow of Vesuvius, invasions, World War II—everybody seems to mess with Naples."

ARRIVAL AND GETTING AROUND

Naples International Airport (NAP), also known as **Capodochino**, mainly services connections from other European cities, but there are also a handful of direct flights from New York and a few Middle Eastern cities. It's located about five miles from the city center; a metered taxi will take fifteen to thirty minutes, depending on traffic, and will cost about 20 euros/US$22; tipping is not customary, but it is increasingly common among Western tourists; a 10 to 15 percent tip will be appreciated.

There are also shuttle and city buses to get you to and from town. See www.unicocampania.it for schedules, routes, and fares.

Napoli Centrale is the city's main train station, centrally located in Piazza Garibaldi, with connections to the rest of Italy and beyond. You can also depart and arrive in Naples by boat via cruise ships or ferries at Stazione Marittima, which is centrally located.

Naples is an occasionally steep but visually striking pleasure to explore on foot; if you're so inclined, metered taxis queue at most piazzas throughout the city. Connect to Naples's subway system beneath Napoli Centrale or at other points in the city. There are also municipal bus, tram, and funicular systems; check www.anm.it for information.

EATING THE HISTORY OF ITALIAN AMERICAN CUISINE

"What Naples is, is damn beautiful. And old. Being old, it can claim responsibility for a number of iconic innovations of Italian culture, like pizza, a slab or a round of dough, covered with tomato sauce, cheese, and maybe some other stuff. Simple, right?

"A lot of what I grew up eating was Neapolitan pizza. What do they mean by that? In 2004, the Italian Ministry of Agriculture actually laid out regulations for how a Neapolitan pizza must be made—dimensions, thickness of crust, ingredients, even cooking temperature. And this place, **Pizzeria Pellone**, is, by Neapolitan general consensus, an excellent example of industry standard, and even one of the very best at making this, pizza margherita, classic minimalist." Pellone also traffics in a fried pizza—really a fried calzone—stuffed with ricotta and crisp fried pork shards.

PIZZERIA PELLONE: Via Nazionale 93, 80143 Naples, Tel +39 081 553 8614, www.pellonepizzeria.it (average pizza about 7 euros/US$8)

"'Everything but anchovies' types: prepared to have your minds changed, and possibly blown, at **Al Convento**, a restaurant located in a former convent in the small town of Cetara, where *alici* are the local specialty and stars of the menu by chef Pasquale Torrente.

"We're talking stuff that in no way resembles the oily, salty, stinky goop you may know from days of college desperation. White, almost sweet, marinated anchovies; anchovy with slow-roasted tomatoes, and fried with onions," as well as anchovy meatballs stuffed with

smoked mozzarella, a variation on eggplant parmigiana stuffed with anchovies, and linguine puttanesca with, naturally, fresh anchovies.

AL CONVENTO: Piazza San Francesco 16, 80410 Cetara, Tel +39 089 261039 (average entrée about 35 euros/US$39)

After diving for fresh sea urchins under a threatening sky (and eating them alfresco, straight from the catch), chef Rocco Iannone took Tony back to his restaurant, **Pappacarbone**, for a spontaneous lunch, informed by what was fresh and on hand: deep-fried local octopus, grilled caciocavallo cheese with fava beans, artichokes, spring onions, and pancetta, and *spaghetti di frutti de mare* with two types of local clams. Iannone thrilled Tony with his pasta-cooking technique, removing the pasta from the boiling water and finishing it in the pan with the seafood, wine, stock, and aromatics. **"It's all the difference in the world when you finish the pasta in the sauce and it takes that stuff in. That's magic."**

PAPPACARBONE: Via Rosario Senatore 30, 84103 Cava de' Tirrena, Tel +39 347 797 0604, www.ristrorantepappacarbone.com (tasting menu 70 euros/US$78 per person)

ROME

"As so many have found throughout history, it's easy to fall in love with Rome. She is seductively beautiful. She has endured and survived many things. What's left of her former glories, her days of empire, are in ruins, but those ruins continue to enchant us. You fall into a trance here. You think, no matter what, this beautiful dream will last forever—and then, suddenly, shit gets real.

"Before World War I, Benito Mussolini was considered a buffoon and a crackpot. A short-tempered, ever-pontificating, soapbox orator from the small town of Predappio. In time, though, the country was divided and in crisis. It saw itself as besieged by enemies within and without. It needed someone who said he could make Italy great again. He was a man on a horse saying, 'Follow me.' And they did. When Fascists marched on Rome, the prime minister resigned and Benito Mussolini was appointed leader by the king. It can happen anywhere. It happened here. Nearly a century later, this is what he left behind: the Rome that many Romans still live in today.

"No matter whose Rome it is—yours, mine, or Federico Fellini's, it's beautiful, as beautiful as everybody says it is. To me, it's not the big things they tell you about—the sculptures, the imposing squares and buildings, the monuments—though they are amazing. It's the little things, the tiny details, the improbable awesomeness of every little damn thing."

ARRIVAL AND GETTING AROUND

Rome's **Leonardo Da Vinci-Fiumicino Airport (FCO)**, is "about twenty miles from the center of Italy's capital city, but it might as well be another planet," said Tony, opening *The Layover* after a very early morning landing from New York. Fiumicino is Italy's largest airport, a major European hub with flights to and from all parts of the globe.

"Fiumicino Airport has the usual assortment of transportation options. The easiest, but pricier, would be a taxi straight into town to your hotel. That's a flat fare of [48 euros/US$53.50]. There are shuttle buses for about fifteen bucks [13.50 euros] which should take about forty minutes, but traffic can be unpredictable. I opt for the [Leonardo] express train this time around. Twenty dollars [18 euros] and only thirty minutes. It's supposed to be fast, efficient, easy, but honestly, as I stare down yet another endless walkway, I begin to regret my decision. Don't do this, man. Take a cab, especially if you have luggage." Italian drivers do not expect a tip, but you may round up to the nearest euro.

Rome has a second, much smaller airport, the one-terminal **Ciampino Giovan Battista Pastine (CIA)**, which mostly serves low-cost airlines and their flights within the European continent. It's about seven miles outside the center of the city, with metered taxis available for a 30 euro (US$34) flat rate, and direct bus connections to Rome's centrally located Termini station, for 6 to 10 euros/US$5.50–$11 each way, with tickets available in the arrivals hall.

Tony wasn't a big fan of **Roma Termini**, Italy's largest train station—**"The massive transportation hub of Rome, and the center of suckdom, as far as I'm concerned. It has all the charm of New York's Penn Station, which is to say, none at all."** Since he made that harsh declaration in 2012, however, Roman authorities have made some improvements to the station, which now has an above-average food court, Mercado Central, and a slightly less chaotic parking and exit situation on the streets outside.

Rome's public transportation options include a three-line metro system, buses, and trams. A ride on any of them is 1.50 euro/US$1.67, with integrated fare cards available for purchase in metro stations and many convenience stores and newsstands.

Taxis queue at ranks located in many of the city's best-known *piazze* (squares); be sure to take only those that are officially licensed, which are white cars with roof signs and telephone numbers on the side of the car, and functioning meters. The most notorious taxi rip-offs happen outside Termini. If you're far from a taxi rank, you'll need to call for a car (or have an Italian do it for you); in this case, be advised that the meter starts when the driver accepts the ride, not when you enter the vehicle. A typical ride will cost between 6 and 20 euros/ US$7–$22, and a 5 to 10 percent tip for good service is appreciated. And of course, in most weather, Rome is a gloriously walkable city, with plenty to see and eat along the way to your destination.

SLEEPING IN ROME

"I suggest the Centro Storico or historical center in the city, so you're within walking distance of all the good stuff that you want to at least lay eyes on. Hotels are expensive, so book early if you're shooting for lower-price pensiones, as they tend to fill up quickly."

Just outside the Centro Storico, in the neighborhood called Monti, which was once a red-light district, there are a number of clean, quiet, and reasonably priced pensiones, among them the forty-one-room **Hotel Raffaello**, located in a nineteenth-century building whose interior has been updated with a small elevator that stops on the half floor. The private baths are relatively large, the linens are crisp, the interiors are classic and charming (if slightly dated), and the staff is friendly and accommodating. It's a short walk to the nearby Cavour stop on the metro B line, and the Colosseum and Roman Forum are also within walking distance, as is the aforementioned Termini station.

"On the other hand, if you want to blow it out and live large and pay big-time for the privilege, the Hotel de Russie is swankadelic, discreet, and it's right down the street, yet comfortably insulated

from, the Spanish Steps. But again, it's expensive." Built in 2000, the 120-room hotel is warm and stylish, with a terraced garden and courtyard, spa, hammam, hair salon, and an excellent food and beverage program. It's family friendly, and the concierge staff is among the best in Rome.

HOTEL RAFFAELLO: Via Urbana 3, Rome 00814, Tel +39 06 488 4342, www.hotelraffaello.it (rooms start at about 75 euro/US$83 per night)

HOTEL DE RUSSIE: Via del Babuino 9, Rome 00187, Tel +39 06 328 881, www.roocofortehotels.com (rooms start at about 450 euro/US$500 per night)

EATING IN ROME

You may believe that you're in Rome for the antiquities, the modern art and culture, to learn the language—but, really, it's the food, and the way in which it's prepared, and shared, consumed, and celebrated for its elemental perfection. Don't waste time or space on a large breakfast; Italians stick to a cornetto (a sweeter, softer, and less-buttery croissant-like pastry) and an espresso or cappuccino, in anticipation of lunch and dinner.

"What's a Roman specialty you might have for, say, a light lunch or a snack? Well . . . score yourself some porchetta. This is **I Porchettoni**, and they are not fucking around. The pride of Rome, porchetta is a whole deboned pig stuffed with herbs, spit roasted, and generally served with a pitcher of ice-cold Italian beer." I Porchettoni is a *fraschetta*—a simple, tavern-like restaurant with communal, paper-covered tables, sturdy glassware, and plastic plates—of the type found in the nearby hill town of Ariccia. In addition to the excellent porchetta, there are classic pastas (*spaghetti cacio e pepe*, *penne arrabiata*, and on Thursdays only, gnocchi), main dishes (Roman-style tripe, grilled sausages, steaks, milk-braised pork), and house wines and beers.

I PORCHETTONI: Via dei Marrucini 18, 00185 Rome, Tel +39 06 4958598 (no website) (two-course meal with wine about 25 euros/ US$28 per person)

"Welcome to **Roscioli**, a family empire of the old, good stuff. In English, we can only say, 'deli,' only it's not really a deli, it's a treasure trove of salumi, cheese, tuna. Words fail here. It's also a bakery, and more. They've got master-crafted breads, and pizza bianca. The bread, just listening to it makes your dick stand right up. And of course, prosciutto, prosciutto, prosciutto. Jesus Lord, this is good."

Roscioli has a handful of storefronts within walking distance of one another, serving various functions: a high-end deli with restaurant service for lunch and dinner; a bakery with extraordinary breads and pizza sold by weight (*al taglio*); and a café. The prices are a bit high, and the stores can be a bit cramped, but the quality of the food, beverages, and service more than balances out the experience.

ROSCIOLI SALUMERIA CON CUCINA (RETAIL DELI AND RESTAURANT): Via dei Giubbonari, 21, 00186, Rome Tel +39 06 6875287, www.salumeriaroscioli.com (prices vary; typical meal 40 to 50 euros/US$44–$55 per person)

ANTICO FORNO ROSCIOLI (BAKERY WITH SANDWICHES AND PIZZAS): Via dei Chiavari 34, 00186 Rome, Tel +39 06 686 4045, www.anticotfornoroscioli.it (prices vary; pizzas about 8 euros/US$9 per kilo)

ROSCIOLI CAFFÈ (ESPRESSO BAR WITH PASTRIES, SANDWICHES, WINE, AND COCKTAILS): Piazza Benedetto Cairoli 16, 00186 Rome, Tel +39 06 8916 5330, www.cafferoscioli.com (prices vary; coffee and a pastry about 4 euros/US$4.50)

Outside the Centro Storico, Rome is full of the kind of low-key but high-quality trattorias that Tony loved for their reliably classic fare and relaxed atmosphere. Case in point:

"Betto e Mary is an unassuming, typically Roman, and definitely not touristy neighborhood place. The owner sits down like an old friend, and tells you what they got, asks what we feel like, and soon, there are antipasti of fried broccoli and mushrooms, eggplant with olives and peppers, roasted red peppers with pignoli nuts and *nervetti"*—a traditional Milanese preparation of chopped and slow-cooked tendon, cartilage, and meat from beef shin or calf's foot—**"which is tender, tender, veal-tender. Next, a very old-school dish: shaved horse meat with arugula and Parmiggiano. Oh, stop it. We may not eat horses in the United States, but we kill them by the droves and sell the meat to Canada—hypocrites. Then, rigatoni with oxtail ragù. Pretty much mention oxtail, and ragù, and I'm ready to slit somebody's throat for a bite. Oh, and fettuccini with artichoke and sweetbreads. Nice, nice, nice."**

BETTO E MARY: Via dei Savorgnan 99, 00176 Rome, Tel +39 06 6477 1096 (no website) (dinner about 20 euros/US$23 per person)

Although Tony didn't personally visit them, the following three trattorias offer a similar experience and have classic Roman food that's confirmed to be equally as good as, if not better than, what's found at Betto e Mary. Reservations are highly advised at each.

Dar Moschino is a warm, lively, family-run restaurant that's been in operation for forty years in a quiet pocket of the Garbatella neighborhood, south of the city center. The wood-paneled room is full of racehorse imagery, and the decor and service have changed very little over the years, to the delight and comfort of the regulars who populate its close-set tables. The house specialties include *gricia* (rigatoni with guanciale, grated pecorino cheese, and cracked black pepper), Roman-style stewed tripe, tender veal meatballs, and *rabbit* *alla cacciatora*, with which you should order a side of the perfectly cooked potatoes.

Piatto Romano is the local joint for its Testaccio neighbors; service is warm and efficient. Here, the *rigatoni con la pajata*, in which veal intestines, filled with mother's milk, are cooked in a piquant tomato sauce, is not to be missed. The owners often supplement the regular menu with esoteric garden greens they've grown themselves nearby, including malva and ramolaccio, or black radish leaves.

In Trastevere, **Tavernaccia da Bruno** is the place for straightforwardly excellent food and friendly service in a warm, bright room. It's been in the same family for fifty years, serving Roman classics that are flanked by some dishes common to Umbria and Sardinia, including an outstanding wood fire–roasted suckling pig. On Sundays, do not miss the lasagna bolognese.

DAR MOSCHINO: Piazza Benedetto Brin 5, 00154 Rome, Tel +39 06 513 9473 (no website) (typical meal about 25 euros/US$28 per person)

PIATTO ROMANO: Via Giovanni Battista Bodoni 62, 00153 Rome, Tel +39 06 6401 4447, www.piattoromano.com (typical meal about 30 euros/US$33 per person)

TAVERNACCIA DA BRUNO: Via Giovanna da Castel Bolognese 63, 00153 Rome, Tel +39 06 581 2792, www.latavernacciaroma.com (typical meal about 30 euros/US$33 per person)

Rome is a pizza-mad city, known both for its slices sold by weight (*pizza al taglio*), and the round, thin-crust pies, mostly seen in full-service restaurants, called *pizza tonda*. And then there's **"Pizzarium, [Gabriele] Bonci's place, a departure from the classics."** Bonci is **"a rogue pizzaiolo who's got a tiny and unusually innovative pizza shop near the Vatican where, in the last few years, [he] claims to have invented 1,500 different takes on pizza. Clearly, he's not done yet.**

Here, as with all great pizza, it starts with the dough—a true and noble dough—the best pizza being the end result of an old and well-maintained bacterial culture, a starter. Bonci is using one that's two hundred years old."

One of Bonci's notable combinations: foie gras and cherries. "It's delicious. It's fantastic. The fat from the foie, the sweetness from the cherries—it's amazing." And even the most fervent haters of Hawaiian pizza may find themselves delighted by the Pizzarium version, in which the conventional pineapple and ham topping is saved by the addition of caramelized onion. "That should not have been good. It was really, really good."

It should come as no surprise that Pizzarium is insanely popular, so expect to wait in a crush of tourists at peak hours, but know that it's worth it.

PIZZARIUM GABRIELE BONCI: Via della Meloria, 43, 00136 Rome, Tel +39 06 3974 5416, www.bonci.it (pizza sold by weight; average 10 euros/US$11 per kilogram)

"I'm at **Freni e Frizioni**, or 'brakes and clutches,' an auto repair garage turned bar. There's a free buffet for the college students to fill up on, in between drinks and unintended pregnancies.

"I'm sitting down and relaxing and having a negroni. Actually, I'm going to have a bunch of negronis.

"By the way, when making negronis at home, one-third high-end gin, one-third Campari, and one-third sweet vermouth. I don't really like gin. I don't really like Campari, and I don't like sweet vermouth, but together: your friend.

"The Count Negroni, it is said, invented this fine cocktail in Florence. Unsatisfied with the level of alcohol in his Americano cocktail of Campari and sweet vermouth, he suggested his waiter ratchet up the danger level with the addition of gin. Thus was born a classic, and many incidents dimly, if at all, remembered."

To find a good negroni elsewhere in Rome, Tony's longtime friend and fixer Sara Pampaloni suggests any historic bar in the city center, such as **Canova**, in Piazza del Popolo, or "anyplace where the Campari bottle doesn't last open more than an hour."

FRENI E FRIZIONI: Via del Politeama, 4, 00153, Rome, Tel +39 06 4549 7499, www.freniefrizioni.com (drinks about 8 euros/US$9 each, with buffet included)

CANOVA: Piazza del Popolo, 16, 00187, Rome, Tel +39 06361 2231, www.canovapiazzadelpopolo.it (cocktails about about 10 euros/ US$11 each)

SARDINIA

"What do you do after your dreams come true? I've had three or four full lives already, most of which I was surprised to find I'd survived. This is like a bonus round, undeserved probably, but like some insane pinball machine, life keeps kicking out extra points regardless of how I play it. (I imagine myself, of course, keeling over among the tomato vines in the backyard somewhere chasing a grandchild around with a slice of orange in my mouth.)

"For a guy who so rarely is home, with such a distorted view of what home is or might be to start with, I'm a pretty sickeningly happy guy these days."

This was Tony's uncharacteristically sentimental wrap-up of a very personal episode of *No Reservations*, for which he and his family traveled to Sardinia. His wife, Ottavia, spent summers with extended family on the rather isolated Mediterranean island, and Tony had already grown enamored of the ancient, largely unchanging culture, the importance of the knife in that culture, and, of course, the food.

"This is a hard place—rock and steel—where life was always tough, but tougher for invaders. You need a knife here, and everybody's got one. Things are still made by hand. The old ways, the very fact of its apartness, are honored still. You keep your family close. I come from a small family. Even at holiday meals, it was just me, my father, mother, younger brother, and maybe a cousin once in a while. Maybe that's one reason I've always been kind of bitter about not being Italian American, why I always kind of yearn for that, those scenes in movies where the whole family's sitting around at a long table, kids running around everywhere. Even when they were arguing, that looked good to me.

"Sardinia's the kind of place you better know somebody. The bumper stickers around here proudly proclaim this is not Italy, and they're not kidding. It's six to seven hours by boat west of central Italy, with its own language, its own culture, a tradition of isolation, clannishness, a place where people still only half-jokingly will tell you that there are bandits in the next village.

"European law, the Italian language, the twentieth and twenty-first centuries—they arrived here kind of late, which suits me just fine, because the food, the food is unbelievable. It's everything you love about Italy but somehow more . . . more intense. And it looks like another world.

"A couple of features you should notice straight off, because they're going to appear again and again and again: Meals almost always begin with, in one form or another, homemade and cured meats—a selection of hams, sausages, maybe a little pecorino, this being sheep country. Lots of this stuff, the omnipresent flatbread of Sardinia, *pane carasau*.

"Pasta, or often pastas, usually specific to the area and also always homemade. Then, [an] open hearth or fire, usually with great hunks of meat on skewers sizzling nearby."

ARRIVAL AND GETTING AROUND

The largest of Sardinia's three airports is in the capital, **Cagliari (CAG)**, on the southern part of the island, which is served by a number of regional European airlines. It's a fifteen- to twenty-minute drive from the airport to city center, which will cost about 20 euros/US$22 by metered taxi. Tips are appreciated but not expected. There are also bus services to the city, and about a half-dozen car rental companies if you prefer to drive yourself. There is also a ferry from Naples to Cagliari.

Closer to the places that Tony visited for *No Reservations*, however, is **Olbia Costa Smeralda Airport (OLB)**, on the island's northeast side, which is busiest during the summer holidays, receiving visitors from continental Europe on a handful of regional carriers. Buses transfer passengers to the city of Olbia or to a nearby train station for trips to the south, and taxis and car hires are available. If you have time and the inclination, you can also take a ferry from Rome to Olbia.

WHERE TO STAY

"I'm becoming a regular here at Su Gologone," Tony observed of the hotel where he posted up with his family for the duration of their Sardinia visit. It's a low-key but luxurious Mediterranean-style spa resort located fifteen miles inland from the east coast, in the Barbagia Mountains, with plenty of room to roam and loaf, and a spring-fed swimming pool. **"The restaurant is old school, a place where the food's much admired by locals. This, in a country where eating in restaurants is seen largely as a character flaw."**

SU GOLOGONE: Località Su Gologone, 0825 Olinea, Sardinia, Tel +39 0784 287512, www.sugologone.it (rooms start at about 180 euros/US$200 per night)

AGRITURISMO IN SARDINIA

"I like to think that family-run *agriturismos* are the future of Sardinia's tourism industry. Hell, the whole world's tourism industry. **Sa Rocca is an *agriturismo* built, cave-like, back into the rocks. What is an *agriturismo*? I think it's like the greatest institution ever. Basically, a funky little place in either a home, a farmhouse. . . . They appear all over Italy and Sardinia, where the small, usually set menu is explicitly local. It's fantastic. You can easily eat your way from town to town, all across the country, scarfing up local specialties."**

For Tony, Ottavia, and the extended family, who visited the restaurant, which is also open to those not staying in one of the modest but comfortable rooms on site, this included Sardinian ham, similar to Italian prosciutto but cut thicker; hand-rolled strands of pasta called *maccheroni stabusa* in tomato sauce; roasted sheep cheese with local honey, and, a particularly decadent specialty, **"*capretto arrosto stidiale*, which I'm gathering means 'baby goat, spit-roasted over the open fire,' but here it's basted with the drippings of flaming lardo, chunks of lightly cured seasoned and herbed pork fat that gives the goat a dark, golden color and crispness and intense flavor unlike anything else."**

AGRITURISMO SA ROCCA: Strada Nebida—Buggerru S.P. 83, km 13, 09016 Nebida, Sardinia, Tel +39 0781 183 6196, www.agriturismosarocca.it (rooms average 67 euros/US$75; entrées average 18 euros/US$20).

"For a typical workingman's grab-a-bite joint, there's **Zia Forica.** In a culture not known for fast food, this is about as quick as it gets, a place where you can drop in, grab a couple of small plates, maybe a quick donkey steak, and move on. I came for the snails, and the artichokes, and the *cordula*," a hyperlocal specialty composed of baby lamb or goat intestines braided around an array of other organ meats from the same animal, either spit-roasted or slow-braised with peas.

ZIA FORICA: Corso Margherita di Savoia, 39, 07100 Sassari, Sardinia, Tel +39 079 233556 (no website) (entrées average 7–9 euros/US$8–$10)

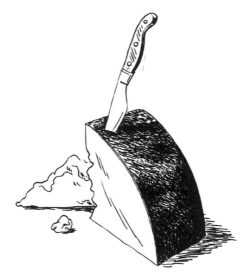

JAPAN

OSAKA: CITY OF EXCESS

"Welcome to Osaka, the hardworking, fun-loving capital of the Kansai region of Japan. It is Tokyo that Osaka is most often compared to. Where Tokyo is seen as sophisticated and a bit reserved, Osaka is considered earthy and direct. More important to me, though, is that history and geography have conspired to make Osaka the culinary heart of Japan. From ancient times, Osaka's location on Japan's inland sea, and proximity to the best farmland, made it known as the nation's kitchen.

"Over time, Osaka developed a large merchant class. Merchants had always been looked down on by Japanese society, but laws enacted in the late sixteenth century made it official, by giving them the lowest social status, and prohibiting showy displays of wealth in the clothes they wore, the houses they built, pretty much everything but food and entertainment—so a town full of merchants were forced to spend all of their money eating, drinking, and having fun. And so was born the idea of *kuidare*. Strictly translated, it means to bankrupt oneself with food. But in common usage, it's any extended period of eating and drinking to excess, preferably concluded by falling over."

GETTING THERE

Osaka has two airports. **Kansai International (KIX)**, situated in Osaka Bay, about twenty miles south of the city center, handles international flights and several daily connections to points within Japan. The Nankai Airport Express train (1,075 yen/ $10 USD) and the Rapi:t airport express train (1,500 yen/about US$14), both operated by the private Nankai Electric Railway, can be accessed from the second floor of the passenger terminal, and will take you to Nankai Namba Station, actually a massive complex of stations, with connections to the metro, Japan Rail (JR), and the highway bus terminal. There are also limousine buses with several designated drop-off points at city hotels and landmarks (1,700 yen/about US$16), as well as taxis (about 10,800 yen/US$100). Tipping taxi drivers is not part of Japanese culture; your exact change will be returned to you, or you may round up to the nearest hundred yen as a means to avoid unnecessary small change, if paying in cash.

Itami Airport (ITM), also called **Osaka International** (despite handling only domestic flights), is about six miles north of the city center, which can be reached by bus (500–900 yen/US$4–$8), limousine bus (2,100 yen/US$20), monorail (325 yen/about US$3) or taxi (5,500 yen/US$50).

Once in town, your best bet for seeing this massive city, third in size only to Tokyo and Yokohama, is the extensive and easy-to-navigate subway system or JR Loop Line train. Signs and announcements are in English, making the system far easier to navigate than the bus system.

OSAKA IS A BASEBALL TOWN

"Americans think they own baseball. I mean, the so-called World Series barely acknowledges *Canada*. But Japan has played the game since 1873. And it is hands-down the most popular spectator sport in the country.

"American players of the Japanese game complain about certain technical differences—a smaller ball and a bigger strike zone—but it's the cultural values that really throw them.

"American baseball heroes seek to differentiate themselves from their teammates by pursuing high statistical averages, the big home run that wins the game. Japanese baseball heroes make sacrifice bunts to load the bases. Serious personal sacrifice for the good of team wins the highest praise here. And the Japanese fan clubs, the *oendan*, define high praise by outrageous costumes, disciplined chanting, and sheer acoustic volume.

"**Gosakudon** is one of a number of baseball-themed restaurants in this town dedicated to Osaka's own Hanshin Tigers. Nothing reinforces the second-city status of Osaka like its baseball rivalry with the Tokyo Giants. The relationship is not unlike the New York Yankees–Boston Red Sox rivalry, with the Tigers taking the Red Sox role of having rabidly enthusiastic fans and facing endless heartbreak against the more-powerful, better-funded Giants."

Gosakudon specializes in sushi, grilled seafood skewers, and beer, and the atmosphere is lively and welcoming whether or not it's game day.

GOSAKUDON: 13–1 4 Horikoshicho, Tennoji Ward, Osaka, Osaka Prefecture 543-0056, Tel +81 50 3466 5529, www.gosakudon-tennoujikouenmae.gorp.jp (average meal 3,000–3,500 yen/US$28–$32)

OCTOPUS ALL AROUND

Among Osaka's best-known specialties are *takoyaki* (spherical fried octopus dumplings), *okonomiyaki* (a griddled savory pancake stuffed with any number of meat, fish, and vegetable variations), and *horumonyaki* (various organ meats, grilled on skewers).

"Good takoyaki can be had all over Osaka day or night. We selected **Pizza Ball House** for its disturbingly surrealist window display [in which a model octopus cooks octopus-containing *takoyaki*]. Fortunately, octo-cannibalism is the sort of thing that leaves me morally outraged without actually ruining my appetite." Guests have the option to cook their own *takoyaki* at the table, customizing the ready-chopped add-ins like scallions or cheese, or let the expert staff do the work.

TAKANOTETSU PIZZA BALL HOUSE: 1–10, Kakudacho, Kita Ward, Osaka City, Osaka Prefecture, Tel +81 06 6345 0301, www.takonotetsu.co.jp (*takoyaki* and other dishes 640–1,030 yen/ US$6–$10)

"The pride of the Kansai region is *okonomiyaki*. Calling it, as people do, a Japanese-style pizza, pancake, or omelet really doesn't do it justice. *Okonomi* means 'whatever you want,' and *yaki* means 'grilled.' So, after laying down the foundation batter, made of flour, grated yam, water, and egg, you can fit in pretty much anything. There are many regional variations to this dish, but as you might expect, Osakans favor an all-at-once, anything goes, freestyle approach. Would you like some bacon with that? Did I mention that it's usually topped with a sweet sauce and Japanese mayonnaise?" Like *takoyaki*, *okonomiyaki* is ubiquitous in Osaka; Tony had his at **Fukutaro**.

FUKUTARO: 2-Chome-3 17 Sennichimae, Chuo-ku Osaka 542–0074, Tel +81 6 6634 2951, www.2951.jp/en/ (*okonomiyaki* sets 900–1,800 yen/US$10–$20)

"*Horumonyaki*: the ancient art of barbecued cow and pig organs. This is a workingman's meal in Japan, and **Horomunyaki Dojo** is a workingman's restaurant. Tripe, some liver, tongue, face, cheeks . . . oh that's kidney . . . and the hometown favorite, most popular: fat. I hated all of this when I was a child, hated all of this. Now it's my favorite. Any great cooking culture uses all these parts. I love this place."

HOROMUNYAKI DOJO: 3-2-23 Ebisuhigashi, Naniwa-ku, Osaka, Tel +81 6 6631 3466 (plates 300–800 yen/US$2.75–$7.50)

TOKYO

Tony returned to Tokyo again and again, reveling in the knowledge that, no matter how much time he spent there, he would only ever scratch the surface of its vast offerings.

"What do you need to know about Tokyo? Deep, deep waters. The first time I came here, it was a transformative experience. It was a powerful and violent experience. It was just like taking acid for the first time. Meaning, What do I do now? I see the whole world in a different way.

"I often compare the experience of going to Japan for the first time, going to Tokyo for the first time, to what Eric Clapton and Pete Townshend—the reigning guitar gods of England—must've gone through the week that Jimi Hendrix came to town. You hear about it, you go see it—a window opens up into a whole new thing. And you think, 'What does this mean? What do I have left to say? What do I do now?'"

ARRIVAL AND GETTING AROUND

Tokyo is served by two international airports, **Narita** (**NRT**) and **Haneda** (**HND**). Narita is the larger of the two, with many more international flights landing each day, and fares into Narita tend to be lower than into Haneda, though it's a longer ride (thirty-seven miles from Narita to Tokyo Station, versus fourteen miles from Haneda) into town, by Japan Rail train, limousine bus, or a private car arranged by your hotel.

Two systems, the **Tokyo Metro** and **Toei Subway**, constitute the city's vast subway system, which is impeccably punctual, fast, safe, and clean, with signs and announcements in English as well as Japanese. The Tokyo Metro website (www.tokyometro.jp/en/) has a downloadable user's guide, and there's also a comprehensive free app that contains maps, schedules, fare information, and more; the **Toei Subway** website (www.kotsu.metro.tokyo.jp/eng), while less comprehensive, is also full of useful information. The simplest way to use both systems interchangeably is by purchasing a reloadable Pasmo card from any station's ticket office or vending machine.

Taxis in Tokyo, though not cheap (rates are on par with those in Manhattan, Paris, and other expensive Western cities), are impeccably clean, easily hailed, and accept cash and credit cards; gratuities are not expected, though you may round up to the nearest hundred yen as a means to avoid unnecessary small change, if paying in cash.

WHERE TO STAY

Tony took enormous pleasure in a stay at the quietly luxurious **Park Hyatt Tokyo**, comprising the top fourteen floors of a fifty-two-story Shinjuku skyscraper, whose star turn in the 2003 feature film *Lost in Translation* cemented its place in the hearts of well-heeled visitors to the city. A drink at the New York Bar may have long ago become a tourist cliché, but it remains a lovely way to enjoy a well-mixed drink and take in the vast nighttime view. In the morning, you can have a full Japanese breakfast and perhaps, on a clear day, a view of Mount Fuji from the forty-seventh-floor swimming pool. The concierge office is indispensable for securing restaurant reservations, return transfer to the airport, and, if you're so inclined, train tickets to other parts of Japan.

PARK HYATT TOKYO: 3-7-1-2 Nishishinjuku, Tokyo, 163-1055, Tel +03 81 3 5322 1234, www. hyatt.com/en-US/hotel/japan/park-hyatt -tokyo/tyoph (rooms start at about 65,000 yen/US$600 per night)

EATING AND DRINKING

"Maybe the most important thing you need to know about Tokyo, from my point of view, is—basically every chef I've ever met, if you asked them, 'If you had to spend the rest of your life in one country, eating one country's food for the rest of your life, where would that be?' They're all gonna say the same thing: Japan. Tokyo. Period.

"For me, that's an argument ender. It is a humbling experience. You come here, and you see how much precision, how much perfection is possible, with so few components. And you come away from that changed, and a little frightened.

"There's an exceptional example in the Shinagawa area, the restaurant called **Toriki**, owned by Mr. and Mrs. Aihara, to satisfy one of my personal obsessions: really, really good yakitori, which is essentially little bits of mostly chicken, often on skewers. Toriki is unusual in that they prefer to use an electric grill over the traditional charcoal, believing that the consistent 900-to-960-degrees Fahrenheit heat makes a better product." Mr. Aihara cuts the pieces from the whole birds (which he slaughters himself) as the orders come in.

TORIKI: 3-11-13 Hatanodai, Shinagawa-ku Tokyo, Tel +81 3 3785 8472, www.toriki.jpn.org (average dinner 4,000—10,000 yen/ US$38–$93)

"Down a flight of stairs next to a subway entrance, in the cellar of an unimpressive-looking office building, you'd never know it from looking at it, but **Sukiyabashi Jiro** has three Michelin stars, and is considered by many to have the best sushi in the world.

"Jiro Ono continues to strive for perfection in sushi. What's the difference between utility sushi and perfection? Ingredient, technique, timing. Every item is served at exactly the right time, and temperature, and stage in its preparation, which requires of the diner, as perfection must, a certain respect. Simply put, it means to do it right. I ate a fifteen-course three-star meal—the best sushi of my life—in twenty minutes. There are *don'ts*: You don't use anything but your fingers. You definitely don't use soy sauce or additional wasabi. It comes the way he says it should be. That's the way you eat it."

SUKIYABASHI JIRO: 4-2-15 Chuo-ku, Tokyo Tsukamoto Sogyo Building B 1st Floor, Tokyo, Tel +81 3 3535 3600, www.sushi-jiro.jp (set price 33,000 yen/about US$300)

"And then there is **Ginza Sushi-Ko** in Tokyo. The original. A hundred and thirty years old, and for all that time, this, in one form or another, is how the day started: scaling and gutting the fish, prepping the kitchen. Young Masa [Takayama, of New York's Masa] was first hired here as an apprentice by Shokunin Toshiaku Sugiyama. This is his son, Mamoru Sugyiyama, who runs Sushi Ko today. The fourth generation to uphold the standards and family tradition."

For his visit on *Parts Unknown*, Tony enjoyed "seared horse mackerel over green onion and ginger drizzled with house-made soy; maguro, [or] bluefin tuna prepared in classic *zuke* style; *tamago-yaki* with lots of shrimp eggs."

GINZA SUSHI-KO: 7-7 Ginza 7-Chome, Chuo-Ku, Tokyo, Tel +81 3 3571 4558, www.ginza-sushikou.sakura.ne.jp (15,000 yen/about US$140 for lunch; 25,000 yen/about US$233 for dinner)

ENTERTAINMENT, TOKYO STYLE

In densely packed Shinjuku you'll find the seedier side of Tokyo—its nightlife, cheap eats, and hordes of party people.

"The Yakuza—that's the fraternal organization prominent in the entertainment and financial services sector, as they say—are said to, um, *supervise* things here in Shinjuku: principally, your arcades, gambling, pachinko, adult entertainments, your porn shops and sex clubs, along with other ancillary services."

One such entertainment opportunity: the nearly seizure-inducing multimedia dance, music, puppetry, and general weirdness show executed twice nightly at **Robot Restaurant**, of which Tony was sincerely enamored, despite its extreme tourist kitsch.

Robot Restaurant is perhaps the most brightly lit and noisy attraction in the impossibly garish Kabukicho district, a subdivision of Shinjuku. **"This is where the subterranean life, the repressed id of the Japanese male, and some females, too, comes out to play. Prepare yourself for the greatest show in the history of entertainment. I've seen Jimi Hendrix. I've seen Janis Joplin. I've seen David Bowie— Diamond Dogs. I've seen Colleen Dewhurst and Jason Robards in *Moon for the Misbegotten*, directed by José Quintero, on Broadway. This—this was the greatest show I've ever seen in my life. It had it all. It was the greatest show in the history of entertainment."**

ROBOT RESTAURANT: 1-Chome-7-7 Kabukicho, Shinjuku-ku, Tokyo, Tel +81 3 3200 5500, www.shinjuku-robot.com (entry ticket 8,000 yen/about US$72; food 1,000–1,500 yen/about US$10–$15)

Just a few blocks from Robot Restaurant you'll find the comparably dark and quiet warren of bar-lined streets known as the Golden Gai. **"This is long my favorite place to drink in Tokyo—there are hundreds of microsize bars, each different from the other, with their** own micro crowd. I love it here—**Bar Albatross**—a few seats, strong drinks, the definition of a hole in the wall.** The Albatross bar staff is friendly, especially toward solo drinkers and English speakers; brace yourself for feline taxidermy, disco balls, crystal chandeliers, and other oddities of decor.

BAR ALBATROSS GOLDEN GAI: 1 Chome-1-7 Kabukicho, Shinjuku-ku, Tokyo 160–0021, Tel +81 3 3203 3699, www.alba-s.com (Drinks 5,000–12,000 yen/US$4.50–$11)

KENYA

"Kenya is as distinct and different from other nations in Africa as Texas is from Mars, with its own problems and its own kinds of awesomeness. It's dynamic, it's changing, and it's incredible.

"Shit runs deep here. Meaning—best scientists can tell—it all started for us in this neighborhood: tribes of hunter-gatherers, the Bantu and Nilotic peoples, Arab and Persian traders, the Portuguese merchants, the Omani, all left their mark. But the British Empire's hold, from 1895 to 1964, is perhaps most deeply felt.

"The British system of education, governance, justice, along with, to a certain extent, its values, were imposed on a native people, and laid, for better and worse, much of the foundation for modern Kenya. It did abolish slavery, for instance. It did build a modern infrastructure. It was also completely and fundamentally exploitative, often violent, and, well, racist, favoring white settlers, landowners, and foreign entrepreneurs in every possible way. Kenya existed to make white people from far away rich.

"But, in 1963, Kenya won its independence, and elected its first president, Jomo Kenyatta, and since that time, has fought an uphill battle to shake the last vestiges of colonial rule while hanging on to what worked. Things are, by most accounts, going well. Today's Kenya is phenomenally beautiful. There is a growing middle class, a highly rated educational system, and an enthusiastic and multilingual professional sector."

ARRIVAL AND GETTING AROUND

Arriving in Nairobi, you'll fly into **Jomo Kenyatta International Airport (NBO)**, originally called Embakasi for the suburb in which it's located, but renamed in 1978 for Kenya's first president and prime minister. It's the hub for Kenya Airways, and it serves flights to and from many African destinations and a handful in China, the Middle East, Europe, and a single flight to and from JFK Airport in New York City.

Arrange a car service in advance with your hotel, or solicit an official taxi from the marked queue outside arrivals. Car rentals are available at the airport, and there is also a network of inexpensive buses. The airport is about ten miles from the city center, and a cab will cost about 2,000 Kenyan shillings/about US$20, depending on your destination. Taxi drivers do not expect tips, but will not be offended if you round the fare up to the nearest hundred shillings.

In Nairobi, people move around via *matatus*, an informal system of minibus taxis operating over a wide geographic area of the city and suburbs. Be warned: their reputation for safety and comfort is not great. There are a number of bus lines, privately owned, with centrally located terminals in the city center. Fares for *matatus* and buses tend to range from 50 to 200 shillings/US$0.50 to $2. Taxis are a more reliable, if slightly more expensive, option, with typical fares costing 300–1,000 shillings/US$3–$10.

FIRST MEAL IN NAIROBI

"*Nairobi* means 'cool water' in Maasai. It's the capital of Kenya, with 6.5 million people living in the metro area. It grew up around a British railroad depot during the colonial era, halfway between other British interests in Uganda and the coastal port of Mombasa."

The largest neighborhood in the city is Kibera. **"Kibera is massive—around 172,000 people live here. A sprawling warren of homes, places of worship, and small businesses competing for an edge. It houses a great part of Nairobi's labor force. Meaning, no Kibera? The city grinds to a halt."**

Stop by **Mama Oliech's**, a small, local chain that distinguishes itself through the use of local wild fish from Lake Naivasha, not the Chinese farmed tilapia that is far more ubiquitous in Nairobi. Mama Oliech herself died recently, but the business lives on. What

to order? "Tilapia from Lake Naivasha, fried, then cooked with tomato and spices, served up right: on the bone, with an ice-cold Tusker beer."

MAMA OLIECH'S: Marcus Garvey Road, Nairobi, Tel +254 701 707070 (typical plate 350–680 shillings/US$3.50–$7)

ON SAFARI

"A few hours' drive from Nairobi, it's another world. The Africa of dreams, of films, the natural world—but a world under constant threat. **Lewa Wildlife Conservancy** seeks to address the problem of keeping all this alive and safe without excluding or marginalizing the people who've lived here for centuries. That is a delicate balance: man and nature; how to responsibly care for one without negatively affecting the other, in a world of ever-decreasing resources. The fact of the matter is, these magnificent animals would most likely be gone without the intervention of man. People pay a lot of money to come see these animals. Without that money, the overwhelming likelihood is that they would have been wiped out long ago."

Lewa is situated on part of a former cattle ranch, the land having been set aside in 1983, at the request of the Kenyan government, as a refuge for the severely endangered rhinoceros population, which has rebounded from an initial 15 animals to the current 169. Lewa also provides protected habitat for zebras, elephants, lions, cheetahs, hyenas, leopards, and wild African painted dogs.

Luxury accommodations and expertly guided safari outings bring in the necessary funds to keep the programs running; a conservation education program that welcomes over three thousand schoolchildren a year, free of charge, is a way of educating the next generation about the importance of wildlife protection.

"Poaching is, of course, an ever-present danger to both the animals at Lewa and the people who look after them. With 62,000 acres to cover, Lewa's antipoaching program is necessarily aggressive, inclusive, and cutting edge, relying on local trackers, advanced tracking technologies, and, perhaps most important, good community outreach and intelligence gathering. If the local people are not on your side, you are at a serious disadvantage."

LEWA WILDLIFE CONSERVANCY: Tel. +254 64 31405 www.lewa .org—Contact administrators via the website, telephone, or specialty tour guides to arrange a visit.

LAOS

As a student of twentieth-century American history, especially the intrigues and secret activities of the US government, Tony was enchanted by Laos (officially, the Lao People's Democratic Republic), a country he first visited, with *No Reservations*, in 2008, and returned to in 2016, for *Parts Unknown*.

"Laos was once a storybook kingdom of misty mountains and opium; at one time a protectorate of France; a mysterious, landlocked nation bordered by China, Thailand, Cambodia, and, as fate would have it, Vietnam.

"In the early 1960s, three idealistic young CIA officers arrived in Laos, a sleepy country of barely over two million people, mostly rice farmers. Their mission? Stop the spread of Communism. Recruit and train hill warriors to fight a shadow war against the North Vietnamese and the Pathet Lao [Communists]. The war in Laos was secret. The Russians knew about it. The Chinese knew. The Vietnamese, the Laotians certainly knew. The only people who didn't were the American public and Congress.

"The United States flew more than a half a million missions over this tiny Southeast Asian nation, dropping more bombs here than were dropped on Germany and Japan combined in all of World War II. What happened here, presumably in the cause of freedom of democratic Western values, resonates still. An estimated 30 percent of the bombs dropped on Laos failed to detonate. These and other UXOs

[unexploded ordinances] remain in the ground and continue to take lives and limbs. Since the war in Vietnam ended, and we left our secret war here behind, twenty thousand people, many of whom were not even alive during the conflicts, have been killed or maimed."

GETTING THERE

From the States, you can fly, after a connection or two, into **Wattay Inernational** (**VTE**) in Vientiane, the nation's capital, which shares a border with Thailand. Wattay had a massive renovation in 2018, and the airport is served by Lao Airlines, AirAsia, China Eastern Airlines, China Southern Airlines, Thai Airways, and Vietnam Airlines. To get to the city center, arrange transport in advance with your hotel, or find the airport taxi counter in the arrivals hall. You'll need to buy a coupon for transport; it's 57,000 lao kip/about US$7 for a sedan, or 66,000 kip/about US$7.50 for a van. The trip is about three and a half miles and should take about fifteen minutes. For 15,000 kip/about US$1.50 there is also a shuttle bus between the airport and the Vientiane bus terminal, which takes thirty to forty minutes. See www.vientianebus.org.la for all details.

You can also fly into the smaller **Luang Prabang International Airport** (**LPQ**), whose domestic and international flights share one terminal, served by Bangkok Airways, Lao Airlines, and Vietnam Airlines. The airport is about two and a half miles from Luang Prabang city center; a taxi will cost about 62,000 kip/about US$7.

For those with plenty of time in Southeast Asia and a multicountry itinerary, there are ways to travel to Vientiane by train from Bangkok, Hanoi, and Phnom Penh, though the itineraries are too complicated and changeable for our purposes here; best consult Rome2Rio.com or your most trusted guidebook or internet travel nerd for specifics.

WHERE TO STAY

In Luang Prabang, Tony was enamored of his suite at the immaculate, hushed **Amantaka** hotel, housed in a restored century-old French colonial building surrounded by mango trees, with high-end dining, impeccable service, a tranquil pool, and an in-house spa.

AMANTAKA: 55/3 Kingkitsarath Road, Ban Thongchaleun, Luang Prabang, Tel +856 71 860 333, www.aman.com/resorts/amantaka (rooms start at about 8 million kip/US$900 per night)

While visiting the Plain of Jars (see page 184), Tony stayed at **Auberge de la Plaine des Jarres**, a collection of fourteen Swiss Alpine-style cabins arranged on a hillside and surrounded by conifers. Although fairly rustic, it's considered the nicest local option, with an on-site French-Lao restaurant, excellent views, and fireplaces in each room.

AUBERGE DE LA PLAINE DES JARRES: Domaine de Phouphadeng, Phonsavan, Tel +020 235 3333 (rooms about 450,000 kip/US$50 per night)

VISITING LUANG PRABANG

"Luang Prabang, Laos's ancient capital, is a sleepy city of ornate palaces and temples. This town enthusiastically observes Wan Awk Phansa, a big party marking the end of Buddhist Lent. The whole thing culminates on the last full moon in October, with a fire lantern festival; it's the symbolic casting away of your sins."

Tony was joined in Luang Prabang in 2016 by James Syhabout, a chef with Lao roots, born in northern Thailand, and coauthor, with

John Birdsall, of the cookbook *Hawker Fare*, which Tony published under his imprint.

When visiting Luang Prabang, Syhabout said, finding where to eat is a matter of paying attention. "There aren't really *restaurant* restaurants. The places I like to go are more like little pop-ups in people's homes—a storefront at the bottom of the house, and the family lives upstairs. There are a lot of places like that in town. On the main corridor, go where the crowds go. If you see four police officers or construction workers crouched up on plastic stools at a noodle stall, that's the place to go."

PLAIN OF JARS

The **Plain of Jars** is a collection of thousands of massive limestone cups whose origins remain unknown, scattered over a wide area of Laos's Xiangkhoang Province. It's no surprise that the plain, which is reminiscent of Stonehenge or Easter Island, but far less visited, piqued Tony's interest.

"From the first time I ever read about Laos, the Plain of Jars sounded so mysterious and enticing. You want to know, right away, 'What does that look like? Where is it? *What* is it?' The very name resonated in my overheated imagination as a young man reading of Colonel Kurtz–like spies leading opium-growing hill tribes in a battle, in a secret conflict."

Because of the preponderance of UXO in the area, only a handful of Plain of Jars areas have been meticulously cleared and declared safe for visitors. To get there, take a short, daily flight to Phonsavan from Vientiane or Luang Prabang, or a long public bus or minibus ride— eleven hours from Vientiane, eight hours from Luang Prabang.

Once in town, charter a *sorngtaaou* (a pickup truck fitted with benches), rent a motorbike, or arrange a tour, generally via minivan, with a local travel agency or guesthouse, of which there are a handful of sparse but clean and serviceable options.

LEBANON

BEIRUT

In the history of Tony's televised pursuits, Lebanon plays an outsized role. In 2006, he visited Beirut and managed to film for two days before war erupted between Lebanon and neighboring Israel. The crew continued to document, as best they could, the experience of sheltering in a luxury hotel in one part of the city while a war raged a few miles away and various Western governments scrambled to evacuate their stranded citizens. After about ten days, the crew boarded a US Marine Corps ship bound for Cyprus and flew home from there. As Tony was fond of retelling, it was on that first day back in the United States that his daughter was conceived, so Lebanon was a personally meaningful place, to which he returned twice.

Tony was perpetually surprised by and smitten with Beirut:

"It was so much more sophisticated and tolerant and beautiful than I thought it was going to be; but much more importantly . . . people are proud of their food and their culture and their country. I mean, everyone's been through here: the Greeks, the Romans, the Phoenicians, the French, so I always knew this was going to be a good place to eat.

"Back in the '60s, it was known as the Paris of the Mediterranean, a lotta different groups, languages, interests, religions, sex, organizations, political factions, a lotta problems. But somehow it seemed, for a while, to be working. It's a big, beautiful city with a lot going on, two worlds, sleek, flashy, trendy, and consumeristic, body worshipping, well dressed, chic, glittery—and, ten minutes away, poor, still

bomb damaged. Hezbollah everywhere, refugee camps. Christians, Jews, Shiite Muslims, Sunni, Druze, Maronites. Gulf State money flowing in, Syrian agents, tourists, models, nightclub promoters and DJs, Western entrepreneurs.

"You hear Arabic, English, French interchangeably still. For whatever reason, even with all the problems and all the terrible things that have happened here over the years, I step off the plane in Beirut and I feel strangely, inexplicably comfortable, happy, at home."

As of this writing, Beirut is reeling from the combined effects of deep political unrest, the COVID-19 pandemic, and a hugely destructive explosion at the Port of Beirut in August 2020 that killed nearly two hundred people, injured thousands more, and left hundreds of thousands homeless. In short, current conditions are far from ideal for tourism in Lebanon, but we remain hopeful that this resilient country will overcome these latest challenges.

ARRIVAL AND GETTING AROUND

Beirut-Rafic Hariri International Airport (BEY) is the country's sole operating commercial airport, named for the two-time prime minister who was instrumental in ending the fifteen-year civil war and helping to rebuild the battered capital, and who was assassinated in 2005. Middle East Airlines, the Lebanese national carrier, has its hub at BEY, and a few dozen other carriers operate flights between major European, African, and Middle Eastern destinations.

The Lebanese pound has been in a free fall since the politically turbulent beginning of 2020; as of this writing, an official airport taxi, marked with an airplane logo and queued outside the arrivals area, will cost about 15,000 pounds/about US$20, and you should plan to tip about 10 percent on all taxi rides. Be aware that Beirut traffic is horrendous, public transport is nearly nonexistent, and that it often may make more sense to walk if you're within a half mile of your destination.

EATING IN BEIRUT

(Note that all of the following businesses were heavily damaged in the August 2020 explosion, though building efforts are underway.)

"Le Chef is a legendary spot in Beirut, famed for its simple, straightforward, home-style classics. Everybody comes here.

"You know, it's exactly the sort of place that we like to do on the show. It was that nice mix of old-school, new-school neighborhood. Really good food, very traditional."

Of special note are the hummus with pine nuts and ground lamb; the *maghmour*, sometimes called Lebanese moussaka, which Tony described as "a **velvety eggplant dish with tomatoes, chickpeas, and onion,"** and the kibbeh formed into disks or wedges, baked with olive oil, and served with *fattoush*, a salad of fried flatbread, vegetables, herbs and sumac dressing.

Le Chef: Gouraud Street, Beirut, Lebanon Tel + 961 1445 373 (no website) Typical dinner and drinks, about 20,000 pounds/US$13 per person

"Kamal Mouzawak created and runs Souk El Tayeb out of a parking lot in central Beirut. The idea: to bring farmers and artisanal producers, from all over Lebanon, together in one place.

"Down the road is Tawlet, Kamal's restaurant commissary concept, a sort of utopian showcase for the artisans at the market, [in which] a rotating cast of cooks and specialists take over the place, a different one each day, providing fresh, specifically regional foods." Among the daily buffet-style offerings, one might find labneh, kibbeh, lahmadjoun, fava bean salads, or whole sparrows cooked in butter, spices, and molasses.

SOUK EL TAYEB: Beirut Souks, Tel +9611 442 664, www.soukeltayeb.com (prices vary)

TAWLET: Beirut Sector 79, Naher Street 12, Tel +9611 448 129, www.tawlet.com. Lunch buffet about 49,000 pounds/US$33 per person

MACAU

"Macau: Chances are, if you've never been there, you have no idea what it might look like. For me, it was always the place firecrackers came from, and little else. I was vaguely aware it was Chinese, kind of, and later I became aware that it was somehow Portuguese, too.

"In fact, it was settled by the Portuguese in the sixteenth century, when Portugal pretty much ruled the sea. The first and last European colony in China, a trading port, spices and flavors from all the other Portuguese colonies in Africa, India, and the Strait of Malacca, mixed with European and Chinese, and, well, what came out the other side was unique. To be Macanese is to be neither Chinese nor Portuguese, but something singular and complex.

"On the south coast of China, thirty-eight miles west of Hong Kong, Macau is no longer run by trading, or firecrackers, or the Portuguese, or even the Chinese, really, who got it back in 1999. It's the great god of gambling who rules this tiny island." (Technically, Macau is a special administrative region of the People's Republic of China, with a separate government and a capitalist economy, fueled by legal gambling and its associated tourism.)

"Millions of gamblers pour in here every year; most of those gamblers are Chinese; and most of them, from the mainland. Everything is about gambling, and more specifically, luck in Macau. The whole place is geared toward the feng shui of the big score."

ARRIVAL AND GETTING AROUND

Macau International Airport (MFM) is served by about two dozen regional carriers, and serves flights between Macau and mainland China, Taiwan, Seoul, Manila, Bangkok, Singapore, and other destinations. There are public Transmac bus routes from the airport (see www.transmac.com.mo), and Express Link shuttle bus service to the New Macau and Taipa ferry terminals (see www.macau-airport.com).

A taxi from the airport to the major hotels takes about ten minutes, and costs about 73 patacas, about US$9. Tipping isn't customary in Macau taxis, but it's appreciated if you round up to the nearest pataca.

WHAT IS MACANESE CUISINE?

To get to the heart of Macanese cuisine, visit **APOMAC**, a civil servant's retirement club (the name stands for Associação dos Aposentados, Reformados e Pensionistas de Macau) with a canteen that's open to the public. **"This is an old-school favorite specializing in Macanese fare. When the Portuguese got here, and when they continued to come, they had already been everywhere. They'd been to Brazil. They'd been to the New World. They'd been all over Africa and India."**

The resultant Macanese cuisine, as served at APOMAC, is an amalgam of dishes cooked in olive oil and seasoned with soy sauce, heavy on grilled seafood, stews, and curries. Try the *minchi*, in which minced pork or beef is seasoned with Worcestershire sauce, soy, brown sugar, pepper, cinnamon, and curry powder, and served with stir-fried or deep-fried cubed potatoes, white rice, and a fried egg. The room feels like an absolute time capsule from the 1950s, with dark wood paneling and warm, friendly service.

APOMAC Macau: Sidonio Pais Avenue, No 49-B, ground floor building, China Plaza, Tel +853 2852 4325, www.apomac.net (set meals about 55 patacas/US$7)

NOW FOR SOME THRILL-SEEKING

If you're ready to tap into your sense of impulsive adventure, there's no better way than by bungee jumping off the 1,109-foot high Macau Tower.

"I don't know why I wanted it, or what possessed me, once I saw people plunging from the top, to decide that I, too, wanted to leap from the world's highest bungee jump. Let me tell you the hard part: The hard part is not jumping into space from high over the city. The hard part is that shaky metal walkway you've got to creep out on, feet tied together, into the cold drizzle, your legs shaking and every nerve ending sending messages to your brain that say, 'Go back. Go back.'

You *want* to jump at that point, get it over with. Then they drop those cables, and you feel a tug. And you hear the countdown. And you drop, face forward, through space. And for six long seconds, but strangely not long enough, you're swimming through air, and life don't hurt anymore."

MACAU TOWER CONVENTION AND ENTERTAINMENT CENTER: Largo da Torre de Macau, Tel +853 2893 3339, www.macautower.com.com (bungee jump is about 3,600 patacas/ US $450)

LIVE TO TELL, EAT SOME PORK

"And then, it's time for pork. The wheel, the internet, the pint glass, the electric guitar: these were all important inventions that made the world a better place to live in, but we must add another innovation— the pork chop bun. The product of genius, and a distinctly Macanese creation, which will live in history.

"Oozing fried pork chop in delicious bread? Here at **Tai Lei Loi Kei** in the village of Taipa, they do one of the better, some even say the original version, as evidenced by the packed house, eagerly enjoying juicy, savory deliciousness." The bone-in chop is marinated in warm and savory spices, deep-fried, and served in a sliced Portuguese roll. (Note to cooks: there's a recipe homage to it in our 2016 cookbook, *Appetites*.)

TAI LEI LOI KEI: Rua Correria da Silva, No 35, Taipa, Tel +853 2882 7150, www.taileiloi.com.mo (pork chop bun about 44 patacas/ US$5.50)

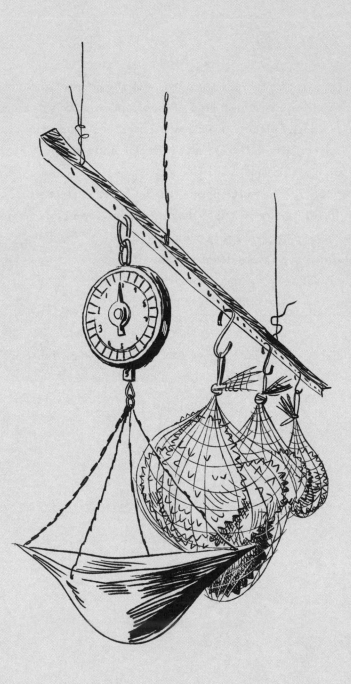

MALAYSIA

BORNEO ADVENTURE: KUALA LUMPUR, KUCHING, IBAN LONGHOUSE ON THE SKRANG RIVER

"Kuala Lumpur rises out of steaming, equatorial Southeast Asian jungle. [It's] Malaysia's capital city, a chaotic, multiethnic, multicultural, modern metropolis of Malay, Chinese, and Indian."

Tony first visited Malaysia in 2005, and he returned in 2015, tracing the same path—Kuala Lumpur, Kuching, and up the Skrang River by boat to an Iban longhouse—to "fulfill a decade-old promise to my ex-headhunter friends to return for Gawai, the annual Iban rice harvest festival."

He also had another, more personal reason for repeating the journey. "I was in a weird place in my head when I first came here. Personally, professionally—everything in my life was changing. I was in this sort of nowhere land between [my] previous life and whatever came next. I'm retracing my steps in a lot of ways, to see if it still hurts."

ARRIVAL AND GETTING AROUND KUALA LUMPUR

Kuala Lumpur International Airport (KUL) is your most likely point of entry into Malaysia. There are currently no direct flights from the United States, but there are plenty of direct flights from major European and Asian hub cities on Cathay Pacific, Emirates, All Nippon Airways (ANA), Delta, British Airways, and other major carriers.

The airport is about twenty-eight miles from the city center of Kuala Lumpur. A metered taxi or airport limousine will cost about 85 Malaysian ringgit/US$20 for an approximately fifty-minute ride. Taxi drivers do not expect tips, but you may round up to the nearest even amount. The KLIA Transit and KLIA Express trains both take passengers between the airport and KL Sentral station for about 42 ringgit/US$10 per person, but you will need to transfer to the city metro to get to the city center, which can be a difficult proposition with luggage.

It's easy to hail a taxi in Kuala Lumpur, but make sure your driver turns on the meter—some drivers try to negotiate a set price for tourists that will almost certainly be higher than the metered fare. For a daily-hire driver who takes you to multiple destinations, a tip of 25 to 50 ringgits is appropriate. Kuala Lumpur has a robust light rail transit system, consisting of three lines. Extensive information and links to route maps, along with plenty of other useful information about travel in Malaysia, can be found at www.wonderfulmalaysia.com.

INK IN KUALA LUMPUR

Tony got one of his first on-camera tattoos in Malaysia. **"My friend Eddie David is a legendary tattoo artist here in Kuala Lumpur. He is also a full-blooded member of the Iban, one of the oldest tribes in**

Malaysia. At his shop, **Borneo Ink**, Eddie tattooed me with an Iban-style ouroboros, a symbol of a snake eating its own tail: life, death, the eternal ebb and flow."

BORNEO INK: 8-3, 3rd Floor, Jalan 27/70a, Desa Sri Hartamas, 50480 Kuala Lumpur, Wilayah Persekutuan Kuala Lumpur, Tel +60 3 2300 1151, www.borneoink.com (prices vary)

AN AUNTY IN KAEL

Once a Malaysian film actress, **Aunty Aini** has long presided over an eponymous and well-loved *kampung*-style restaurant. **"The charming and, for lack of a better word, fabulous Aini was an actor in the Malaysian film scene, who now runs a very successful *kampung*-style restaurant, specializing in beloved village or country classics, all of them prepared with a staggering finesse and precision. This is delicious, delicious food."** Expect a range of *laksas*, curried stews, soups, and noodle dishes, and do not be put off by (but do not waste your time ordering from) the Western menu, a concession to timid tourists and, perhaps, their children.

AUNTY AINI'S GARDEN CAFÉ: Batu 16, Jalan Sepang Kampung Chelet, Nilai 71800, Tel +60 6 799 1276 (dishes 8–39 ringgit/US$2–$10)

LAKSA IN KUCHING

"After a two-hour flight from Kuala Lumpur, I land in Borneo, third-largest island in the world, divided among Malaysia, Brunei, and Indonesia.

"Kuching, capital of the Malaysian Sarawak, is a sleepy city with a colorful, nineteenth-century boy's adventure story history: pirates, headhunters, opportunists; [it's] the former domain of Sir James Brooke, an Englishman who came to be known as 'the White Rajah.' For a century, generations of the Brooke family ruled Sarawak as an independent kingdom. They created their own army, the Sarawak Rangers, who also acted as the rajah's personal guard.

"Tomorrow, I follow the pavement as far as it goes, and then it's boats the rest of the way. But first, breakfast, and fortunately I know exactly where to go. Kuching is famous for one of the most delicious, spicy morning treats, the weapons-grade plutonium of breakfasts.

"Behold *laksa*!

"It starts off benignly enough, with a generous serving of *bee hoon* noodle, fried egg, shrimp—but what comes next takes this dish to a whole new level: a spicy, fabulous, hearty hellbroth of coconut milk, curry, Sarawak hot chili peppers—together it's a liquid whose flavors combine to create a scorchingly hot, yet delicious, assault on the senses. It's a masterpiece of pain and pleasure."

Note that **Choon Hui Café**, also known as Choon Hui Kopitiam, is strictly a breakfast joint that operates from 6:30 a.m. to 12:00 noon, and is closed on Mondays.

CHOON HUI KOPITIAM: 34, Jalan Ban Hock, 93100 Kuching, Sarawak, Tel +60 82 243 857 (dishes 5–11 ringgit/US$1–$3)

ON TO THE LONGHOUSE

Four hours by car from Kuching and another three to four hours by open boat on the Skrang River, Tony's journeys to the Iban longhouse were, in a sense, his own *ba jelai*, a journey of discovery that's a rite of passage for Iban men.

He observed, in 2005, "I love this part of making television. I love the idea of the Iban *ba jelai*. And maybe my own journey—milking a television career so I can go to cool places—is not too far from their custom. I like to think so, anyway. As I head upriver, I think about all the places I've been, and where I've yet to go. This is not the Garden State Parkway, friends. As we continue upriver, we move farther and farther away from the world I know, and toward someone else's. It's thrilling to not know where you're going."

Should you wish to experience a night or two in an Iban long-house, there are some communities that will welcome overnight guests, for a fee, with details organized by local travel agencies or the Sarawak Tourism Board (www.sarawaktourism.com), including a translator-guide to facilitate communication. Do your research to find a reputable agency, and be prepared for a lack of modern facilities and privacy and an abundance of insects. Inquire ahead of time about what gifts from the outside world would be most appreciated, and to whom they should be given upon arrival.

PENANG

"When I first fell in love with the East, deeply and hopelessly, it was while watching delicate fingers opening a *nasi lemak*. Like origami, a sexy little package of rice and *sambal*, shrimp paste and chilis, wrapped beautifully in banana leaf. That was it for me. From then on, there was no going back. I felt, seeing that for the first time, I need more of this."

"This" was Malaysian food. Tony and the *No Reservations* crew visited Penang in 2012, drawn by the promise of a vibrant street food scene born of Chinese, Malay, and Indian cultures, ingredients, and techniques blended together on this island off the northwest coast of peninsular Malaysia.

"This part of the world really messed me up. It's these condiments here, the chilis, the *chili padi* [Thai chilis]. Once you have that, there's no going back. They open up the nether regions of your palate, which hitherto you didn't know existed."

ARRIVAL

Penang International Airport (PEN) is located at the southeastern end of the island. There are daily flights to and from peninsular Malaysia, Singapore, Thailand, Philippines, China, Japan, and Indonesia. A bus system, Rapid Penang, gets passengers from the airport to various points on the island, for a few Malaysian ringgit (less than US$1), but taxis will take you in a more direct fashion, for 20–50 ringgit/US$5–$12.

HIT THE GROUND EATING

While groups of tourists swarm the Kek Lok Si temple complex, head straight for a nearby fix at **Penang Air Itam Laksa**, a stall that's been in operation since 1955. Fishier, herbier, and more tamarind-soured than the Kuching *laksa*, the local *assam laksa* may inspire a reverie.

"**Every time I come to Malaysia, there's one thing I gotta have: *laksa*. It's everything I love in one bowl. Strong fish stock, almost like a southern French fish stock, made from mackerel, I believe. If you like noodles and spicy stuff that comes in a bowl, you would really like this. Imagine a world without traditional fast food outlets clogging up our mini-malls. Imagine we have individually owned and operated joints, serving stuff like this all over America. Can you imagine how delicious that would be?**"

PENANG AIR ITAM LAKSA: Jalan Pasar, Paya Terubong, 111500 George Town, Palau Pinang, Tel +60 12 500 7063 (bowl of laksa 5 ringgit/US$1.25)

"**Street by day, food wonderland by night**": welcome to **New Lane Food Stalls**. Here you'll find *char koay teow*, which Tony's guide, the local food writer Helen Ong, described as "lard, prawns, noodles, bean sprouts, chopped garlic, ground chili—and then the really special ingredient is the sauce. It's not just plain old soy sauce. Every store has its own secret recipe. But the secret of a good *char koay teow* is the heat of the frying pan."

NEW LANE FOOD STALLS: Lorong Baru, George Town, 10450 Pula Pinang, Tel +60 16 443 7463 (prices vary)

MEXICO

Tony made a handful of visits to Mexico over the years, seeking to shine a light on a complex culture that's often compressed into a single distorted dimension on the American side of the border. He sought to disentangle the myths from reality, and help tell a few stories from the daily lives of ordinary Mexicans, living under an openly corrupt government, in a society profoundly affected by narcoviolence and economic injustice.

"Americans love Mexican food. We consume nachos, tacos, burritos, tortas, enchiladas, tamales, and anything *resembling* 'Mexican' in enormous quantities. We love Mexican beverages, happily knocking back huge amounts of tequila, mezcal, and Mexican beer every year. We love Mexican people—as we sure employ a lot of them. Despite our ridiculously hypocritical attitudes toward immigration, we demand that Mexicans cook a large percentage of the food we eat, grow the ingredients we need to make that food, clean our houses, mow our lawns, wash our dishes, look after our children. As any chef will tell you, our entire service economy—the restaurant business as we know it—in most American cities, would collapse overnight without Mexican workers.

"We love Mexican drugs. Maybe not you personally, but 'we,' as a nation, certainly consume titanic amounts of them—and go to extraordinary lengths and expense to acquire them. We love Mexican music, Mexican beaches, Mexican architecture, interior design, Mexican films.

"So why don't we love Mexico?

"Look at it. It's beautiful. It has some of the most ravishingly beautiful beaches on earth. Mountains, desert, jungle. Beautiful colonial architecture, a tragic, elegant, violent, ludicrous, heroic, lamentable, heartbreaking history. Mexican wine country rivals Tuscany for gorgeousness. Its archeological sites—the remnants of great empires, unrivaled anywhere."

MEXICO CITY

"Mexico City, known in these parts as the Distrito Federal, or DF: Home to nineteen million people, and the second-largest city in the world. It alone tries to keep much of the country employed, responsible for a fifth of the nation's economy, and nearly a fifth of its total population. As an ongoing enterprise, it shouldn't work, but somehow it almost does."

ARRIVAL AND GETTING AROUND

Mexico City International Airport is also known as **Benito Juárez International Airport (MEX)**, named for the man who was president of Mexico from 1861 to 1872. Juarez, considered a national hero, pushed back against foreign occupation of Mexico and sought to strengthen constitutional support for a federal democratic republic. MEX is the busiest airport in Latin America; it's the hub for Aeroméxico, along with Interjet, Volaris, and Aeromar airlines.

MEX is about seven miles from the center of Mexico City. Officially licensed taxis in the ranks outside the terminals charge a flat rate of 250 pesos/about US$13 for transfer into the city. Pre-purchase a voucher from the Transporte Terrestre booth before entering the taxi line. Within the city, you can hail a metered taxi on the street, which will run about 15 pesos/US$0.75 per mile; those taxis dispatched via telephone or smartphone app tend to have a better repu-tation for safety, at about 30 pesos/US$1.50 per mile.

You may take a bus from the airport; tickets are 30 pesos/about US$1.50, and the ride takes about thirty minutes. See www.metrobus.cdmx.gob.mx for routes and timetables from the airport and for use of the extensive bus and metro system within the DF.

There is also a metro stop within walking distance of terminal 1; tickets are 5 pesos/about US$0.25, and the ride takes forty to fifty minutes, depending on your destination.

EATING IN MEXICO CITY: BEYOND MOLTEN CHEESE

"Mexican food is about taking the time to do it right, about hours of slow simmering. It's about hands, people making things, everything, by hand, that day. It's about people talking to you with their food, telling you something about themselves, their country, their area, their town, their family. And it's about some of the best, fastest-served street food in the world. And yes, there will be tacos."

The hands of chef Eduardo Garcia, once a young cook at New York's Le Bernardin and now a business owner in his hometown, have made a particular impact on Mexico City's culinary landscape.

"Eduardo Garcia has hacked his way up the ladder to become chef-owner of the city's hottest restaurant. Garcia runs Maximo Bis-trot with his wife, Gabriella. Here's the kind of extra helping of crap you gotta deal with if you run the hottest restaurant in Mexico City: In 2013, the spoiled daughter of the head of Mexico's consumer pro-tection agency walks in and demands a table when there's, unsur-prisingly, no table available. When Garcia says, 'Sorry, no can do,' she pulls a 'You know who I am?' and then calls daddy, and gets the health inspectors in to shut the place down."

Fortunately for Garcia, the story blew up via social media, embarrassing the government and forcing a quick reopening. As for the food:

"**Right now, a defiant, young, creative generation of Mexican chefs like Eduardo are performing some of the most exciting new cooking anywhere on earth—a mixing of the very old and traditional, with the very new,**" including, in the case of Maximo Bistrot, confit of suckling pig, topped with salsa and served on a warm tortilla, and abalone with chilis, lemon, and brown butter: simple, balanced, elegant, and modern.

MAXIMO BISTROT: Tonalá 133, 06700 Ciudad de Mexico, Tel +52 55 5264 4291, www.maximobistrot.com.mx (appetizers 120–300 pesos/US$7–$16, entrées 310–530 pesos/US$16–$28)

"**In a cantina, the snacks are free. The more you drink, the more you get, which offers a powerful incentive for conviviality.**" Tony was initially surprised by the civility on offer, along with the customary free food, at **Cantina La Mascota**. Some may argue that the price of the food is built into the drink prices, which are slightly higher than the average, but you'll likely agree that the sum experience is greater than its parts.

"**When I hear the word** *cantina*, **I think, naturally, a filthy saloon clogged with lying drunks, toothless prostitutes, and stray dogs. I deliberately avoided shaving for two days, so I could blend. But no: this place is decidedly nicer than the Peckinpah films had led me to believe, though breakfast still starts with tequila.**"

A typical La Mascota snack might include "**carnitas: tender, juicy stewed and pulled pork, loaded onto a warm tortilla and eaten immediately, the hot juices running down your chin, while the brightly flavored salsa hits the back of your throat.** *Mas tequila y mas comida*— **fava bean and cactus soup. It's delicious, and it's free.**"

CANTINA LA MASCOTA: Mesones 20, Centro Histórico, 06010 Mexico City, Tel +52 55 5709 3414 (no website) (beer about 95 pesos/US$5; whisky and tequila about 155 pesos/US$8. **NOTE:** The food is free but it's expected that you will tip the waiters who deliver it to your table, separately from those who bring you drinks.

There are some cities (Paris, Rome) in which Tony advises not to bother with breakfast, so as to leave valuable real estate for lunch and dinner. In Mexico City, breakfast, or at least one breakfast, is highly advised.

"**It's 5:30 in the morning in Mexico City, still dark outside, but we gotta get up early if we don't want to be standing on line for this place. Fonda Margarita is a family-style joint famous for its breakfasts. [This] place has been serving really good food for a really long time.**"

Check out the "**giant earthenware cauldrons of slowly bubbling meat and beans, simmered over beds of charcoal.**" Fonda Margarita has "**all the indicators of greatness—long communal picnic tables, minimalist decor, menus on the wall, and the heady aroma of what is unmistakably home cooking. *Huevos e frijoles*, eggs and beans served straight up or on fried tortillas for the *huevos rancheros*. It's a simple thing, you might think, but the beans, the beans. . . . Back home, a stew might be the last thing you'd think of at this hour of the morning. But here, given the all-too-rare opportunity to range freely through all these soulful wonderfully old-school grandma dishes— pork loin in salsa verde, beef in a dark chili sauce, pigs' feet, stewed lamb and fried *chicharrón*, pork skins in the same vibrant green tomatillo sauce, tortitas, little pork meatballs with spicy jalapeño tomato sauce—no way you don't want everything.**"

Fonda Margarita serves breakfast only, till 11:30 a.m., to locals and tourists in more or less equal measure.

FONDA MARGARITA: Adolfo Prieto 1364B, Tlacoquemecatl de Valle, Mexico City, Tel +52 55 5559 6358 (no website) (main dishes 45–65 pesos/US$2.25–$3.50)

"**In Mexico City, as in any enlightened culture, street food is king. From a cart on a corner, rough additions to existing restaurants and businesses, or just a grill under a tarp, head for the streets if you're looking for the good stuff.**"

As it's been over a decade since Tony took to the streets of the DF with a camera crew in tow, you'd be well advised to check in with a trusted street food source to find out who's currently doing the best stuff, and where. However, as of this writing, the following two street food purveyors are still at it, and doing it well:

"**One must not, when in Mexico City, one must not miss tacos al pastor, the most famous and typical dish of Mexico City. At El Huequito, they churn out thousands of these bad boys every day.**" The operator shaves pieces of adobo-spiced pork off a rotating spit, loads it into a warm tortilla, and tops it with salsa verde. In business since 1959, El Huequito now has a number of sit-down establishments in Mexico City, but word on the street is that the original tiny stand is the best of the bunch.

EL HUEQUITO: Ayuntamiento 21, Mexico City, Tel +52 55 5518 3313, www.elhuequito.com.mx (tacos about 20 pesos/US$1)

Along with local guide David Lida, Tony enjoyed *quesadillas azules* (blue quesadillas), prepared by street food legend **Doña Anastasia**.

"**Doña Anastasia's hands grow bluer as the day wears on, forming and cooking her amazing blue corn tortillas, filling them and cooking them on her *comal*, as she has every day for the last eight years.**" She fills each one to order: "**There's sausage, brains, and beef, but David and I go for the sautéed spinach and zucchini flowers. The taste of this thing [is] sublime. Every tortilla of blue corn masa, made fresh** right here. Out of this world. Best tortilla ever. There's not even any pork in it."

DOÑA ANASTASIA: Corner of Bajío and Chilipancingo, Monday through Friday, in the Roma Sur neighborhood (quesadilla about 20 pesos/US$1)

OAXACA

"In Oaxaca, ancient indigenous traditions and ingredients define not only the mescal, but also the food. I haven't been anywhere in Mexico where the cooking is better than here. As much as we think we know and love it, we have barely scratched the surface of what Mexican food really is. It is *not* melted cheese over a tortilla chip. It is not simple, or easy. It is not simply 'bro food' at halftime. It is, in fact, old; older even than the great cuisines of Europe and often deeply complex, refined, subtle, and sophisticated."

ARRIVAL AND GETTING AROUND

Xoxocotlàn International Airport (OAX) is a one-terminal airport that handles flights to and from within Mexico, along with Los Angeles, Houston, and Dallas flights. It is located about six miles south of Oaxaca's historic center; a private cab ride takes twenty to thirty minutes and will cost 150 pesos/about US$7.50; a shared airport van is 48 pesos/US$2.50; for either choice, buy a ticket inside the terminal and tip 10 pesos for good service.

Oaxaca is a pleasantly walkable city, with lots to see (and eat) along the way. For longer distances, hail a standard taxi or ask your hotel to call one for you. Not all drivers use the meter, so ask that your driver turn it on, or agree on a rate up front. Oaxaca has a few bus routes, but the buses are privately owned, and information about schedules, routes, and fares can be difficult to come by.

"LIKE LYON IS TO FRANCE, OAXACA IS TO MEXICO"

"When we're talking about Oaxaca, this is a deep, really sophisticated cuisine. What people miss is how really deep and really sophisticated the sauces here can be. Like Lyon is to France, Oaxaca is to Mexico, in my experience.

"Alejandro Ruiz Olmedo is one of Mexico's best chefs. Olmedo's cooking—his focus, his passion—has very old, very deep roots. He started cooking young. When he was twelve, his mother died, and it fell on him to raise, and feed, his five siblings. Today, he draws much of his inspiration from Central de Abastos, Oaxaca's central market."

In 2013, for *Parts Unknown*, Tony walked the market, which sprawls over several blocks, in a series of tented lanes and semi-enclosed built spaces, where vendors sell fruit, vegetables, herbs, meat, eggs, spices, roasted crickets, and cheeses, along with a huge selection of stewed, roasted, and barbecued meats, tacos, quesadillas, stews, soups, sandwiches, fresh-squeezed fruit juices, baked goods, and much more. It would be easy to make an entire day of a market visit. Seek out, as Tony and Alejandro did, *tlayudas* with zucchini flowers and string cheese cooked on a clay comal, *barbacoa* tacos, and consommé, washed down with fruity Jarritos soda or a cold beer.

CENTRAL DE ABASTOS: Juárez Maza, 68090 Oaxaca, Tel +52 951 278 7315 (no website) (prices vary)

It's worth hiring a driver to take you outside the city, to Restaurante Tlamanalli, in **"the quiet little town of Teotitlán del Valle, about fifteen miles outside Oaxaca. It's a town where the arts, crafts, and traditions of the pre-Hispanic Mexico are celebrated, and packaged for consumption. Abigail Mendoza and her sister Refina are Zapotecan: original people from Mexico, before the Spanish. Before the Aztecs. This is her restaurant, where Abigail has been grinding corn by hand, making masa, and moles like this, the ridiculously faithful, time-consuming, difficult traditional way she was taught to make these things, and the way she's been making them since she was six years old."**

Among the wonderful things on the menu are **"*seguesa*, a mole-and-chicken dish. This mole sauce, like a lot of the real old-school moles made by masters like Abigail, uses thirty-five different kinds of chili peppers, and takes more than two weeks to make. And another Zapotecan classic, *chile agua*; a simpler dish of cow and pork brains, cooked with chilis, tomatoes, and *yerba santa*. I mean, that's as old school as it gets."**

RESTAURANTE TLAMANALLI: Teotitlán del Valle, Oaxaca 70420, Tel +52 951 524 4006 (no website) (typical meal about 350 pesos/ US$18 per person)

MOROCCO

TANGIER

"When I was an angry young man, disillusioned with the world, disenchanted with my generation, disappointed by the 'counterculture,' and looking for role models, William S. Burroughs's paranoia and loathing, his antisocial appetites, his caustic, violently surreal wit, and his taste for controlled substances seemed to perfectly mirror my own aspirations.

I wanted to write. I wanted to be apart from everything I grew up with. In short, I wanted to be elsewhere. And the Tangier—the 'Interzone' that Burroughs described—where he'd found himself exiled, strung out, writing the pages that eventually became *Naked Lunch* sounded, to my naive young mind, like an exotic paradise."

Governed by a handful of European nations from 1923 to 1956, Tangier was at that time a place where behaviors, proclivities, and appetites that may have been frowned on elsewhere were permitted, giving rise to an affordably hedonistic city full of expats, set somewhat apart from the Arab and Berber cultures that continue to define the rest of Morocco.

"At the northern tip of Africa, a short ferry hop from Spain, Tangier was a magnet for writers, remittance men, spies, and artists. Matisse, Genet, William Burroughs—many have come this way, staying a while or hanging around. But no one stayed longer, or became more associated with Tangier, than the novelist and composer Paul Bowles. In works like *The Sheltering Sky*, he created a romantic vision of Tangier that persists even today, a dream that has become almost inseparable, in the minds of many, from reality."

Like Haight-Ashbury in San Francisco or the Times Square of New York's seedier, darker era, Tangier's time as a freewheeling playground for artistic deviants has long passed. The reigning king, Mohammed VI, has poured about US$1.1 billion into developing the port, which is now the largest in the Mediterranean.

However, the fact remains: "There is no place like it in the world. It looks, smells, sounds, and tastes like no other city. It is all too easy to lose oneself in the romantic ideal—more difficult to assess the place as it is: an increasingly modern port metropolis situated only a short boat ride from Europe. It's probably a good idea to do both: Live the dream for a bit. But keep your eyes open. And be careful. As you'll see, many visitors came to Tangier for a short vacation and remained for life. It's that kind of place."

ARRIVAL AND GETTING AROUND

Tangier Ibn Battouta Airport (TNG) serves flights to and from other cities within Morocco, select European cities, and Istanbul; the largest carriers to Tangier are Air Arabia Maroc, Royal Air Maroc, and the discount airline Ryanair. To get from the airport to the city center, you can arrange private transport in advance, rent a car, or take what's known as a "grand taxi," a six-seat vehicle whose driver may opt to fill the car with passengers before leaving the airport. It's an approximately thirty-minute drive to the city center or tourist zone, where most of the hotels are located. The fare is government-regulated at 250 Moroccan dirhams/about US$26; a tip of 5 to 10 dirhams is appropriate for good service.

There are, of course, various ferry options between Spain and Tangier; the most direct route, and the one with the greatest frequency of departure, is between Tarifa and Tangier. One-way travel is about 415 dirhams/US$43, round trip is about 740 dirhams/US$75, and takes an hour each way.

Moroccan train service is said to be the best in Africa, so you may wish to arrive in Tangier via the national railway, administered by Office National des Chemins de Fer (ONCF). Buy tickets at www.oncf.ma, or in a station, where there are manned booths and an increasing number of ticket machines. Be sure to purchase tickets to Tanger Ville station, not Tanger Morora, which is a few miles out of town.

Once in town, Tangier is a walkable if occasionally quite steeply graded city. Taxicabs exist but do not abound, so plan ahead, or work closely with your hotel staff if a car is a must.

CAFÉ CULTURE, PRESERVED IN AMBER (AND SMOKED)

Although the literary glory days were over decades ago, and the growing port has brought new affluence and purpose to sleepy Tangier, some things haven't really changed—namely, the café culture, centered on sweet mint tea or coffee, and, in some places, hashish.

"The Grand Socco is the gateway to the Medina, where you can find the Kasbah—which means 'fortress,' by the way. The Port of Tangier is to the east. And right in the middle of it all, the Petit Socco. What Uncle Bill Burroughs called 'the last stop,' the meeting place, the switchboard of Tangier. Reasons for settling in Tangier diverge. But everyone, sooner or later since the beginning of memory, comes to Café Tingis." Largely unchanged since Burroughs's time, the café is furnished in a fashion that borders on derelict. You're there for the outdoor people-watching, a cup of tea or extremely strong coffee, and atmosphere; go elsewhere for a meal.

CAFÉ TINGIS: Rue Almohades, Tangier (no phone, no website) (coffee and tea about 10 dirhams/US$1.10)

And, at **Café Baba,** in the Kasbah and also largely unchanged since it opened in 1943 (though there is now a flat-screen TV showing soccer games and the like), you're also there for the tea, and perhaps to soak up the ancient memory of visits from the Rolling Stones, the Beatles, and the Clash. Or, sure, you may be there for the openly accepted smoking of hashish, which creates **"a thick, slow-moving haze of smoke that smells like my dorm room, 1972,"** as Tony put it. Fans of Jim Jarmusch may recognize Café Baba from a scene in his 2014 vampire film, *Only Lovers Left Alive.*

CAFÉ BABA: Rue Zaitouni, Tangier, Tel +212 699 309943 (coffee and tea about 10 dirhams/US$1.10)

"Tangier is situated at the chokepoint between the Atlantic Ocean and the Mediterranean Sea. The Moroccan coast is a rich fishing ground, and a lot of people make their living from the sea." The local seine-haul fishing method, in which a weighted net is dragged along the ocean floor, scooping up everything in its path, yields a variety of seafood, some of which is sold to Mohammad Boulage, the chef and owner of **Le Saveur de Poisson.**

"Boulage is from the nearby Rif Mountains. And he sources a lot of his stuff, his produce and his greens, from there. The back room of the place is dedicated to sorting and drying various herbs, which he blends into a secret mix he claims has all sorts of healthy and boner-inspiring benefits. Look, if every dish I've been told over the years was gonna make me 'strong' worked, I'd have a permanent pup tent going on down there, so I take all that with a grain of salt."

Dinner at Le Saveur de Poisson is a multicourse affair, starting with an appetizer of olives, roasted walnuts, fresh-baked bread, and **"a pulpy purée of figs, raisins, strawberries, full of Mohammad's potent herbs and spices, of course."**

The main event is a seafood tagine that varies daily, depending on what's been brought in, but it often includes shark, squid, and monkfish, **"slowly cooked over charcoal in the classic clay pot that gives it its name. The tagine's dome top is supposed to force the condensation back into the dish and keep it moist and tender."**

After the tagine, there's usually a whole fish or fish kabobs, and a dessert of fruits and nuts, sweetened with honey. **"This is the Tangier version of farm-to-table. . . . Spectacular. This is a good value; eccentric and delicious."** Le Saveur is well known; reservations are strongly suggested.

LE SAVEUR DE POISSON: 2 Escalier Waller, Tangier, Tel +212 5393 36326 (no website) (multicourse meal about 195 dirhams/US$22)

MOZAMBIQUE

In Mozambique, Tony found a beautiful, welcoming country where there was often not enough food, money, or work, especially the deeper into the interior he traveled.

"In 1975, the newly independent Mozambique looked forward to a brighter future. But this was not to be. Yet rather than giving up after enduring a sixteen-year civil war—one of Africa's most brutal and senseless—the country picked itself up and began the enormous, daunting task of rebuilding, well, everything, from the ground up.

"There are very few places left in this world like Mozambique. The climate is nice. The people are really nice and the food is extraordinary.

"Yet today, Mozambique is barely a pit stop on the tourist trail. It was with all this in mind that I arrived on my first visit to this East African country of twenty-three million people.

"Mozambique, it should be pointed out, is a darling of the World Bank. It's seen as an African success story, and the fact is, things are good, very good, here, compared with how things have been in the past. Five hundred years of truly appalling colonialism, eighteen years of enthusiastic but inept Communism, and a brutal and senseless sixteen-year civil war ending less than twenty years ago left Mozambique with a devastated social fabric, a shattered economy, and only the memory of an infrastructure.

"Shockingly, people here, throughout the country, after being relentlessly screwed by history, are just as relentlessly nice."

And about the island of Ilha de Mozambique, Tony remarked, "There are very few beautiful corners of the globe unmarked by the comfortably clad feet of tourists. Ilha de Mozambique seems to be one of those places. Set out on the turquoise water of the Indian Ocean, this island strip of sand and rock was the first European settlement in East Africa. Vasco da Gama landed here in 1498 while sailing the trade winds in search of the spice route to India. But before him, there'd been Greeks, Persians, Chinese, Arabs, and Indians come down from the gulf or across the Indian Ocean. . . . Spend enough time on the island, and the rest of Africa can feel like a different continent. Ilha de Mozambique [is] a ruin really, a shell of its former glory, a crumbling monument to a colony built on the backs of the occupied and enslaved. Once storybook mansions, promenades, decaying, beautiful, but sad."

The island is inhabited by about 18,000 people, most of whom are quite poor. Should overseas hotel developers set their sights on the island, a few would get jobs, but many would just be in the way:

"If tourists come, where will all the people living on the island—most in dire and decidedly untouristy conditions—where will they go? They'll have to be relocated, of course, seen as inconvenient to the common good."

ARRIVAL AND GETTING AROUND

Mozambique has three international airports, the largest of which is **Maputo International (MPM)**. Maputo is Mozambique's capital city, in the country's southern coastal section. MPM mostly handles flights to and from other parts of Mozambique and other African nations, but there are also connections to Doha, Istanbul, and Lisbon. The airport is less than two miles from the city center; a taxi will cost about 600 Mozambican metical/about US$10, and should take about twenty minutes. Many taxis do not use meters, so agree on the fare before you depart; to a metered fare, add about 10 percent tip. Some hotels will send a shuttle to the airport, with prior arrangement.

Nampula International Airport (APL), in the country's northeast, is the closest to Ilha de Mozambique, the tiny, largely undeveloped island connected to the mainland by a road bridge. Nampula services flights from Nairobi, Johannesburg, and within Mozambique; upon arrival, arrange for a taxi to take you on the two-and-a-half-

hour drive to the Ilha, which should cost about 3,000 metical/about US$50 each way. Accommodations on the island itself are limited to a few hostels, so it's best to arrange a stay on the mainland and visit the island by day.

EATING IN MOZAMBIQUE: WORLD INFLUENCE, COASTAL ABUNDANCE, AND PIRI-PIRI

Having traveled to many other points on the continent, Tony declared the food he enjoyed in Mozambique **"the best food I've had in Africa."**

Numerous cultural influences can be seen, felt, and tasted on Mozambican tables: **"Brazilian spices, Indian curries, the best of Africa and Asia, Arab traders, a dizzying Afro-Portuguese, Latin American, pan-Arab, Asian mix. And along much of the coast of Mozambique, through good times and bad, what they always had was an abundance of incredible seafood. In addition to the abundant use of coconut milk, it's the beloved local hot pepper, *piri-piri*, that makes the food uniquely Mozambican."**

Beira, a centrally located port city, is **"a place that shows its history—the scars are everywhere."** At a casual restaurant called **Copacabana**, experience one of Mozambique's most famous meals. **"*Piri-piri* chicken is arguably the national dish. You find it all over—restaurants, street corners, beach shacks like this one,"** surrounded by **"sand, salt air, the sound of waves in the distance, the smells of grilling poultry, and spice of charcoal,"** and, the reward, **"the chicken. They continuously baste that grilling chicken with the *piri-piri*. Tangy, slightly tart, elements of citrus—they dole this shit out like it's pure cocaine. I mean, there's never more than a tiny little bit** in there. What is this precious substance? Peanut oil, lemon juice, minced garlic, tomato—but it's the *piri-piri* pepper that gives this stuff its trademark burn."

Cyclones Idai and Kenneth struck coastal Mozambique about a month apart, in March and April 2019; the effect on Beira was particularly devastating. Copacabana, a vulnerable thatched-roof structure with no walls to speak of, sustained heavy damage, but fortunately has been renovated and reopened at the same location.

COPACABANA: Avenida de Bagamoyo, Beira, Mozambique 2678, Tel +258 82 6480673 (no website) (about 1,700 metical/US$15 per person for food and drinks)

MYANMAR

The very first episode of *Parts Unknown* was shot in late 2012, in Myanmar, a country that had been closed to outsiders for decades, and was on the cusp of a new, more open era. Tony and his production crew arrived just days after the departure of President Barack Obama, the first-ever sitting US leader to visit.

"For almost one hundred years under British rule, this was [the capital, Rangoon. In 1948, after helping the British fight off the Japanese, and with a new taste for self-determination, the country gained independence. After a decade of instability, however, the military consolidated power and never let go.

"Elections? They came and went, the results ignored, opposition punished or silenced entirely. Burma, now Myanmar, where Orwell had once served as a colonial policeman, where he'd first grown to despise the apparatus of a security state, became more Orwellian than even he could have imagined; [it was] a nation where even having an opinion could be dangerous.

"Just as the door is opening, my crew and I are among the first to record what has been unseen for decades by most of the world. Meanwhile, this Southeast Asian country of eighty million people is collectively holding its breath, waiting to see what's next."

ARRIVAL

Yangon International Airport (**RGN**) has no direct flights from the States, but there are plenty of connections from Doha, Singapore, Seoul, Hong Kong, Bangkok, and other Asian hub cities. The airport is about ten miles from the city center. Arrange for ground transportation with your Yangon hotel, or take a metered taxi; either trip will take from thirty to fifty minutes, depending on traffic. A taxi from the airport to your hotel should be about 10,000 Myanmar kyat/about US$7. Tipping is not customary, but you may round up to the nearest whole number.

NOTE: Foreign visitors, and foreign capital, have streamed into the country since the release of Aung San Suu Kyi and the end of military rule in 2011, but since 2016, tourism has been slowed by news of ethnic violence and the displacement of Rohingya Muslims in Rakhine State, at the hands of the police and military. Newly constructed hotels are largely empty, and outside tightly designated zones, visiting remains a dangerous and, in some cases, expressly forbidden proposition. Consult the advice of the US State Department, or the advice of your country's embassy or mission, before planning travel.

THREE CLASSICS IN YANGON

Tony's preferred place to stay was **the Strand**, a relic of British colonial rule, built in 1901. Much like its grand counterparts in Singapore, Phnom Penh, Saigon, and Bangkok, the Strand has seen decades of high grandeur and extreme neglect. After a 2016 renovation, it's currently operating in the former camp.

THE STRAND: 92 Strand Road, Yangon, Tel +95 243 377, www.hotelthestrand.com (rooms start at about 500,000 kyat/US$300 per night)

"Of course, morning in Yangon has always been about tea. It's black, Indian-style tea, usually with a thick dollop of sweetened condensed milk." Tony's go-to spot for tea and a hearty breakfast in Yangon was **Seit Taing Kya Tea Shop**. "In the back, a cauldron of salty little fish bubble over hardwood coals. Fingers work mountains of sweet bean, one of the fillings for the variety of pastries that are stuffed, shaped, and put into an old stone oven. In another corner, the heartening slap of fresh bread, pressed against the clay wall of a tandoor. And, of course, eggs bob and spit in the magical hellbroth of fish, spice, and herb. Mohinga? This, I must have." Rice or rice noodles are added to the broth, along with any combination of crispy beans, cilantro and other herbs, lime wedges, and bits of fried offal.

SEIT TAING KYA TEA SHOP: 44 Ma Po Street, Myenigone, Sanchaung Township, Yangon, Tel +95 1535564 (tea about 700 kyat/US$0.50; typical plates 1,500–2,000 kyat/US$0.75–$1.50)

Yangon's **Morning Star Tea House** is the place to find "the must-have, bone-deep, old-school favorite around here, *lahpet thoke*, the salad of fermented tea leaves. I know—that does not sound good—but you'd be wrong to think that. Take the fermented tea leaves, add cabbage, tomatoes, and lots and lots of crunchy bits, like toasted peanuts. Season with lime and fish sauce."

MORNING STAR TEA HOUSE: Saya San Road, Yangon (no phone, no website) (*laphet thoke* about 1,500 kyat/US$1)

TRAIN TO BAGAN, AND THE TEMPLES

"The night express to Bagan: six hundred kilometers of what will turn out to be kidney-softening travel by rail. But Bagan, Myanmar's ancient capital, I've been told, is a must-see. Out the window, the modern world seems to fade away, then disappear altogether, like the

last century never happened, or even the century before that. We're traveling across the largest mainland nation in Southeast Asia."

If you decide to travel by rail, your trip may well proceed like Tony's did, at a comically slow pace, with many local stops, gradually picking up alarming speed for a railway with a less-than-stellar safety record. A journey meant to take ten hours may well take twice that time; any discomfort can be eased by a steady stream of beer, snacks, and the kind of dark jokes made in the face of one's own potential demise. Tickets for this and other journeys can be purchased in advance at Yangon's Myanmar Railways booking office between the hours of 7:00 a.m. and 3:00 p.m., or via a reputable travel agency, often for an additional fee.

As for the Bagan temples, pagodas, and monasteries themselves, built over one thousand years ago, in a period of two and a half centuries as a paean to Theravada Buddhism, Tony and Philippe Lajaunie, his sidekick and former boss at Les Halles in New York, found them

refreshingly devoid of tourist hordes in 2012. "You'd expect this, an ancient city of nearly unparalleled size and beauty, to be overrun with tourists, souvenir shops, snack bars, tours on tape. But no. . . . For the most part, you're far more likely to bump into a goat than a foreigner. Over three thousand pagodas, temples, and monasteries remain today. Inside almost every one of them, a Buddha figure, each one different."

The beauty, the scale, the physical manifestations of religious faith—it's a powerful experience, and one that Tony rightly pointed out was made possible, in part, by "slave labor. I'm thinking, 'You build this many temples, thousands of them, in a relatively short period of time? You know, chances are somebody was working for less than minimum wage, let's put it that way.'"

After your temple visit, head to **Sarabha** for a different kind of paradise. "This is the best restaurant in the country so far. Nestled among the temple ruins, [here] you're more than likely to catch a very enticing whiff. Slow-simmered curry, served with a side of sour soup made from roselle leaves. With it, you get fried, ground chilies, pickled bean sprouts—you get the idea."

SARABHA: Taunghi Villae of the Nyaung Oo Township, Tel +95 9968 172009 (entrées 5,500–8,500 kyat/US$3.50–$5.50)

NIGERIA

LAGOS

"Lagos: Nigeria's megacity. One of the most dynamic, unrestrained, and energetic expressions of free-market capitalism and do-it-yourself entrepreneurship on the planet. Buy, sell, trade, hustle, and claw. Make your own way, any way you can. They say you have to have three hustles.

"With a ridiculously overburdened infrastructure, [and] a history of egregiously bent leadership, they long ago learned, ain't nobody going to help you in this world. Pick up a broom, a hammer. Buy a taxi, a truck. Build a bank, a billion-dollar company, and get to work."

This strategy, as Tony observed, can pay off unevenly for Nigerians, as exemplified by the aggressively upscale "Victoria Island, the garden of dreams, where the winners work and play." Those who have benefited most from the moneymaking sectors of the Nigerian economy—oil, agriculture, and financial services—live there.

And, on the income spectrum's inevitable other end is Makoko, a sprawling city within a city, on the edge of the gulf, about which Tony said, "This used to be a little fishing village. People started showing up, no plan, build your own house."

Most of Makoko's 100,000 residents navigate its watery lanes via dugout canoe. To outsiders, it's a slum and an eyesore, but it's also a living testament to do-it-yourself Nigerian ingenuity, with fresh

water, electricity, schools, hotels, hospitals, barbershops, and gro-
cery stores. The government, no surprise, seeks to raze the un-
planned, unregulated and untaxed community, to clear the way for
hotels and other big-money businesses. Under similar threat is Computer Village, a chaotic hub of electronics sale and repair businesses
that's said to generate US$2 billion in annual sales; Nigerian officials
announced plans in 2017 to move the market to the city's outskirts,
citing traffic congestion and pollution.

"Public money is generated in Lagos, not so much by oil but by
the free market—a Wild West free-for-all of private enterprise. Who
really runs the streets, the de facto front line of law and order, are
area boys. An area boy's crew levels street taxes on, well, everything.
Reporting to their regional boss, a king of boys. Taxis, buses, any tar-

get of opportunity pays. Police, politicians, business leaders. Everybody gets their piece of the action. It's a daily fact of life in Lagos."

Femi Kuti, son of the late legendary musician Fela Kuti, explained, "If you wanted to go for election, you needed to see all the area boys. You have to give a lot of money for him to get all his gang members to vote for you. And if you do a good job in dealing with this, you probably would win."

"I hate to talk Nigeria down, because you hear all these things all the time," said Kadaria Ahmed, a journalist and editor. "Yes, there is corruption, it is about corruption; it's about the fact that the resources that are supposed to be used for people aren't being used for people. Years of military rule meant that people were brutalized. There was a fight against thinking. You saw a decline in education. That continued for thirty years.

"The biggest obstacle in this country is the political class," said Ahmed, "because what we have in Nigeria, if you lose elections, you then jump to the other party. And you win elections. And if you lose, you go back to this other party. So it's the same people. They're going to fight tooth and nail to stay in office. And to keep the system the way it is."

ARRIVAL AND GETTING AROUND

Murtala Mohammed International Airport (LOS) is the country's largest international airport, serving flights to and from other parts of Nigeria; many African nations; and select Middle Eastern, European, and US cities, including New York and Atlanta. It is the hub for Arik Air, a Nigerian airline; several major world carriers also operate flights, including British Airways, Emirates, KLM, and Virgin Atlantic.

LOS is located about ten miles from Lagos city center, a trip that will take at least an hour, and up to three, depending on traffic, which can be fierce. Most sources advise arranging transport to your hotel ahead of time, to avoid the gantlet of drivers, money changers, and others who will swarm you upon exiting the terminal, especially if you look unsure. Arrange a shuttle from your hotel, if possible. Otherwise, rideshare services like Uber do operate in Lagos, and there are unmetered taxis available. You'll need to negotiate the fare ahead of time, and pay in advance of the ride, which should be about 11,000 Nigerian naira/US$30. Tips are not necessarily expected, but a 10 percent tip for good service will be appreciated.

A TASTE OF LAGOS IN A *BUKA*, OR "MAMA PUT"

The term *buka* is used to denote a casual, open-sided restaurant found throughout Nigeria. Generally operated by women, these restaurants serve hearty fare and tend to specialize in one type of dish, though the menus are extensive. *Bukas* are also colloquially known as "Mama Put" restaurants, given that the food is so good, a regular customer might request that the proprietor, a.k.a. the "Mama," put some more on his plate.

"Good cooking takes time. As more and more Lagotian men and women enter the workforce, fewer and fewer cook the old way: long, low and slow preparations that could take hours." *Bukas* fill this need for comfort and tradition on the plate.

Stella's Kitchen, in Computer Village, has a reputation for cleanliness, and for being slightly pricier than the typical *buka*. The kitchen specializes in pounded yam, which goes nicely with its *egusi* soup, thick with goat, melon seeds, and chilis in a fish stock base.

Be sure to also plan a meal at **Yakoyo**, whose Yoruba-language name translates to "stop by and be full." The house specialties include Jollof rice and *amala*, made from sliced raw yam that's been pounded into a flour and steamed. Dunk balls of it into a soup of crayfish, chilis, locust beans, and jute leaves, and do not skip the roasted goat.

STELLA'S KITCHEN: 16 Francis Oremeji Street, Ikeja, Lagos (no phone, no website) (full meal about 2,000 naira/US$5.50)

YAKOYO: Olabode House, 217 Ikorodu Road, Ilupeju, Lagos, Tel +234 807 538 5987 (no website) (full meal about 2,000 naira/US$5.50)

OMAN

Tony and the *Parts Unknown* crew traveled to Oman in late 2016, by which point Tony had been traveling the world for fifteen years; jaded traveler though he might have been, he was floored by Oman. In planning this chapter, he said, "Let's do as much as we can there. I really love that place. I want to encourage people to go there."

"You probably can't find it on the map. It has incredible beaches. Mountains. Pristine desert. It practices a tolerant, nonsectarian form of Islam. One of the most beautiful, most friendly, generous, and hospitable places I've ever been. I'm talking about Oman.

"Oman defies expectations. It shouldn't, according to the cruel logic of the world, exist. But it does, and it's incredible. The sultanate of Oman is an absolute monarchy. [It's] a predominantly Islamic state, and a vital strategic choke point in the world's oil supply. It is surrounded by some of the trickiest and most contentious powers in the region. And yet, here it is, relatively small, tolerant, welcoming to outsiders, peaceful, and stunningly beautiful. But Oman is facing uncertainty, with succession issues and dwindling oil reserves. The question of what's next is a big, if often, unspoken one.

"Oman, it should be understood, sits at the top of the Indian Ocean rim. The empire once stretched from Pakistan to East Africa, with important trade routes that reached from southern Africa all the way to the China Straits, Indonesia, and deep into East Asia.

Modern Oman is a fraction of that size now, but its DNA, culture, cuisine, and to some extent, attitude toward the outside world is a reflection of that history.

"In the 1930s, Winston Churchill switched the [British] Royal Navy's mode of power from coal to oil. And suddenly, everything changed. They needed oil, which made Oman vital not for its limited oil resources, but for where it is: the Strait of Hormuz, the Persian Gulf's femoral artery. Twenty percent of the world's oil flows through there, making it one of, if not *the*, most strategically important waterways on the planet.

"Sultan Qaboos bin Said al Said is the much-admired and enigmatic absolute ruler and monarch. He's presided over everything Omani [since 1970]. In that time, he has raised the nation, literally, from a dusty primitive backwater to a modern, functioning, largely secular society. . . . Usually, one-man shows are not a good thing. I mean, historically, seldom does that work out. But you look around and see how the country is doing now—it's pretty impressive.

"Oman ain't your system, and it ain't my system, and it's far, far from being either perfect or a Western-style democracy, but there is a palpable pride here in the collective identity of being Omani. Notably as well, the sultan has placed emphasis on the role of women, decreeing, at least as a matter of policy, equal access to education, to work, to political office." Note: The sultan died in January 2020 and his cousin Haitham bin Tariq has assumed the role of Oman's leader.

ARRIVAL, GETTING AROUND, AND ACCOMMODATIONS

Air travelers from abroad will almost invariably arrive at **Muscat International Airport (MCT)**, about twenty miles from the nation's capital, Muscat. It is the hub for Oman Air, with flights within Oman and the Middle East, and many destinations on the Indian subcontinent, Africa, Asia, and Europe.

There are red-and-white metered taxis available for hire from the Mwaslat desk within the arrivals hall. There are also taxis queued outside, but note that they are not required to use meters, so it's best to agree on a fare before your trip. The average taxi from the airport to a Muscat hotel is about 12 Omani rials, or about US$30. Tipping is not expected but is appreciated. A number of private shuttle services and hotels operate buses between the airport and hotels as well, and you may also rent a car at MCT.

Once in Muscat, you can get around by taxi or on local buses, called *baizas*, which are orange and white. Passengers commonly share taxis to keep costs low. Oman's railroad system, as of this writing, is still a work in progress.

HOTELS: A LITERAL PALACE, A MOUNTAIN RETREAT, A DESERT OASIS

While using Muscat as a home base, Tony stayed at **Al-Bustan Palace**, a Ritz-Carlton resort between the al-Hajar Mountains and Sea of Oman that was originally built as a palace for Sultan Qaboos bin Said al Said. There's a serious spa on site, multiple outdoor pools, beach

˙service, kayaking and snorkeling, a Chinese fine-dining restaurant, a major breakfast buffet, and the kind of refined service and lavish interiors you'd expect from such a place.

AL-BUSTAN PALACE: Quron Beach/PO Box 1998, Muscat 114, Tel +968 24 799666, www.ritzcarlton/en/hotels/oman/al-bustan (rooms start at about 150 rials/US$400 per night)

"As one moves away from the coast, and into the interior, everything changes. This is the country's more conservative core, its spiritual center. Uniquely, Oman is neither Sunni nor Shiite, but rather Ibadi: a very old and particularly tolerant nonsectarian form of Islam. This is a distinction we in the West would be wise to notice. Islam is not a monolith; it comes in many forms.

"Ibadi theology arguably forms the backbone of many of Oman's codes of conduct. It places value on concepts like politeness, acceptance, unity, and understanding. Perhaps as a consequence of that,

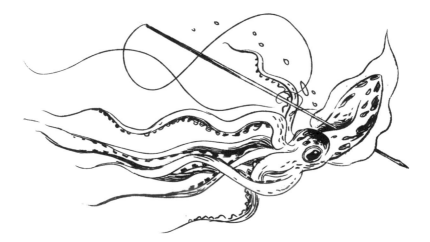

the sultanate embraces grace and tact as a matter of foreign policy. Internally, too, Oman has avoided radicalism and sectarian violence. It is considered shameful, by Ibadi teachings, to draw blood over religious conflicts, unless attacked.

"The terror and bloodshed in neighboring Yemen feels very far away up here—Jabal al-Akhdar, the Green Mountain."

While visiting al-Jabal al-Akhdar, two hours' drive inland from Muscat, **Anantara al-Jabal al-Akhdar Resort** offers super-luxury accommodations, built 6,500 feet above sea level on the Saiq Plateau of the mountain for which the place is named. The property is situated on the edge of a canyon, with superb views from almost any point, especially an infinity pool built into the cliff's edge, and a viewing platform named for a onetime visitor, the late Princess Diana. Guided hikes and cultural tours, extensive spa options, cooking and fitness classes, numerous dining options, and the kind of calm, luxurious isolation that its location provides are among the many reasons that Tony was wild for the place. Note that the mountain road is sufficiently steep that only 4×4 vehicles may make the ascent; the resort offers a chauffeured ride up the mountain from the base, a thirty-five-minute drive, for a fee.

ANANTARA AL-JABAL AL-AKHDAR RESORT: PO Box 110 Postal Code 621, al-Jabal al-Akhdar, Nizwa, Tel +968 25 21 8000, www.anantara.com/en/jabal-akhdar (rooms start at about 200 rials/ US$500 per night)

"One hundred and thirty miles south of Muscat, the pavement ends and you hit this: Sharqiya Sands, on the edge of Rub' al Khali, the largest sand desert in the world. Once you get up into soft sand, things change, everything changes, you change. This is the traditional domain of the Bedouin, who, for thousands of years, moved across this harsh, dry, seemingly endless landscape, making it their home."

While spending time in Sharqiya Sands, make your home at **1000 Nights Camp**. It's one of very few permanent settlements in the region, which allows visitors to become immersed in life among the sand dunes, with some measure of comfort, ranging from traditional Arab-style tents (arrayed around a shared bathroom facility) to more spacious and luxurious tents, to a freestanding house option.

1000 NIGHTS CAMP: PO Box 9, Postal Code 115, Mandinate al-Sultan Qaboos, Tel +968 9944 8158, www.thousandnightsoman.com (rooms/tents start at about 100 rials/US$250 per night)

EATING IN OMAN: REFLECTIONS OF EMPIRE

"The food of Oman is a mix of flavors and ingredients and tastes from Arabia, and from all over Oman's former empire." The common elements of the Omani diet include rice dishes, dates, a light brew of coffee mixed with cardamom and rosewater called *kahwa*, grilled or roasted meats and seafood, flatbreads, and vegetables cooked with cloves and coconut. The cuisine is clearly influenced by the ingredients and techniques found on Zanzibar, which was once part of the Omani Sultanate.

"**Bait al-Luban** is an old boardinghouse turned restaurant, where you can try dishes like *pakora* and *kashori*, which both came back from India; *chapati* from East Africa; and *shuwa*, Oman's classic special-event dish. They do one version or another of this all over the world, but *shuwa* is special. They slather a goat with a spicy paste consisting of cumin, coriander, red pepper, cinnamon, cardamom, and nutmeg, then wrap the meat in palm or banana leaves, dig a hole, throw in some meat, and cover it up and leave underground for a day or two over hot coals."

BAIT AL-LUBAN: Al-Mina Street, Muttrah Corniche, Muscat, Tel +968 24 711842, www.baitalluban.com (entrées about 6.50 rials/ US$17 each)

PERU

LIMA

For *Parts Unknown*, Tony combined a visit to cosmopolitan Lima, the gastronomic capital of South America, with a visit to a remote cacao plantation. Tony had gone into the high-end chocolate business with Eric Ripert, and he wanted to meet the people at the beginning of the supply chain, in Marañón Canyon.

"Peru is a country that's historically driven men mad: mad for gold, for coca, for its magical, ancient history. But now, there's something else drawing outsiders to its hidden mountain valleys. We love this stuff. We obsess about it, gorge on it, and fetishize it. I'm talking about chocolate. Once a common treat, it's now becoming as nuanced as fine wine, making the pursuit of the raw good stuff all the more difficult.

"A prophet once said, 'Don't tell me what a man says, don't tell me what a man knows. Tell me where he has traveled.' I wonder about that. Do we get smarter, more enlightened as we travel? Does travel bring wisdom? I think there's probably no better place to find out than Peru. Ever since Pizarro came looking for gold, people have been drawn to Peru. Born of an uneasy mix of Spanish and indigenous influences, today it's a land of extreme contrasts: present versus past; verdant jungle, snow-capped mountains, vibrant cities; the assimilated and the not. It's often those very contrasts that draw people here."

ARRIVAL AND GETTING AROUND

Jorge Chávez International Airport (LIM), named for a well-known aviator of the early twentieth century, is the country's main international airport. It services flights from within Peru and South America, Central America, and a handful of North American and European cities.

Airport Express Lima is an air-conditioned bus service (with Wi-Fi and a toilet!) that will get you safely from the airport to one of seven stops at hotels in Miraflores, which is the district you'll almost inevitably be staying in. Buy a ticket inside the airport; it's about 25 Peruvian sol/US$8 one way or 50 sol/US$15 round trip. You can also take a taxi (but not Uber, which has been banned from the airport and is considered unsafe) to your hotel. The airport is twelve miles from Miraflores; a taxi will take about thirty minutes and cost 50 to 60 sol/US$15 to $18. Taxi drivers do not expect tips.

Within the city, you can take your chances with a taxi, though apart from a few established companies, taxis are largely unregulated and unmetered, so prepare to negotiate a price and, in some cases, give the driver directions, as many people come from the rural regions looking for work, and there is no barrier to entry as a taxi driver. Lima has an official bus system, El Metropolitano, and an unregulated network of minivans, called *colectivos*, that are dirt cheap, but slow, unregulated, and not really for the casual, skittish, or non-Spanish-speaking visitor.

CEVICHE AND ANCIENT EROTICA IN LIMA

"Lima is the cultural hub and culinary capital of a country that has exploded in the last decade, with scores of world-class chefs, cooks, and restaurants. It has long been considered to be one of the best

food scenes in all of South America. There are so many products in Peru that are unfamiliar to people in the States. When you eat this food, it's not 'kind of like' anything. It's really all its own. Chinese and Japanese immigrants came to Peru in great numbers in the nineteenth and twentieth centuries, as contract laborers and farmers. And their influence is felt here, particularly in the food, to a greater degree than anywhere else on the continent. It's that influence, and the ingredients of Amazonia and the Andes, that really distinguishes the food here as something special—flavors you find no place else on earth."

For an intimate lunch in Lima, it's hard to do better than a visit to **Chez Wong**—literally the home of chef Javier Wong, who has been serving ceviche in the tiny six-table restaurant in his home for thirty-five years. He works with a network of a dozen or so fishermen, and the restaurant serves lunch only, with Wong himself cutting and seasoning all the fish.

"**The whole place is served whatever menu he's doing that day— the same for everybody. And today, the flounder he got from the market is particularly nice, so that's what we're getting.**" Wong might typically make octopus and flounder ceviche: a *tiradito* of flounder with pecans, lime, aji limon, and sesame oil. (Eric Ripert remarked that he planned to adapt the ceviche for his menu at Le Bernardin, back in New York.) And don't miss the more offbeat offerings, like *queso fresco* with pineapple. "**This shouldn't be good, but it is.**"

CHEZ WONG: Enrique León García 114, 15043 Lima, Tel +51 1 4706217 (no website) (entrées about 85 sol/US$25 each)

After an obligatory spin around the gold and other pre-Columbian artifacts housed within the impressive **Museo Larco**, you may wish to check out the Erotic Gallery, in which are displayed many fine examples of pre- and post-Columbian pottery and other works, featuring all manner of humans and animals engaged in various acts of sexual congress. "It sounds about as much fun as an all-nude renaissance fair, but is actually pretty cool. Turns out, things could get pretty interesting back in the day. Oh yeah, those guys could get crazy, get wild, and apparently, very kinky. Nothing new under the sun that these pre-Columbian horndogs didn't think of first."

MUSEO LARCO: Avenida Simón Bolivar 1515, 15084 Pueblo Libre, Lima, Tel +51 1 4611312, www.museolarco.org (adult general admission 30 sol/US$9)

CUSCO AND MACHU PICCHU

To visit Machu Picchu, you must first travel from Lima to the high Andean city of Cusco.

"In its streets, tourists rub shoulders with traditional Andean people, while gawking at Spanish colonial buildings built atop Inca stone ruins. It's a great place to introduce oneself to both the beauty and the uneasy contrasts of Peruvian history—and to the uneasy breathing at high altitude."

While it's about 350 miles as the crow flies between Lima and Cusco, the driving distance is nearly double that, given the layout of the roads that avoid going directly over some treacherous mountain terrain. There are tourist-oriented bus lines that make a three-day journey of it, traveling in a southern loop and stopping overnight along the way, which will give you plenty of time to acclimate to the altitude change (Lima is at about 500 feet above sea level, while Cusco is at 11,000 feet). There are also "fast" buses, making the journey in a more direct way, in twenty-two hours, but they have a dodgy reputation for unsafe driving and even armed hijackings.

The flight from Lima to Cusco's **Alejandro Velasco Astete Airport (CUS)** takes just over an hour; there are a handful of Peruvian airlines serving this route. Be prepared for some altitude shock upon arrival. Arrange for an airport transfer to your hotel inside the airport for about 50 sol/US$15, or take your chances with the drivers outside the airport, which will cost between 15 and 35 sol/US$4–$10, depending on your negotiating and language skills.

As in Lima, Cusco can be navigated on foot, by taxi, bus, or *combi* van.

To complete your journey to the Machu Picchu citadel site, you may either take a train (information at perurail.com), or book a guided trek with a reputable tour company.

ROOM TO BREATHE IN A CUSCO HOTEL

While in Cusco, you'll find comfort and easy breathing at the **Belmond Hotel Monasterio,** "a four-hundred-year-old Jesuit seminary turned five-star hotel. Its period decor is a powerful reminder of the Spanish presence. Spiritual enlightenment—that's what the conquistadors convinced themselves they were bringing to the Incas. They claimed to be waging a war for souls. But here in the rarefied air, the war I'm waging is to suck in a decent breath. The hotel spares no effort, trying to help by pumping pure oxygen into the rooms."** The hotel has no pool or gym, but there are four courtyards, two high-end restaurants, a consecrated chapel, and breathtaking works of art from the seventeenth century.

BELMOND HOTEL MONASTERIO: Calle Plazaleta Nazarenas 337, Cusco, Tel +51 84 604 000, www.belmond.com/hotels/south -america/peru/cusco/belmond-hotel-monasterio (rooms start at 1,000 sol/US$300 night)

PHILIPPINES

MANILA

After some increasingly urgent entreaties from Filipino fans, who had grown frustrated with him passing up their country, year after year, in favor of other corners of Southeast Asia, Tony first visited the Philippines in 2008, for season 5 of *No Reservations*, and returned seven years later with *Parts Unknown*.

"The history of the Philippines is long, complicated, extraordinarily violent, and hard to quantify or describe in a neat little paragraph. From indigenous Polynesian peoples, waves of Malay and Chinese settlers and traders, and colonizing Spanish and Americans, it's a big and deeply personal story when it comes to America.

"The Philippines paid a very heavy price during World War II. Between the Japanese occupiers and our bombers, Manila was pretty much leveled. They tend to like us in the Philippines, in the measured way one likes someone who's set you free from an enemy but flattened your country while doing it. The way Manila looks today is a product of those times and those postwar values, and an enormous American military presence."

GETTING THERE

Fly into **Manila Ninoy Aquino International Airport (MNL)**, so named for the former Philippine senator Benigno "Ninoy" Aquino, who was assassinated there in 1983, upon his return from exile in the United States. Aquino was a vocal critic of President Ferdinand Marcos, an authoritarian who ruled from 1965 to 1986, after finally being swept from office by the People Power Revolution that saw him replaced with Corazon Aquino, Ninoy's widow.

From the airport, it's about eight miles to downtown Manila; a metered taxi will take thirty minutes to one hour (or more, in evening rush hour), and will cost about 200 Philippine pesos/US$4, plus a customary 10 percent tip for good service. For 150 pesos/about US$3, there are also buses that make several drops in the city.

Think twice about renting a car; traffic in metro Manila is impossible, and you're better off not contributing to the legendary gridlock.

PORK

"So, every Filipino I know in the States, and everybody who came up to me in the airport, the first thing that they mentioned was, 'You're gonna eat *sisig*?' The fierce love, the misty-eyed reminiscences of Filipinos in the United States looking back on the food of their country—*sisig* always comes up first, and most emotionally, and I completely understand why.

"For me, the 'come to mama' moment is that most-loved of Filipino street foods, the strangely addictive, sizzling-hot mélange of hacked-up pork face. A crispy, chewy, spicy, savory, and altogether damn wonderful mélange of textures that just sings. Everything I like, on a smoking hot sizzle platter. Oh, sweet symphony of pig parts, oh yes."

For a first taste of the real deal, seek out **Aling Lucing's Sisig** stall in Angeles, a city in Pampanga Province, about fifty miles northwest of Manila. The proprietor, Lucia Cunanan, died in 2008, but her daughter Zenaida carries on in her wake, though now from the other side of the street. Claude Tayag, who was one of Tony's on-camera guides in 2008, advises that there are a number of other branches bearing the Aling Lucing name, but they are unaffiliated with Lucia's family. (See Claude Tayag's essay, "Busting the *Sisig* Myth," on page 256.)

Upon his return in 2015, Tony meant to explore outside Manila, but the soggy rage of Typhoon Nona kept him and the crew grounded in the city, where he enjoyed another round of *sisig*, this time at **Super Six Bar & Grill**, where he indulged in a typical pork-induced reverie: **"Hot sizzling pig face with a runny egg on top, and bitch, you better ask somebody, because nothing is getting in between me and this spicy, chewy, fatty goodness."**

ALING LUCING'S SISIG: Glaciano Valdez Street, Angeles, Pampanga, Tel +63 45 888 2317 (no website) (*sisig* platter 200 pesos/about US$3.75)

SUPER SIX BAR & GRILL: 533 Remedios Street, Malate, Manila, Luzon 1004, Tel +63 2 400 7956 (typical plate about 200 pesos/ US$3.75)

"It is true that I lie to my daughter and tell her that Ronald Mc-Donald has been implicated in the disappearance of small children. That I sneer at fast food—revile it at every opportunity—but I am also a hypocrite, because to me, the Filipino chain Jollibee is the wackiest, jolliest place on earth. There are over nine hundred of these things, all over the seven thousand–plus Philippine Islands, and a whole lot more, internationally, wherever there are homesick Filipinos."

JOLLIBEE: many locations, www.jollibee.com.ph/stores/metro -manila/ (two-piece chicken meal about 160 pesos/US$3)

Busting the Sisig *Myth*

BY CLAUDE TAYAG

Of all the Filipino dishes known to foreigners, it seems *sisig* has fast replaced *adobo*, *pancit* (noodles), and *lumpia* (spring rolls) in popularity. But what exactly is *sisig*?

According to the Center for Kapampangan Studies, at Holy Angel University in Angeles City, Pampanga [Philippines], the word *sisig* appeared in a 1732 Pampango-Spanish dictionary; it was defined as "a salad served with vinaigrette."

During that era, pregnant women commonly ate fresh fruits or vegetables (unripe papaya, green mango, guava, banana heart) dipped in vinegar and salt, to satisfy a craving for something sour. As the pregnancy progressed, the expectant mother would be fed a concoction of boiled pig's ears, again soaked in vinegar; the cartilage was believed to help make the growing fetus's bones stronger. These two elements together compose *sisig babi*; how it became a favorite appetizer of menfolk on a drinking spree is anybody's guess.

The present-day sizzling *sisig* is a fine example of how one person can steer the culinary landscape of a locality, then a province, an archipelago, and the world. In the early 1970s, Lucia Cunanan of Angeles City was just one of a dozen of barbeque vendors by the city's railroad track, selling grilled chicken and a combination of boiled pig's head, sliced and flavored with *sukang sasá* (nipa palm vinegar), onions, salt, black pepper, and chili that together was known as *sisig*.

According to Lucia's daughter Zenaida, one evening, her mother accidentally burned an order of pig's ears on skewers. Rather than throw it away, she chopped it up and served it like the boiled *sisig*, flavored with vinegar, calling it her "new" version of the centuries-old recipe. It became an instant hit with the locals, and this grilled version became known as Aling Lucing's *sisig*.

Around 1976, another Angeleño, Benedict Pamintuan, opened a beer garden, Sisig Benedict, serving grilled *sisig* on a hot skillet, which gave it an added crunchy finish. At that time, sizzling *sisig* was popular only among us locals, and the occasional accidental tourist.

In 1980, my brothers, Mario and Abong Tayag, together with our cousin Dan Tayag, opened Trellis Restaurant in Quezon City. Among other Pampango specialties, they served Benedict's version of sizzling *sisig*, with the addition of chopped boiled chicken liver. Trellis was at the forefront of the restaurant-grill genre, and it helped the sizzling *sisig* craze catch on in the metropolis.

In October 2008, Tony interviewed me for the Philippine episode of *No Reservations*, and had his first bite of *sisig*. It was love at first bite: **"It's got everything I love about food—sizzling pork bits, with all that good, rubbery, fatty, crispy. And it goes wonderfully well with beer,"** he wrote on his blog, and the world took notice of this Pampango delicacy.

My last encounter with Tony was in Manila, in June 2017, where he was a guest speaker at the World Street Food Congress. In an interview for my TV show, *Chasing Flavors*, he said, "Sisig is the breakaway dish that catapulted Filipino cuisine to mainstream America."

Nowadays, it seems that just about anything chopped and served on a sizzling plate is called *sisig*—but nothing beats the genuine article, in all its pork fat glory. Just don't forget to add acidity from vinegar or calamansi, some chili, and a bottle of subzero San Miguel beer. Bon appétit!

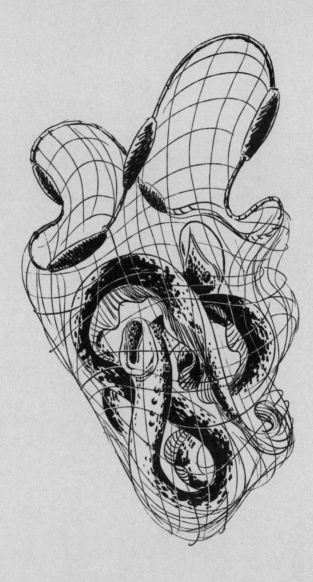

PORTUGAL

Tony first learned about Portugal and its food as a young dishwasher and cook in Provincetown, Massachusetts, where much of the population of restaurant workers, fishermen, and their families were of Portuguese descent.

"Portugal—sandwiched between Spain and the Atlantic Ocean, and tiny as countries go—has had an outsize impact on the world. During the 'Age of Discovery,' the Portuguese went to sea in great numbers, gained fame as navigators, shipbuilders, explorers. They conquered a large part of the world, their empire stretching from Brazil to Africa to the East Indies.

"Everything old is new again. [Or] maybe not. I come close sometimes to believing nothing actually changes. Back in the beginning, fresh out of the kitchen when I first went out into the world to figure out how to make television, I came to northern Portugal. Little did I know what I would find."

He learned that the chunky, fiery kale, potato, and chorizo soups and stews he'd come to associate with continental Portugal were in fact endemic to the Azores, an archipelago in the North Atlantic, an autonomous region of the country with its own distinct culinary and cultural traditions. Most of the people whose cooking Tony had loved in Massachusetts were immigrants from the Azores, where, in search of the differences between continental and island Portugal, he shot an episode of *No Reservations*. That episode was perhaps most notable for his bemused on-camera reaction to the strong smell of the sulfurous hot springs (**"like a wet fart"**), in which a local cook hard-boiled an egg for him.

LISBON

ARRIVAL AND GETTING AROUND

Lisbon, the capital of Portugal, is considered the gateway to the country. Its airport, **Humberto Delgado or Lisbon Portela**, is known simply as **Lisbon Airport (LIS)**; it's served by all major US carriers, TAP Air Portugal, the nation's flag carrier airline, and all the major European carriers. There's an airport shuttle bus (Aerobus, which costs 4 euros/US$4.50 and takes about forty-five minutes), the city metro (1.45 euro/US$1.60 for a thirty-five-minute ride, which includes a necessary transfer), and taxis, which will cost about 20 euros/US$22 for the approximately six-mile, twenty-minute ride to the city center from the airport.

Lisbon has several train stations, the largest of which is Gare do Oriente, a modernist beauty designed by Santiago Calatrava, the renowned Spanish architect. The city has a four-line metro system, Lisbon Metro.

EATING IN LISBON: MINIMAL FUSS, MAXIMUM PLEASURE

"Lisbon: it's an old city, the heart of the Age of Discovery, once the world's richest empire. There's history here, lots of it. It's a beautiful city. Lisboetas, as the locals are known, like their food. They talk about it a lot, and have strong ideas about what visitors should eat and where. Ramiro is one of those places that locals love, have always loved, and always will love. It's chef friendly, with the kind of straight-ahead meals that chefs tired of sauce and garnish crave. It's

a barrage of minimalist seafood of maximum quality. They don't do a lot to their fish here. Start with the seafood, end with the steak sandwich." Ramiro is a busy three-story establishment with few frills, though the service is friendly and polished, and the food is simple and impeccable.

You can make an epic meal of their goose barnacles, shrimp, langoustines, clams, and, for dessert, a garlicky slab of steak, seasoned with mustard and sandwiched on a roll, along with plenty of beer.

RAMIRO: Avenida Alimante Reis no. 1, 1150–007 Lisbon, Tel +351 21 885 1024, www.geral24128.wixsite.com/cervejariaramiro/copia-home (typical meal for two 75 100 euros/US$83–$111)

"Whenever possible, I like to eat where I can also fill all my fishing tackle needs: **Sol e Pesca**, in the crummy part of town—a strip populated by cruiser-weight hookers with bad dentistry. Along with my love of fishing tackle, I have recently acquired a true and deep love for really good stuff—eel, sardines—that comes in cans."

There's also several varieties of tuna and tuna roe, horse mackerel, octopus, squid, and more, served with bread and wine. Tony ate and drank among the rods, nets, and reels with Pedro Gonçalves and Tó Trips of **Dead Combo**, "one of the best and most interesting bands in Lisbon," whose music scored the entire episode.

SOL E PESCA: Rua Nova de Carvalho 14, 1200–019 Lisbon, Tel +351 21 346 7203 (typical meal 20–30 euros/US$22–$33 per person)

PORTO

ARRIVAL

Porto Airport, formally known as **Francisco Sá Carneiro**, is also a hub for TAP Air Portugal, and is serviced by a handful of European carriers. The city metro system, Metro do Porto, takes riders between the airport and the city center for about 3 euros/US$3.35, and there are a handful of shuttle bus services of varying rates, as well as metered taxis, whose fare to the city will be about 25 euros/US$28.

Porto Campanhã is the train station serving the main railway lines in and out of the city; the far more beautiful, elaborately tiled Beaux Arts **São Bento** station is the hub for a number of suburban train lines.

DRINKING FOOD

"What do you do when left with nothing but guts and hooves and odd bits? Figure out how to transform them into delicious, delicious things, of course." At this, the Portuguese excel.

"A meal here is, generally speaking anyway, not light. The Portuguese like pork; they like it a lot." Start with *patinhas*, or small whole sardines, and then *tripas à moda do Porto*: a classic dish of beef tripe, beans, and various pork parts (**"sausage, bacon, pig's ear, cured and smoked"**) at the homey but polished **A Cozinha do Martinho**.

A COZINHA DO MARTINHO: Rua da Costa Cabral, 2598, Porto, Tel +351 91 959 5316 (no website) (typical meal about 30 euros/ US$33 per person)

Porto has no shortage of the kind of fatty, meaty late-night foods with built-in appeal to those who may have had a few drinks of an evening. **"Those who know me even a little bit are familiar with my unholy attraction to the mutant hot dog,"** said Tony, by way of introducing the *cachorro*, a hot sandwich of fresh sausage, cheese, and spicy sauce on a thin, crusty Portuguese roll, toasted and cut into tapas-size portions, all the better for efficient, relatively mess-free eating, and best served with a cold Super Bock beer, at **Cervejaria Gazela**. It's a busy, popular place, but it's worth the wait for a seat at the bar, a counter, or one of a handful of small high tables. There's also a simple steak sandwich on offer, for the spice or pork averse, and crisp, golden fries.

CERVEJARIA GAZELA: Travessa Cimo de Vila 4, 4000–171 Porto, Tel +351 222 054 869, www.cervejariagazela.pt (this is the original location; the newer, larger outpost is at Rua de Entreparedes, 8–10, 4000–434 Porto, Tel +351 221 124 981 [same website as original location]) (hot dog, 3 euros/US$3.30)

"**Meat, cheese, fat, and bread—it's an immortal combination.**" Fewer dishes demonstrate this better than Porto's other signature sandwich, the *francesinha*, a sort of turbocharged croque monsieur, doused in a rich, meaty beer-and-tomato sauce (the exact components of which are a secret jealously guarded by each sandwich maker), and best eaten with a knife and fork.

"**[It] translates as 'little French girl,' but I understand she's not so little. It weighs, like, a ton: bread, ham, steak, sausage, and a bit of linguica. What a construction.**"

CAFÉ O AFONSO: Rua da Torrinha 219, 4050–610, Porto, Tel +351 22 200 0395 (no website) (sandwiches 10 euros/US$11.10)

SINGAPORE

Discussing Singapore in 2017, Tony wrote, for *Food & Wine* magazine, "While I am generally either bored to tears or scared shitless by places where the streets are too clean, everyone behaves well, and the trains always run on time, I make a big exception when it comes to the city-state of Singapore. It could be the roaring heat and humidity, which render the sharp edges of the shopping mall/nanny state a little fuzzy. It could be the wealth of legal vices that begin to balance out the illegality of chewing gum, littering, and public dissent. Or it could be that I'm in love with so much of the food, that great democratizer, especially that which is served within the fragrant confines of the famed hawker centers, which the government would like to begin replicating by the dozen.

"Spotless, efficient, safe, protected, controlled, a utopian city-state run like a multinational company. Welcome to 'Singapore Incorporated.'"

The land now known as Singapore was in fact an important trading port as far back as the thirteenth century. Established as a British colony and essential trading post in 1819 by Stamford Raffles and the British East India Company, Singapore has been an independent entity since 1965.

"Helmed by its first prime minister, Lee Kuan Yew, tiny Singapore famously went from a third-world outpost to a first-world nation in a single generation. By some measures, Singapore is a welfare state, taking care of the less fortunate—but at its heart, it's a cold-blooded meritocracy. You follow the rules—and there are many—work hard, and you will have a good life. That's the message.

"For a state where an ounce of weed can put you in the jug for up to ten years, and the same weight of dope can mean death, and where chewing gum is indeed illegal, a surprising number of vices are allowed here. Drinking age is eighteen. Prostitution is legal, with sex workers getting regular medical checkups. There are casinos and strip clubs. The government seems to understand that, along with a certain amount of repression, safety valves are required. Get drunk, get laid, and you are less likely to be difficult. Perhaps that's the thinking? Or maybe it's just business."

ARRIVAL

"**Singapore Changi Airport (SIN)** is one of the very few airports in this world where you actually might want to arrive early. You've got the usual perks of a good airport—hotels, day rooms, shopping, the stuff you might actually want to buy. There's edible food and in pretty decent variety. Here, it goes way further, seriously: there's a free movie theater, free internet, reclining chairs, smoking lounges, a super slide, indoor gardens, a children's play area, TV and entertainment lounges, 3-D experience zone, rooftop swimming pool, rain forest lounge with Jacuzzi massage, napping facilities and shower, hair and beauty services, the butterfly garden perhaps we'd like to visit, or the koi pond . . ."

On the ground in Singapore, where it's nearly always hot and humid, one can do worse than to rely on robustly air-conditioned public transport, known here as Singapore Mass Rapid Transit (SMRT), to get from place to place. There are train and bus lines that carry passengers between the airport and city center, for about $2 Singapore/US$1.50 for a forty-five-minute ride.

"Back home, I don't look forward to the subway; I try and avoid it. Here, it's clean, like nearly everything in Singapore, shiny and new. And most importantly, cool." It is also extensive and efficient.

Single fares are calculated based on route and distance, starting at about SG$0.75/about US$0.50 and topping out around SG$3/about US$2.15. One-, two-, and three-day unlimited cards are available for tourists. SMRT also administers the city-state's bus service and even its taxis; a taxi ride from airport to hotel should take about thirty minutes, and cost about SG$30/US$22.

Singapore is also, in theory, a walkable city, though the average temperature is 88°F and it rains about ten days out of every month, so, as they say, your mileage may vary.

And finally, a word to the wise. "Despite all my trips here, I don't think I've ever seen a cop, but know this: when they say, 'No drugs in Singapore,' they are not kidding, and I mean really, really not kidding. You bring drugs, even a bag of weed in here with you, you are easily the dumbest person alive."

HOTEL

"I'll tell you right up front. I stay at the **Grand Hyatt** because I've been put up here regularly for years, and at this point, they treat me good—*real* good."

Sometimes, pure luxury rules the day. The most lavish and spacious suites here are outfitted with their private sauna and steam room, but even the most modest room at the Grand Hyatt is tranquil and elegant, as are the public spaces. The hotel has its own indoor waterfall, plus the requisite spa, outdoor pool, and plenty of dining options.

The hotel's restaurant, StraitsKitchen, is also particularly impressive. Skilled cooks prepare and present Malay, Chinese, and Indian hawker-style dishes in distinct open kitchens under one roof, a conceit that could smack of Disneyfication if done wrong—but at the Grand Hyatt, it's done right.

GRAND HYATT SINGAPORE: 10 Scotts Road, Singapore 228211, Tel +65 6416 7016, www.hyatt.com/en-US/hotel/singapore/grand-hyatt-singapore/sinrs (rooms start at about SG$380/US$280 per night)

FOOD, OR, WHY YOU'RE HERE

"New York may be the city that never sleeps, but Singapore's the city that never stops eating. For a gastrotourist, somebody who travels to eat, any kind of serious eater, Singapore's probably the best place you can go for maximum bang in a minimum period of time. In this one tiny city-state, which you could cross by car in like, forty-five minutes, you could find more variety, more options, more specialties from many lands (and cheap!) than just about anywhere else: Chinese specialties from regions all across China, and down the straits; Malay cooking; Indian.

"There's something for everybody, and Singaporeans love their food, and they're refreshingly not snobby about it, but they get it. Fancy restaurant or tiny hawker stand, whoever's got it good is what matters. Worst thing that can happen to you in Singapore is you get a mediocre meal, but even that is unlikely."

THE MIGHTY HAWKER CENTERS OF SINGAPORE

"The hawker centers of Singapore were a shrewd strategy to incorporate and control what was once a chaotic but pervasive culture of street carts."

A little history: From the mid-1800s, Singapore street hawkers—either walking the streets, set up in place, or going door to door—sold everything from cooked food, produce, meat, and hot drinks to cigarettes, household sundries, and services like haircutting and tinsmithing. It was a low-investment way to make a living or supplement a household's income, but it was not without its attendant issues: namely, street congestion, sometimes-dodgy sanitation, and trash.

By the 1930s, there were an estimated six thousand licensed hawkers, and another four thousand unlicensed. To address the aforementioned quality-of-life issues, Singapore's government undertook a decades-long plan to further regulate street hawkers, eventually constructing the hawker centers frequented by Singaporeans and hungry visitors. To date, the government oversees 114 hawker centers, with plans to build another 20.

"The centers are covered structures, still open to the air, but in stalls with regulated running water, refrigeration, and strict rules of food handling. So, basically, you don't have to worry about getting poisoned.

"There's all sorts of good shit you can have for breakfast. Remember, this is a culture where there's no shame in a big bowl of steaming noodles or *laksa* first thing in the a.m. Stall after stall, often organized by nationality: Chinese over here, Malay halal here, Indian over there. Every owner or operator has one or two individual specialties. That's what they do—what they do best.

"Breakfast options at a place like this one are pretty vast. *Tiong bahru* boneless chicken rice, *teck seng soya* bean milk, *min nan* pork ribs prawn noodle, and the famous *kampong* carrot cake." This special dish is a savory steamed cake of fresh and pickled daikon and rice flour, diced and stir-fried with eggs and seasonings. The "white" version is more delicately seasoned with white pepper and scallions, while the "black" version is cooked with a thick sweetened soy sauce. Your options are limitless, but start at the hawker center **Tiong Bahru** with *chwee kueh*, an order of steamed spherical rice cakes topped with sweet and salty pickled radish and optional chili sauce.

TIONG BAHRU FOOD CENTRE: 30 Seng Poh Road, Singapore (no phone, no website) (prices vary by stall)

"Most hawker stalls are family-run operations, and **Whampoa** is no exception. What's unusual is that Li Ruifang left her white-collar job to work alongside her parents, bucking a trend that has left the hawker centers with an aging workforce, unable to replenish generations of expertise with new blood." The signature dish—a combination of substantial yellow wheat noodles and thinner *bee hoon*, or rice vermicelli, tossed with whole prawns and a rich and spicy *sambal* gravy and topped with crisp bits of shallot—is made using a recipe that hasn't changed since the 1950s, when Ruifang's grandfather began the business.

Whampoa is part of the bustling Tekka Food Centre, which includes a wet market, the hawker center, and various dry-goods shops. Located in Singapore's Little India, it's heavy on prepared dishes from the subcontinent, so leave some room for world-class *biryani*, *dosas*, and much more.

545 WHAMPOA PRAWN NOODLE: 665 Buffalo Road, Tekka Food Centre #01–326 Singapore 210665 (no phone, no website) (dishes SG$3–$4/US$2–$3)

The **Tanglin Halt Original Peanut Pancake** stall specializes in a sweet, chewy pancake, made with a hand-whipped wheat flour dough that's studded with ground peanuts leavened with naturally occurring yeast, filled with more peanuts and cane sugar. **"These guys are famous for handpicking, roasting, and grinding their own peanuts, something most other operations take a shortcut on."** There are also round pancakes filled with sweetened pastes made from black sesame, yam, pandan, red bean, and salted green bean. The stand opens at 3:30 a.m. on Tuesday, Thursday, Saturday, and Sunday only, and often sells out before the official 11:00 a.m. closing time, so check your days, set an alarm, and don't be late.

TANGLIN HALT ORIGINAL PEANUT PANCAKE: 48A Tanglin Halt Road, Singapore 148813 (no phone, no website) (peanut pancake SG$0.80/US$0.58; various round pancakes SG$0.90–$1.20/ US$0.70–$0.90)

In the mood for a more substantial meal, the kind of breakfast that will send you back to bed, or help you sleep on a long flight home? Stop at the Hong Lim Hawker Centre for a favorite:

"Oh here it is, the mighty *char kway tiao*. I eat it every time I'm in Singapore. It's just about the unhealthiest breakfast you could have; it's literally like lard, crispy lard bits, healthy cockles, shrimp paste, a whole lot of noodles. And it's, like, *legendarily* fattening; originally created to feed laborers. So it ain't pretty, not the healthiest of breakfasts, but delicious. If you're looking to fit into that silver lamé Speedo, this will not be option one.

"The problem is, you eat this, and you're surrounded by all these sort of 'Wonders of Asia' in the food court here, and after this, you're kind of done. I don't know how anybody works after this, frankly."

OUTRAM PARK FRIED KWAY TIAO MEE: Hong Lim Complex, 531A Upper Cross Street #02–17, Singapore (no phone, no website) (noodles SG$4–$6/US$2.90–$4.40)

Chicken rice may look a little underwhelming, but it's sublime when done well, and it's among the most well known and well loved dishes of Singapore. **"It's a must-try. You may not like it the best, but it's the dish that just might lead you to understand Singapore better. It's so beautiful, so austere and simple."**

The chicken is gently poached, iced, hung to dry, and served on the bone, with a delicate layer of gelatinous fat suspended between skin and meat. The rice is cooked in chicken broth enhanced with some combination of white pepper, garlic, ginger, lemongrass, pandan leaf, soy sauce, and sesame oil; the dish is most often served with chili sauce, an enriched soy sauce, and pickled ginger, so that you can customize each bite.

A favorite chicken rice spot is **Tian Tian**, whose proprietors have been making the dish in the same way, at the same stall in the Maxwell Hawker Centre, since 1985; they received a Michelin Bib Gourmand designation for their efforts in 2017. The chicken rice is also exceptional at **Chin Chin Eating House**. **"This restaurant has been owned and operated by the same family since 1934. So, there's continuity going for you."**

TIAN TIAN HAINANESE CHICKEN RICE: 1 Kadayanallur Street,#01–10/11 Maxwell Food Centre, 069120 Singapore, Tel +65 9691 4852 (no website) (single portion of chicken rice SG$3.50/US$2.50)

CHIN CHIN EATING HOUSE: 19 Purvis Street, 188598 Singapore, Tel +65 6337 4640, www.chinchineatinghouse.com (single portion of chicken rice about SG$4/US$3; average meal about SG$15/US$12)

Nasi lemak is another classic Singapore dish not to be missed. **"On the way to the airport, the Changi Village Hawker Centre, in a residential neighborhood, has a famously good one. It doesn't sound** like much, but believe me, this is important: egg, fried chicken or fish, *sambal*, and coconut rice from the long, slow-moving line—it's clearly worth waiting for the best. I know from experience, it is.

"This is one of the things I love about these hawker centers. You notice *nasi lemak* sold here, *nasi lemak* sold there. Here is a slow-moving line, in the smoking heat, and a half-hour, forty-minute wait—for the same item they're selling over there? No one on line for that. The people have spoken."

INTERNATIONAL MUSLIM FOOD STALL NASI LEMAK: Changi Village Hawker Centre, 2 Changi Village Road, #01-03 500002 Singapore, Tel +65 8400 6882 (no website) (*nasi lemak* plates SG$3–$4.50/US$2.15–$3.25)

SOUTH KOREA

SEOUL

"So many of the good times traveling this world relate directly to finding a human face to associate with your destination, the food you eat, and the memories you'll keep with you forever. The best times are when it's impossible to be cynical about anything. When you find yourself letting go of the past, and your preconceptions, and feel yourself and your basic nature, the snarkiness and suspicion, the irony and doubt, disappear, at least for a time. When, for a few moments or a few hours, you change.

"Sometimes, something in you needs to be kicked loose from its shell, or through guile and persistence and a fervent belief in something as fundamental as your country and your family and their inherent goodness, someone pulls you out of yourself. In South Korea, Nari Kye did that for me."

Nari, who'd been with Zero Point Zero since nearly the very beginning, did double duty on each of two South Korea episodes, one for *No Reservations*, and one for *Parts Unknown*, appearing on camera to show Tony the place where she was born, and working as a producer behind the scenes. (See Nari's essay about the experience on page 278.)

ARRIVAL

Seoul has two airports: **Gimpo International (GMP)**, originally built as Japanese Imperial Army base in World War II, now serves short-haul flights from Japan and China, along with domestic flights from elsewhere in South Korea; and the vast, modern **Incheon International (ICN)**, for flights from everywhere. The two airports are connected by the Airport Railroad Express (AREX) commuter train, a ride that takes about twenty-five minutes and costs about 4,700 won/US$4. An express AREX line takes passengers between Incheon International and Seoul Station, which takes about forty-five minutes and costs about 8,300 won/US$7. There are, of course, private taxis and group limo buses available for transfer between the airports and the city, and, as of this writing, Uber cars can be summoned via your smartphone in Seoul.

Once in Seoul, your best bet for moving around this city of ten million inhabitants is the excellent, extensive, and inexpensive subway system, whose announcements are made in both Korean and English. Get a reloadable T-money card or a Seoul City Pass and an English map or Seoul subway app like Seoul Metropolitan Subway, Subway Korea, or Explore Seoul. The city's bus system will also get you around cheaply, but is less user-friendly for the non-Korean speaker. Taxis are relatively inexpensive, and good for shorter distances. *Ilban* (regular) taxis are cash only, distinguished by their silver, orange, blue, or white color, and black *mobeum* (deluxe) taxis are generally roomier, accept credit cards, and provide receipts. In both cases, it's wise to have your destination written down in Hangul, the written form of the Korean language, as drivers often don't speak English.

FISH, EAT, DRINK, SING, PLAY

"**Korea is a fish and rice culture. The staggering demand for seafood here goes a long way toward what it means to be Korean. And before the sun comes up, the Noryangjin Fisheries Wholesale Market, Seoul's largest, at nearly 200,000 square feet, and open twenty-four hours, is a great place to start.**" It's cold, wet, and chaotic, so dress and act accordingly: layer up, wear waterproof shoes or boots if at all possible, bring cash, and keep your wits about you, as people are working here. There's a 3:00 a.m. fish auction, and during daylight hours, you can purchase seafood to be cooked for you, or cleaned and sliced sashimi style, in one of the on-site restaurants, for a modest service fee.

NORYANGJIN FISHERIES WHOLESALE MARKET: 674 Nodeul-ro, Noryangjin-dong, Dongjak-gu, Seoul, Tel +82 2 2254 8000, www.susanijang.co.kr (prices vary)

What is *hwe sik*? Nari explains, "It's a company outing, basically mandatory, that consists of three parts called 'cha': (1) *il cha*, (2) *ee cha*, and (3) *saam cha*. If you miss any of these parts of the night out (especially the latter parts), you'll be scorned, teased, and shunned by the office or group of friends. *Il cha* is dinner, usually barbecue; *ee cha* is drinking; and *saam cha* is karaoke.

"Koreans live steadfastly by the 'work hard/play hard' motto, and while all aspects of *hwe sik* are to enjoy, let loose, and get drunk, office politics live on strong. Seniority is everything, so the younger employees pour the drinks and pay the tab. There's a lot of pressure to drink; it can get pretty intense, to the point that younger employees, especially women, have developed clever techniques to fake-drink and not get plastered during these social outings."

Get started with *il cha* at **Mapo Jeong Daepo**, where the house specialty is *galmaegisal* (pork skirt steak), cooked at the table on a

Becoming Who I Am

BY NARI KYE

The South Korea episode of *No Reservations* started as a joke. I was a production manager, and one of my jobs was planning our wrap parties. At the end of season 1, I said, "We're all going to eat Korean barbecue, and drink lots of soju." I got us a huge table in Manhattan's K-Town, and Tony came. We went outside to smoke, and in my drunken soju haze, I said, "Tony, you have to swear you're going to Korea." And he said, "Of course. And you have to come with me."

A few months later, he came into the office and said, **"You should start planning that Korea trip. We're going to visit your family, and you're going to be on camera."** I felt so overwhelmed. I only vaguely remembered our drunken discussion. There were ten thousand things I wanted to do with him, and lists started going off in my head.

I had no idea that this was going to be one of the most important things I'd ever done in my life, that it would change me, fundamentally, forever. I was focused on the planning, and didn't step back and think about the bigger picture.

When we landed in Seoul—it's a fourteen-hour flight, so already we were exhausted, jet-lagged—but because the story arc was that I was visiting my homeland, they started filming in the airport. It was my birthday, and producer Rennik Soholt had arranged for the fixer to bring a cake to the airport. Even after we got to the hotel, exhausted after twenty hours of travel, Tony said, **"We've got to celebrate. It's your birthday."** He ordered a bunch of snacks, bought everyone drinks. We had a really great night, one I'll never forget.

We went to a kimchi farm, where I got to make kimchi with old-school aunties. We visited a soybean factory. We did a BBQ scene at a charcoal factory that also had a sauna. It was amazing.

Tony said, **"I would rather die than do karaoke. You're never going to get me to sing."** But you can't avoid it, especially in Korea.

It would be so rude to skip it. There's this whole process of going out: you need to go eat, you need to drink, and then you need to do karaoke. You *have* to do these things. And so we went, and the scene was ridiculous. And if you watch one of the clip shows, you'll see Tony singing karaoke for the first time! We got him after all.

We also went to the demilitarized zone that has separated North and South Korea since 1953, and Tony walked around with some of the American soldiers. What was really special, the highlight of the whole show, was having my grandfather meet us there, just outside the DMZ. We went fishing, and ate at this little restaurant in the middle of nowhere, and my grandfather told us his whole story, including things that I had never heard before.

My dad's side of the family was from the north, before the country split, and my grandfather had an incredibly harrowing story of escaping to the south during the war, covering himself in mud and hiding in the forest to escape the soldiers. The Communists were trying to recruit him—he was well educated, a smart young man, and they wanted him to join the Party and fight in the war.

He and my grandmother were just married; they'd just had their first child. My grandmother escaped first, in the middle of the night, on a boat, and she almost had to suffocate the baby, because she was crying. They had made plans to meet some day again in the south. And finally, after a year apart, they somehow found each other, and then my father was born, and then the rest of his siblings.

I knew then, hearing this story, making this show, would change me. Back in New York, watching the edit come together, I thought, "This is the greatest thing I've ever done." And I was so grateful to Tony for allowing me to do it. He had no idea—or maybe he did—that he was changing my life, with this one episode of the show.

I moved to the States when I was five, from Korea, and after that, I had a predominantly white, Anglo American upbringing. As a kid who already looked different from everyone else, I was trying to fit in as an American, and was mortified of my Korean heritage. My mom cooked only Korean food. My parents spoke only Korean to me. We watched only Korean television—we would borrow VHS tapes from the Korean supermarket every week. We basically lived in Korea in our house in a very American town.

All my friends were white, blond-haired girls named Jenny and Erin, who would wear their shoes inside their houses, call adults by their first name, and for dinner would have weird things like macaroni and cheese and canned string beans. So, whenever they'd come over to my house, I would run around and hide all the Korean things, because I didn't want them to see how different I was, even asking my mom to attempt to cook American dishes (which she refused to do).

Before making the Korea episode of *No Reservations* with Tony, I was a different person: I was ashamed and embarrassed to be

round charcoal-fueled grill, encircled by a metal gully into which runs the rendered pork fat. A server will add beaten eggs to the well, and guests may add kimchi, scallions, or other bits of *banchan* (the pickled vegetable and fish accompaniments to a barbecue meal).

MAPO JEONG DAEPO: 183–8 Dohwa-dong, Mapo-gu, Seoul, Tel +82 2 3275 0122 (no website) (skirt steak barbecue 12,000 Korean won/about US$10.25)

Next, head to tiny, smoky **Gol Mok Jib**, for kimchi *jjigae* (stew) and Korean drinking games, facilitated by many glasses of beer, soju, and rice wine.

different. I just wanted to fit in. All my life, I felt like I really didn't belong. It wasn't until after that experience that I realized this is what makes me who I am.

Now, if I had to say what makes me a unique individual, it would be, number one, that I'm of Korean heritage—even before being a woman, a mother, a wife. All I want to do now is spread the gospel of Korean culture in America.

I have two kids now, and I speak to them in Korean. I started a Korean Mommy and Me school, to promote the language and teach it to babies. We eat Korean food, and I try to teach non-Koreans about Korean food and Korean culture. Through my work, I'm developing creative content that's centered on Korean culture. Everything I do is through that lens now. Tony was the person who unlocked that for me. He helped me realize what I want to do as a creative person, and as a person, period. *He* fundamentally changed me.

Thank you, Tony.

GOL MOK JIB: 813–11 Yuk Sam Dong, Gangnam-gu, Seoul (no phone, no website) (kimchi *jjiage* about 1,800 won/US$1.50)

And, once you're suitably shit-faced, it's karaoke time at **Junco Music Town**, where you can enjoy squid, M&M's, soft ballads, and many more drinks in the *noraebang* ("singing room").

JUNCO MUSIC TOWN: 1309–5, basement floor, Suh-cho gu, Sucho-dong, Seoul, Tel +82 2595 3235 (no website) (karaoke 5,000–10,000 won/US$4.50–$9 per hour; cooked food 10,000–20,000 won/US$8–$18)

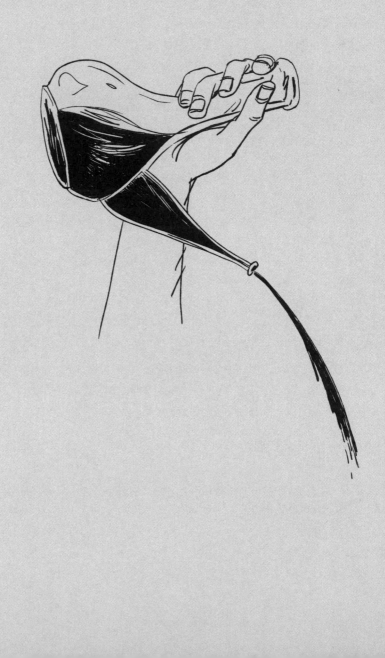

SPAIN

From his first visit to the country in 2002, Tony was riveted by the culinary culture of Spain, where centuries-old tradition bumps up against some of the most modern techniques and ideas in the world, against a backdrop of exquisite natural beauty and several eras' worth of stunning architecture.

BARCELONA

"Outside of Asia, this is it: the best and most exciting place to eat in the world. This is where all the young chefs want to work. This is where all the young apprentices want to do their *stages*. This is where the innovation is, this is where the creativity has been happening. Along the way, they encounter this sort of everyday food of Spain. The simple, good things of Spain that most Spaniards see as a birthright.

"How can ham be this good?! How can something that comes in a can be that terrific? Simple things—an anchovy, an olive, a piece of cheese. Really really simple things, the little things that you see every day here—that's what's cool about Spain."

ARRIVAL AND GETTING AROUND

Barcelona–El Prat Josep Tarradellas Airport (BCN), more commonly known as El Prat, is the country's second-busiest airport after Madrid, and the most common point of entry for travelers to northern Spain.

BCN is located about nine miles from the city center. There are taxi ranks outside each arrival hall; there is a minimum charge of 20 euros/US$22 per trip from the airport, regardless of distance; a typical fare to the city center from El Prat is about 35 euros/US$39. Tips are not expected, but rounding up to the nearest euro, or adding 10 percent for exceptional service, is appreciated.

The number 9 line of Barcelona's metro system, Transports Metropolitans de Barcelona (TMB), stops at both airport terminals. See www.tmb.cat for routes, fares, and schedules. The R2 North train line travels from the airport into the city and to nearby towns. A number of bus lines take passengers into the city, to regional cities, and into parts of southern France, Switzerland, and Andorra.

Barcelona Sants is the main train station for regional and international rail travel; the Renfe train and the city metro both travel between the airport and the train station.

EATING IN AND AROUND BARCELONA

"If I lived across the street from this place, I'd quit my job and just hang out here all day, until all the money was gone. Quimet & Quimet is a four-generations-old tapas bar in the El Poble-Sec neighborhood of Barcelona, which relies heavily on that Catalonian tapas bar staple of canned food." There's an extensive wine selection, along with cocktails and beer, but the real draw are the *montaditos*, or canape-size open-faced sandwiches populated with the likes of *cipriones* (stuffed baby squid), anchovies, mussels, tuna belly, sea urchin, Spanish and French cheeses, pickled vegetables and more, all prepared to order behind the bar—there is no kitchen on site, and it's a tight space, with room for only about twenty guests at a time.

QUIMET & QUIMET: Carrer del Poeta Cabanyes, 25, 08004 Barcelona, Tel +34 93 442 31 42, www.quimetquimet.com (tapas 2–18 euros/US$2.25–$20)

"There is something so liberating, so democratic, so fun about nibbling food this great off a weathered wood bar-top. At its best, it's so many good things at once: a beer or vermouth in hand, lively social setting, a comfortable movable feast where you come and go, eat or don't eat, when you please."

About a half hour's drive outside Barcelona, you'll reach **Taverna Espinaler**. "It looks like a million other old-man bars, a local joint. The uninitiated might be forgiven for being unimpressed. Yet what you're receiving is in fact some of the finest, most delicious, and most expensive seafood in the world. Here, the best stuff comes straight off the boat—and into the can."

About twenty years ago, fourth-generation Espinaler proprietor Miguel Tapias, looking to grow the family business, decided to expand into retail canned seafood, harvested in the cold Atlantic waters of Galicia, so that visitors can now take home razor clams, cockles, mussels, high-quality tuna, and other delicacies available under the family label.

"Rest assured, this stuff bears no relationship to the can of smoked oysters you ate, stoned and desperate, at two in the morning back in college. This is the world's very best seafood, and here's what's so mind-blowing: it only gets better in the can." Seafood this good does not come cheap: a six-ounce can of razor clams can retail for upward of 225 euros/US$250.

TAVERNA ESPINALER: Camí Ral, 1, 08340 Vilassar de Mar, Barcelona, Tel +34 937 591 589, www.espinaler.com (tapas 2–14 euros/US$2.25–$15.50)

SAN SEBASTIÁN

"We could make the argument that there's no better place to eat in Europe than the city of San Sebastián. There are more Michelin-starred restaurants per capita here than anywhere on earth. But even the everyday joints are superb. The love of food, the insistence on the very best ingredients, is fundamental to the culture, and to life here. And it's beautiful, did I say that? It's a beautiful city.

"At the nexus of this culinary capital is the godfather of the new Spanish cuisine, Juan Mari Arzak. He and his daughter, Elena, run the legendary three-star restaurant Arzak. The food is innovative, wildly creative, and forward thinking, but always, always, Basque."

Tony often remarked that, in the course of his television work, he made close friends for a week at a time, but given how often he was on the move, most of those friendships were impossible to maintain. His bond with Juan Mari and Elena was a rare exception.

"My father died very young," Tony said to Elena, while shooting *Parts Unknown*. "But . . . I'd like [Juan Mari] to know that since the first time I came here, I feel like he's looked after me like a father. He's been a loyal and good friend and supporter, and I want him to know I appreciate him."

At the table, any table, with Juan Mari and Elena, Tony reported feeling "a sense of place, a grounding, that feeling of being among friends and, somehow, home. And it's a beautiful thing when the reality lives up to your hopes and expectations; when everything, everything, is as good as anything could be."

On the plate, highlights of an Arzak meal might include lobster with powdered olive oil; an egg poached in chicken stock and seasoned with freeze-dried chicken and its caramelized skin; grilled hake jowls with teff seeds and fresh almonds, served in a bamboo leaf; and white tuna with green melon and jackfruit sauce.

ARZAK: Avenida del Alcalde J. Elosegi Hiribidea, 273, 20015 Donostia, Gipuzkoa, Tel +34 943 27 84 65, www.arzak.es (average meal 242 euros/US$286 per person)

"**Elkano, in the seaside village of Getaria, is a place known and loved by chefs all over the world for what they call their Paleolithic cooking. This is straight-up application of fire and a very few ingredients to make, well, magic of a kind. Rock prawn—the head and body are cooked separately; the body is served nearly raw, what they call semiceviche, while the heads are grilled. Squid, served the paleo way, grilled with an onion–green pepper sauce. And _kokotxas_, about as bone-deep, old-school, fundamentally Basque an ingredient or a passion as there is. The jowls or chins of hake, cooked _pil-pil_ style, in olive oil, and swirled constantly to emulsify the oil with the fish's natural gelatin.**

"**But it's this dish that brings passionate eaters to Elkano from all across the world: the turbot, grilled, and then portioned out methodically by the owner, Aitor Arregi. The idea is to highlight each and every unique bit, and its special characteristics—the light, gelatinous skin, with soft and slightly caramelized flesh; the fat, unctuous** belly; the bones, tiny scraps of the sweetest meats clinging to them. One dish, a mosaic of many distinct flavors and textures, all of them epically delicious."

ELKANO: Herrerieta Kalea, 2, 20808 Getaria, Gipuzkoa, Tel +34 943 140 00 24, www.restauranteelkano.com (average meal 70–100 euros/US$78–$111 per person)

"**Ganbara, my favorite place. I come here every time, like a heat-seeking missile. The house specialty, what they're most famous for, is the be all and end all for me: seared wild mushrooms and foie gras with a raw egg yolk gently draped over the top to sizzle and commingle with the hot fungi.**"

GANBARA: San Jeronimo Galea, 21, 20003, Donostia, Gipuzkoa, Tel +34 943 42 25 75 (tapas portions from 9 to 20 euros/US$10–$22 each)

"**In a perfect world, in another life, I'd live in San Sebastián. All this, all this food, this place, would be a birthright, and somehow Elena Arzak would be my sister, and Juan Mari Arzak would adopt me. I love this man, I adore Elena, and I'm absolutely giddy with excitement that I'm meeting up with them at Bar Haizea, one of their favorite little tapas bars.**" Among the *pintxos* [one- or two-bite snacks] worth sampling are the brick de bacalao (a codfish fritter), stuffed eggs, salmon mousse, and the "**spicy, briny goodness [of] pickled banana peppers and anchovies. Simple, traditional, and unbelievably rewarding.**"

BAR HAIZEA: Aldamar Kalea, 8, 20003, Donostia, Gipuzkoa, Tel +34 943 42 57 10 (*pintxos* 1.50–4 euros/US$1.75–$4.50; *raciones* (plates) 4–14 euros/US$4.50–$15.50; *bocadillos* (sandwiches) 4–5 euros/US$4.50–$5.50)

"It is no exaggeration to say when you're eating at *Etxebarri*, no one else in the world at that precise hour is eating better than you. It is, in every way, extraordinary. And this man is a legend. He is a master of what looks austere and simple, but is, in fact, in almost a Japanese way, fetishistically perfectionist in his treatment of local ingredients."

Victor Arguinzoniz's iconoclastic grill restaurant is located in the Atxondo Valley, about an hour's drive from San Sebastián. In the company of a very small staff of cooks, Victor grills everything over charcoal he has made, from oak wood he has chopped: all kinds of meats, like a Galician beef chop, and chorizo that he's made from Iberian pork loin, as well as prawns, razor clams, local eels in season, and squid served in its own ink, but also tiny new peas in season; Beluga caviar (in a custom-made grill pan, atop seaweed); and even ice cream, whose dairy components are infused with smoke before being turned with sugar and eggs into an ethereal frozen confection.

"Absolutely one of the great meals of my life. I think what you need to understand about Spain is that, in order to understand the new cuisine, the new cooking, you have to understand that all of these guys deeply love this stuff," said Tony, meaning that the new vanguard appreciates the traditional cuisine, adding, "One cannot exist without the other."

ASADOR ETXEBARRI: San Juan Plaza, 1, 48291 Atxondo, Bizkaia, Tel +34 946 58 30 42, www.asadoretxebarri.com (set menu 180 euros/US$200 per person)

SRI LANKA

"Hot. *Relentlessly* hot. Three-showers-a-day hot; three-changes-of-clothes hot. I feel swollen, bloated, queasy, and exhausted, utterly beaten down by the heat. And the madcap daily realities of a South Asian city, the crowded streets, the crush of commerce, the relentless equatorial sun, the humidity and traffic, only add to the sense of unreality." This was Tony's lament, after his first twenty-four hours in Sri Lanka.

The *No Reservations* crew shot an episode in the sweltering, heavily fortified, locked-down capital city of Colombo in 2008, a year before that country's long civil war finally ended. Tony observed: **"There's a quote somewhere, describing the old days of exploration and empire, that 'all Europe has fallen in love with Ceylon.' The Portuguese thought they discovered the Garden of Eden, the crown jewel of the spice trade—cardamom, cinnamon, nutmeg, clove, pepper, mace, ginger—the object of desire of many empires. The Chinese called Ceylon, now Sri Lanka, 'the Land Without Sorrow,' though I doubt anyone would say that today."**

In 2017, Tony returned, this time with *Parts Unknown*, to see what had changed, what had opened up, and what the lasting consequences of twenty-five years of fighting were. He remarked: **"Everywhere you look: construction, expansion, new hotels, foreign money—something that looks a lot like hope. Hundreds of thousands of dead and missing later, the country is at peace, and we can go where we want."**

A LONG CIVIL WAR

"From 1983 until 2009, Sri Lanka's bloody civil war divided the island in two, splitting the country along religious lines: Buddhist Sinhalese majority in the south, versus Hindu Tamil minority in the north. Years of mistreatment and suppression led to the formation of the Liberation Tigers of Tamil Eelam (LTTE), and their campaign to seek an independent state. The conflict ended in 2009, but an enormous number of internally displaced persons remain in refugee camps."

GETTING THERE AND AROUND

Sri Lanka is an island nation just southeast of the Indian subcontinent; glance at a map and it's easy to see where island and continental landmass likely once connected in the Indian Ocean. Colombo is the nation's capital, and **Bandaranaike Airport (CMB)**, some nineteen miles north of the city, is its major international hub. It is served by a few dozen airlines, including Cathay Pacific, Air India, Emirates, KLM, Korean Air, and Etihad Airways. **Mattala Rajapaksa (HRI)**, on the southeast tip of the island, is the secondary international airport, served by SriLankan Airlines, flydubai, and Sriwijaya Air.

While you can rent a car and drive yourself around Sri Lanka, it is a far more relaxing and surprisingly affordable proposition to hire a car and driver. Inquire with your hotel or travel agency. Within cities, taxis and *tuk-tuks* are widely available.

Railroad travel between cities is relatively cheap via the government-run **Sri Lanka Railways**, often quite scenic and a great way to experience Sri Lankan life.

In 2017, Tony and crew traveled by train from Colombo to Jaffna, a ten-hour journey. **"Early morning, Colombo station. The platforms** bustle with a mix of commuters, long-distance travelers, and the occasional tourist. Breaking free from Colombo's gravitational pull, the landscape opens up. Second- and third-class compartments host a mix of people, smells, and slices of life. Commuters get on at one station, off at another. Others like me are in for the long haul. That the *Jaffna Queen* train runs at all is a symbolic move toward reunification. As the fight for an independent Tamil state in Sri Lanka's north intensified, the LTTE destroyed these tracks. For the last two decades of the war, Jaffna was all but cut off from the rest of the world." (See Vidya Balachander's essay on page 296 for more on food in Jaffna and Colombo.)

"Nearing the end of the line, weary passengers awake to find themselves in a different world. Out the window, the air is thick; the smell of salt and sea."

A GOOD OLD COLONIAL HOTEL

"The Indian Ocean crashes against the seawall just outside the windows of the **Galle Face Hotel.** There's a crack of thunder, and lightning lights up the horizon. In the distance, the dark silhouettes of oil tankers from Indonesia and points east scud slowly toward the Persian Gulf and beyond. This is where I wake up every morning; this is where I come home to every night. This hotel is a little creepy, but in a cool, Graham Greene, 'grand colonial hotel in a postcolonial wartime' sort of a way. And yeah, there are sinister-looking guys with guns hanging out at the beach. And yes, there are crows everywhere, hundreds of them. Giant bastards and loud, an army of 'em shrieking and diving right outside your window. And it's up to this guy, apparently, armed with only a slingshot, to keep them away from the guests and their breakfast." Each evening at sunset, a bagpiper plays while the Sri Lankan national flag is ceremonially lowered from its pole between the veranda and the sea; it's a tradition worth witnessing over a gin and tonic from the excellent bar.

GALLE FACE HOTEL: 2 Galle Road, Colombo 3, Tel +94 112 541 010, www.gallefacehotel.com (rooms start at about 23,300 rupees/ US$130 per night)

SRI LANKAN FOOD: PUNCHY FLAVORS AND SHORT EATS

Roasted whole spices tempered in mustard oil; pungent sauces studded with curry leaves and thickened with coconut milk; the springy rice pancakes called hoppers and *idli*; whole fish, river crabs, and hunks of goat or chicken slathered with fiery spice pastes and accompanied by sweet, sour, salty, and spicy condiments, or *sambols*; hot, crunchy, handheld street foods known as "short eats"; rich, sweet custards and shakes flavored with dried fruits and cashews; tea brewed with care in the place where it's grown: Sri Lankan food and drink is, in a word, intense.

If you come to Colombo looking for street food on the street, you'll likely be disappointed: mobile vendors are few and far between, mostly appearing outside known watering holes in the wee hours, clustered on the Galle Road.

But fear not: stretched out between the beach and the street, the **Galle Face Green**, a historic promenade-like park, is home to a long line of mobile food stalls. Offering the likes of fish samosas, *isso wade* (lentil flour cakes with shrimp), grilled seafood, spicy crab, *kottu roti* (griddled roti with vegetables, egg, optional meat and curry sauce), fruits seasoned with salt and chili powder, and packaged snacks, these stalls adhere to halal standards, so no pork and no alcohol (though, if asked, many of the waiters will be willing to subtly procure a beer or two). Look for the stalls with the most robust crowd of locals, and wade in. Most of the action takes place in the evening, as the sun begins to set.

GALLE FACE GREEN NIGHT MARKET, 56 Colombo-Galle Main Road, Colombo (no phone, no website) (costs vary, meal for two with drinks about 3,000 rupees/US$15)

A Bit More about Food in Colombo and Jaffna

BY VIDYA BALACHANDER

Vidya Balachander, a journalist, was a local source of research for the Parts Unknown *episode shot in Sri Lanka in 2017. Born and raised in Mumbai, Balachander spent five years living in Colombo; she now resides in Dubai.*

I write about food. I'm a food journalist. And, specifically, over the last few years, I've tried to specialize in using food as a lens to talk about various other subjects, including, in this country, history and culture.

I used to live in Mumbai. When I moved to Colombo, I wanted to find some sort of anchor there, and food was that anchor for me, because it was familiar. I began my exploration of Sri Lanka using food as my guide. You won't find too much food literature about Sri Lanka at all.

I think the only thing that people knew about Sri Lanka was in the context of war, right? That was all that anybody knew about it. And it was only after 2009, and after the war ended, that the country has sort of come into its own; the people are still discovering things to be proud of, in a sense. And I think you will find that especially in Jaffna, which was so cut off for three decades, that it has almost a sense of confusion about that identity—about what makes Jaffna food special. I tried to find the answer. It was not very easy to find Jaffna food in Jaffna. The war had some bearing on that; it was just never a priority for anyone, eating out. Being in a state of siege, you're always hiding. So the concept of pleasure itself is new.

Things have definitely changed in the last couple of years, albeit slowly. There are more restaurants now that serve "authentic" Jaffna cuisine, and a few places in Colombo even serve northern specialties, such as *odiyal kool*—a fiery seafood stew with crab, prawns, fish, rice, and vegetables such as moringa leaves, thickened with *odiyal maa*, or the dried flour of the palmyrah palm. The north also now has a chain of government-run eateries called Ammachi, which are run by war-affected women and serve South Indian and Sri Lankan snacks at very reasonable prices.

I'm still puzzled by why there isn't a stronger street food culture in Colombo. I mean, there's no reason why there shouldn't be. It's lacking, especially as compared with Mumbai, which has an amazing street food culture. As compared with Bangkok, Singapore, or Hong Kong or Ho Chi Minh City. As opposed to my experiences in all those places, I find that food is quite solitary in Colombo.

But short eats are nice. And the bread vans. My father-in-law lives in Colombo 7 [Cinnamon Gardens], which is the most elite part of town; everybody is kind of hidden behind these walls, and it's only when this bread man comes—and his van plays a familiar tune—that you will find people opening their doors and asking what he has.

Some of the breads are unique to Sri Lanka. There's one that looks like a croissant dusted with sugar on top, but it's much denser, called a *kimbula banis*. *Kimbula* means "crocodile." So, this is one way of creating community. I find that at certain times, this community, on purpose, is so separated. It's only these food interventions that get people out of their homes and to acknowledge one another. I wish there were more of that immediacy of enjoying food. In Colombo, I miss the knowledge that this sandwich guy is really good at this, and everybody will queue up for hours, the way they do in Mumbai.

TAIWAN

Having long heard tell of its excellent street food and extensive night markets, Tony made Taiwan a must-stop for the second season of *The Layover.*

"Taiwan is an alternate-reality version of China—the China that might have been, that never turned its back on traditions: sybaritic, commerce driven, foodie. The area was colonized by the Spanish, then the Dutch. During the Qing dynasty, Taipei became the regional capital of the island. The Japanese dominated for nearly fifty years, starting in 1895, and stayed until 1945, bringing with them a lot of ugly-ass buildings, and some very bad history.

"But Japan left behind a Japantown in Taipei, and an enduring overlay of influence, and an affection for sushi and *izakayas*, and a lot of bars. In 1949, Chiang Kai-shek and his Chinese nationalists (I think you could charitably call them anti-Communists) retreated to Taiwan from the mainland, ceding their country to Mao Zedong. Two million of them flooded Taiwan, many from military or administrative backgrounds. The Chiang Kai-shek memorial in Zhongzheng honors this mercurial general, inarguably the most important figure in Taiwanese history."

ARRIVAL AND GETTING AROUND

Visitors will most likely arrive at **Taiwan Taoyuan International Airport** (**TPE**), an hour and a half west of Taipei, one of the largest and busiest airports in Asia, served by dozens of international, national, and regional carriers. There are two multistory terminals, with a third under construction, scheduled to be completed in 2023. Express and commuter trains, part of the Taoyuan Mass Rapid Transit (MRT) system, run between both terminals and downtown Taipei, with intermittent stops. See www.tymetro.com.tw for routes, schedules, and fares.

Each airport terminal contains a bus terminal with connections to Taipei and other cities on the island, and there are metered taxis queued outside each arrival hall. The city of Taipei is just under an hour's drive, in traffic, from the airport, and will cost 1,200–1,400 new Taiwan dollars/US$40–$45. Tipping taxi drivers is not expected.

The other arrival option is **Taipei Songshan Airport**, officially **Taipei International Airport** (**TSA**), located within the city limits of Taipei; the airport handles flights within Taiwan and a handful of flights to cities in mainland China, Seoul, and Tokyo. Visitors can get to downtown Taipei via the MRT train, city buses, and taxis, which take about twenty minutes and cost about TW$600/US$20.

Once in the city, taxicabs are a relatively cheap way to get around Taipei, and the MRT and bus lines are even cheaper, and easy to navigate.

EATING IN TAIWAN

"Taiwan has some of the most exciting food, particularly when it comes to street food, in Asia. There are a lot of night markets in Taipei—they're famous for them—but this is the one I've been yearn-ing for. Half an hour out of town via commuter train toward the Pacific coast is Keelung, the seaport home to its best night market."

Arrive hungry to **Keelung** (pronounced *Jeelung* by Mandarin speakers) **Maiokou Night Market**, a short walk from the train station and next to the city harbor. Here, you can sample rice pot sticker soup—basically, liquefied rice that is steamed with mushrooms, bamboo shoots, dried tiger lilies, dried shrimp and oysters, and shredded pork; *gua bao*, **"a steamed bun filled with melt-in-your mouth pork belly braised in soy sauce, wine, shallots, and five-spice powder, served with pickled mustard greens, cilantro, and crushed peanuts"**; a rich and custardy variety of the seafood delicacy *uni*, served in its shell; spiced mini hard shell crabs, meant to be eaten whole; king crab steamed and sautéed with shallots and garlic; and *ba-wan*, or Taiwanese meatball, wrapped in a steamed rice skin, along with bamboo, pork, and mushrooms, and seasoned with garlic and soy.

"I'll tell you, I've been to a lot of street markets. This is truly a wonderland. It's the variety here that's really amazing. It's maddening. Really, as far as I'm concerned, we can just check into a hotel next door and spend the rest of the entire show eating my way through here."

KEELUNG MIAOKOU NIGHT MARKET: No. 20 Aisi Road, Ren'ai District, Keelung City, Taiwan 200 (no phone), www.taiwan.net.tw (prices vary)

The other can't-miss market in Taipei is **Raohe Night Market**. "You can shop: the usual T-shirts, cheap dresses, shoes, and plenty of cell phone cases, should you need. You could buy a pet. If you're not a fan of stinky tofu, which is everywhere here, there's delicious steamed blood cake with sweet-and-sour sauce. I'm looking for this *hu jiao bing*, a wheat flour dough stuffed with peppery pork and spring onion, baked in a cylindrical clay oven closely resembling an Indian tandoor." You can find the dish at the Fuzhou Black Pepper Bun stall. Other standouts include oyster omelets, mochi, and pork ribs cooked with medicinal herbs.

RAOHE NIGHT MARKET: Raohe Street, across from Songshan Station, Songshan District, Taipei, Tel +886 2 2763 5733, www.travel.taipei/zh-tw/attraction/details/1538 (prices vary)

"**Din Tai Fung** are masters, and I mean *masters*, of the soup dumpling. It's a chain. By now there's lots of them. Theoretically that should make it not good, right? In fact, when you're talking about a single object of food, there may be things as good in this world, but you can certainly make a very good and very reasonable argument that there is no single better thing in the world than what you are about to see.

"We're talking an object of incredible craftsmanship, and yet something that is reproduced thousands of times constantly, fresh, right beneath our feet, and also in many other outlets. They're all over the place. As far as I know, they're all good, but this—this is the mother ship. This is a great state-of-the-art dumpling. Head-flooding pleasure, unimaginable until you try one. I had my first soup dumpling here years ago, and it was a deeply religious experience. Eat these all goddamned day. This is a must-stop if you come to Taipei, and they know it, and they're prepared."

DIN TAI FUNG, No 194, Section 2, Xinyi Road, Da'an District, Taipei, Tel +886 2 2321 8928, www.dintaifung.com.tw (Ten dumplings for TW$210/about US$7)

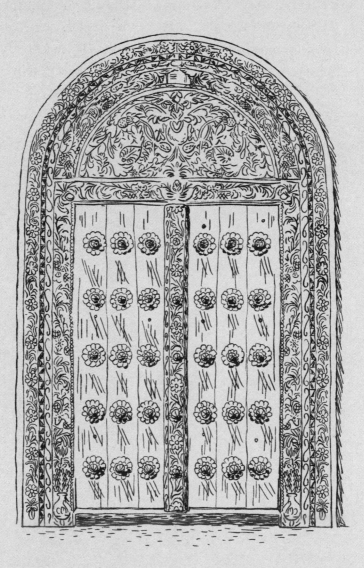

TANZANIA

Intrigued by the Maasai, the wildlife, and the promise of luxury safari lodgings, Tony and the *Parts Unknown* crew visited the East African nation of Tanzania in 2014. There he was confronted with questions about the Western fantasy of Africa: Does it exist, and if so, who may access it, and why?

"It's nuts driving into the Serengeti. After a short while, you actually get used to the *Jungle Book* scene playing out in front of your car. Giraffe and wildebeest, zebra—they all seem to hang out with each other. No conflict at all. Thousands and thousands of wildebeests on their annual migration are everywhere. A big circle, stretched out across Tanzania and into Kenya, in search of prime grazing. It's all about water and grass and a good place to make babies.

"Over the years, my crew and I have shot in Liberia, Ghana, Namibia, South Africa, Mozambique, the Congo, and much of North Africa. But what we've never done was step back to our first impressions, to the Africa of Hollywood films and nature documentaries that many of us grew up with: vast herds of wild animals charging across the Serengeti, lions and giraffes and zebras and hippos, safari gear, Land Rovers, and the equally magnificent 'natives' in their brightly colored robes. Does this Africa even exist? And if so, how? And for whom?

"That Africa, the CinemaScope Africa, *does* exist. You can find it in and around the unspeakably beautiful Ngorongoro Crater, where lions and their traditional adversaries, Maasai warriors, still live much as they did a hundred years ago.

"The lions survive because they are protected. Visiting Tanzania to gaze at and photograph these beautiful but deadly creatures (and other animals) is a major industry, bringing many millions to the country each year. It makes financial sense to protect both animals and the environment they live in.

"The Maasai are herders—and warriors. Their status within their tribe, their image of themselves, is based largely on their traditional roles as defenders of their herds—as warriors, lion killers. Lions eat cattle and goats when they can get them. The Maasai protect and rely on cattle and goats to live. Lions roam over large areas of terrain, competing for food with any number of other predators. Maasai herd their cattle over large areas of terrain. Thus it has been for centuries.

"They are among the last great warrior tribes on earth. Semi-nomadic, they believe that all the world's cattle are a gift of the gods to them. They move with their animals across the Tanzanian plains, setting up homes where they find the best grazing. Their cattle are everything, the wealth of the family, units of currency, givers of milk to live, and, on special occasions, of meat and blood.

"Lions are beautiful living creatures worth many millions of dollars from the thousands and thousands of people from all over the world who want to come to Tanzania and gape at them.

"The Maasai are beautiful living people whom somewhat fewer people from all over the world want to come and gape at.

"You see the problem.

"Many hardworking, well-intentioned people are trying to help resolve this conflict of interest. But it raises, once again, the question we run into frequently in our travels: Whom does the natural world exist for? For the people who live there—have always lived there? Even when they become . . . inconvenient? Or the animals who also have always lived there—but like their adversaries, are under threat, can no longer survive without the intervention of (usually) pale-skinned experts in comfortable shoes?

"It's an uncomfortable question. One would have to be truly monstrous to suggest that one be sacrificed for the other. But the slow grind of history is already making that decision for us—and the outcome is often not pretty."

ARRIVAL AND GETTING AROUND

You'll land at **Kilimanjaro International Airport (JRO)**, which services flights to and from other parts of Tanzania and East Africa, as well as Doha, Frankfurt, and Amsterdam. It's highly advised to arrange your ground transportation in advance with your hotel or safari company; one-way transfers will cost about 690,000 Tanzanian shillings/US$300.

LUXURY AT THE CRATER'S EDGE

While exploring the Serengeti, Tony made his home at **&Beyond Ngorongoro Crater Lodge**, an absolute throwback to colonial days:

"**It's nice, very, very nice, if you find yourself here. A hot bubble bath awaits after a long day in the bush. Perhaps a dry sherry from a cut-glass decanter. The next morning, one rises to breakfast in one's chambers, on the balcony perhaps. Silver service, hot coffee, freshly baked croissant.**" The lodge is composed of eighteen luxury suites, with fireplaces, bathtubs, and Wi-Fi. The rates, which it should be noted are quite steep, include meals, daily wildlife expeditions, laundry, evacuation insurance, and all but the top-shelf booze.

"**The Ngorongoro Crater was once a massive volcano that, somewhere around 2.5 million years ago, collapsed in on itself, creating a caldera, a true lost world. Inside the crater, an entire ecosystem within an ecosystem.**" The crater is twelve miles across at its widest point, surrounded by a forested rim and with an open grassland floor that's an excellent habitat for the aforementioned lions, hippos, and elephants, along with rhinos, leopards, warthogs, gazelles, and buffalo. The shallow Lake Magadi makes an inviting habitat for pink flamingoes.

"**Wildlife pretty much stay put, coming to drink, well, right below my place. Even the toilet has a nice view. Idyllic natural setting and good plumbing? It's pretty much paradise.**" Just be sure to follow the house rules, and don't go wandering around alone, especially at night.

"You don't wanna get lost here. You definitely don't want to be on foot, outside your car, or injured, for instance. Nature, as they say, is a cruel mistress. It takes care of its own, without mercy. The evidence"—meaning carcasses—"of this cruel math called 'survival' is everywhere."

&BEYOND NGORONGORO CRATER LODGE: Ngorongoro Conservation Area, Tel +27 11 809 4300, www.andbeyond.com/our -lodges/africa/tanzania/ngorongoro-crater/andbeyond-ngorongoro -crater-lodge/ (rates start at about 2,500,000 shillings/US$1,100 per person, per night)

TRINIDAD AND TOBAGO

Tony's visit to Trinidad and Tobago, for *Parts Unknown,* was timed to provide a respite from the New York City winter, but still several weeks in advance of the country's legendary Carnival, as he had a well-known aversion to the chaotic tumble of such affairs.

"Trinidad and Tobago: one country, two very different islands, two very different places. One island is what you expected when you arrived wearing flip-flops and a Hawaiian shirt, or greased up in cocoa butter." This would be Tobago. It's the smaller, less-developed, more laid-back, beachier, and more service-oriented of the two islands, distinctly African in its culture. **"Tobago is what you hope for when you waddle away from the buffet on the SS *Norway* cruise ship. Lazy beach days, boat drinks, villas, all set to a calypso beat.**

"The other"—Trinidad, thirty miles to the southwest—**"ain't about that at all.**

"The faces you see in the street are African, Indian, Chinese, and Middle Eastern in features. And every shade of mix in between. This patchwork of ethnic identities and colors is a direct legacy of Trinidad's colonial past." Trinidad is industrialized, busier; it's far more culturally and religiously diverse than Tobago, though there are elements of language, history, and economy common to both islands.

"Located at the southern end of the Caribbean Sea, and seven miles offshore from Venezuela, Trinidad and Tobago have long been important ports of call. Like a lot of islands in the area, everybody's been through there at one point or another—the usual European hunters of fortune. The Spanish came looking for gold. Then the Dutch, French, and British took their turns at the real money of the time: sugar—an economy built on plantation labor and slavery. Finally, the island hit the big money: oil." Trinidad and Tobago remains the Caribbean's largest producer of oil and natural gas.

"No island in the sun is paradise on earth, however it might look from the concrete box, glass cubicles, or wood boxes we may live in. And all the dancing and music and great food in the world could never hold together by itself what would keep us apart. What might look like a utopian stew of ethnicities and cultures living together

under gently swaying palms is, of course, a far more complicated matter. But Trinidad and Tobago has done better than most, and in proud and unique style."

ARRIVAL AND GETTING AROUND

Port of Spain Piarco International Airport (POS) is almost inevitably where you'll arrive by air, though Tobago also has a small international airport, **Arthur Napoleon Raymond Robinson International (TAB)**, known until 2011 at Crown Point International. Piarco is the primary hub for Caribbean Airlines, and both airports serve flights from other Caribbean locales, North America, and a few European cities.

From POS, you can take a taxi to Port of Spain, which is about seventeen miles away. Expect to pay about TT$240/US$35 for a thirty-minute ride, and be sure to look for official licensed drivers, who will be in a uniform of white shirts and dark pants, and who will have official ID badges. It is customary to tip drivers 10 to 15 percent of the total fare.

There is also a bus, operated by the Public Transport Service Corporation (PTSC) of Trinidad and Tobago, that runs hourly from Piarco to City Gate, the main bus terminal, located on the historic South Quay, in what was once the terminal of the now-defunct Trinidad Government Railway system. Purchase TT$27/US$4 one-way bus tickets in the airport terminal's video arcade or newspaper stand, or, for a return journey, at the bus terminal.

From Tobago's airport, official taxis (those whose license plates begin with an *H*) can take you to your hotel or other destination, for anywhere from TT$34 to $475/US$5–$70, plus a 10 to 15 percent tip, depending on your destination.

EATING IN TRINIDAD: THE DOUBLES

"A half century after Trinidad became independent of the British Empire, there are surprisingly few architectural remnants. But the face of the country—and its population—were forever changed when slavery ended in 1834, and Great Britain found itself in need of cheap—if not free—labor to work the plantations. They found it in East India. Between the end of outright slavery and the beginning of World War I, 150,000 indentured servants were brought here from India. Indentured servitude is slavery by another name. The people brought here from India were bought, sold, and treated like property, but were told if they completed five years of often backbreaking labor, they would be set free."

"Among the enduring legacies of this arrangement is the indelible imprint of Indian cuisine on Trinidad; among the most iconic is the fast, hot breakfast sandwich (of sorts) known as doubles.

"People keep coming up to me in the street. First thing they say is, 'Have you had doubles yet?' So I'm eating fucking doubles, all right?

"Doubles are a Caribbean take on the Indian *channa bhatura*: two floppy, tender pieces of soft Indian-style bread, loaded with a wet heap of curried chickpeas, pepper sauce, and mango."

The bread, called *bara*, is deep-fried, the dough sometimes spiked with turmeric, and the chickpea curry, seasoned with cumin, onion, garlic, and curry powder, is called *channa*. Various chutneys of tamarind, cucumber, or coconut may also apply; essential to the doubles experience is hot pepper sauce, ordered in one of three intensities: slight, medium, and hot.

Caveat emptor: the Trinidadian writer and poet Anu Lakhan, who shared her doubles recipe for *Parts Unknown*, warned, "In Trinidad and Tobago, one person's slight is another's trip to the ER."

The whole thing is wrapped in wax paper to keep it all together; extra napkins are highly advised.

As he ate his doubles on a chair outside **U-Wee**, juggling bits to avoid messy spillover, Tony said, **"Structurally, I have questions. I don't want seepage. Seepage is never good,"** conceding as he finished, **"I don't think there's meat in here, and I still like it. I mean, it's really, really good."**

U-WEE DOUBLES & ROTI SHOP: Augustine Street, M9V St. Augustine, Trinidad (no phone, no website) (one doubles TT$5–$8/ US$0.75–$1.25)

UNITED KINGDOM

LONDON, ENGLAND

Tony made London a regular stop for each of his TV series, and he found it a reliable city in which to promote and sell his books. He spent a month living there while shooting the UK version of the cooking competition series *The Taste*, with his colleagues and friends Nigella Lawson and Ludo Lefebvre. His final televised visit, in 2016, just happened to coincide with the Brexit referendum vote, which left Londoners stunned, anxious, and ready to drown their fears and sorrows in the city's legendary pubs and restaurants.

"London, England, the capital city that draws more international visitors than any other city in the world. Bastion of good manners? Not really, nah, not the London I know. In fact, how English is London, anyway? The national dish, more popular than fish and chips by far, is chicken tikka masala, and any notion you might have that English food is bad, that's hopelessly outdated thinking. In fact, London has long been a food capital. Pubs, you know about, and they are truly as fine and wonderful as they are said to be. People here like to drink, often too much, and sometimes admittedly not well.

"You could understand then, perhaps, why London is one of my favorite cities, often a home away from home. A layover here is a chance to see old friends, chefs whom I admire, and, of course, eat the kind of unique and lost food that's hard to find in New York—the very best ingredients, the best possible execution to honor these ingredients, and a love for what it means, has meant, and should mean, to cook and dine as an Englishman."

ARRIVAL AND GETTING AROUND

London has two major airports: **Heathrow (LHR)**, a massive, hugely busy international hub with five terminals, and **Gatwick (LGW)**, also a major international airport, though slightly smaller and less crowded than Heathrow. Both airports have rail links that can bring passengers to and from the center of London for far less money and at a faster rate than a cab, which will cost 45–70 pounds/US$55–$90, plus a customary 10–15 percent of the fare.

The city has a number of major railway stations that serve rail lines stretching into the suburbs and beyond into the rest of Britain, including Waterloo, Paddington, King's Cross, and Saint Pancras, which is the station you'll enter and depart if taking the Eurostar train between London and Paris or Brussels.

To get around London, turn to London's subway system, known as the Underground or the Tube. **"A one-day travel card lasts twenty-four hours, and you can go anywhere, but please move quickly. Do not bring a backpack on a rush-hour train. Always stand up for pregnant ladies, whether it was you that put the bun in the oven or not. Then, the Tube might, just might, be your friend."**

But, if a taxi is more your speed: **"Something you should know—never take a minicab, only black cabs. Black cabs have a meter. You know how much you're paying. Plus, not only do they know where they're going, but they know alternate ways to get there. Minicabs, they pretty much charge whatever the hell they like, and the likelihood that they know where they're going is remote in the extreme."** Black cabs can be hailed on the street, or from ranks outside hotels and major attractions.

HAZLITT'S, "A LISTING SHIP"

"There are certain cities where I have a home base; London is one of those cities. And in the heart of the Soho theater district, in three Georgian buildings that date back to 1718, is a personal oasis of mine called **Hazlitt's**, a boutique hotel that caters to a lot of writers.

"One of the things you need to know about this hotel is everything's kind of on the slant. I always feel like I'm on a listing ship. The doors don't actually meet the floor, and the furniture tilts. That's one of the things I really like about this hotel."

Hazlitt's, which has twenty-three rooms and suites full of antique furniture and art, is also known for its library, with visiting authors, including Tony, often leaving copies of their published works on its shelves. There is no on-site restaurant, but twenty-four-hour room service and an honesty bar (unattended, but outfitted with a pay box and a price list) keep guests well fed and properly hydrated.

HAZLITT'S: 6 Frith Street, W1D 3JA London, Tel +44 20 7434 1771, www.hazlittshotel.com (rooms start at about 320 pounds/US$400 per night)

CUSTOM SHOES

"I've been kind of fascinated with the relationship between English bespoke shoemakers and their clients since seeing Alan Bennett's play *An Englishman Abroad*, a true account of the life of the British spy and trader Guy Burgess in Moscow postdefection. He may have defected to Russia, but he continued to get his shoes made by the same man in London. I found that detail intriguing. What could be so special about them?"

To find out, Tony made his way to the atelier of shoemaker **George Cleverley.**

"**Handmade shoes: it's a huge luxury, but you know, how much is a decent shoe these days? They're ridiculously, stupid expensive. Your shoes'll last forever.**" The shoemakers make an impression of the foot, take meticulous measurements before and during the shoe-making process, and generally take their time to create and deliver a perfectly custom-fitted, classic gentleman's shoe. Mr. Cleverley himself died in 1991, and the business is now run by George Glasgow Sr., who spent twenty years working with Cleverley, along with his son, George Glasgow Jr., and a small team of highly trained craftsmen.

GEORGE CLEVERLEY & CO: LTD. 13 The Royal Arcade, 28 Old Bond Street, London W1S 4SL, Tel +44 20 7493 0443, www.georgecleverley.com (prices vary)

EATING LIKE AN ENGLISHMAN

"**At Sweetings, you're made to feel, I'm told, like you're back at boarding school, minus the caning and the sodomy. Your waiter is your waiter for life. You wait until he and only he has a table. It's a relationship that outlasts some marriages.**"

Enjoy a lunch of mushy peas, scampi, chips, and smoked haddock with poached eggs at **Sweetings**, a seafood institution that's served predictably comfortable English fare (Welsh rarebit, shrimp cocktail, fish pie, cod roe on toast) to the business set since 1889. Sweetings was for many years a lunch-only affair, though the best lunches often extended boozily into the dinner hour; in late 2018, the century-old seafood restaurant in London's financial district finally began experimenting with occasional dinner hours.

SWEETINGS: 39 Queen Victoria Street, London EC 4N 4SF, Tel +44 020 7248 3062, www.sweetingsrestaurant.co.uk/menu (average meal 50–75 pounds/US$65–$95 per person)

"It's a remarkable, if painful, irony that while demand for offal among the working classes has plummeted, on the other end of the dining spectrum, foodies and fine-dining types are shelling out big bucks for ingredients the poor once had to eat. No one has been a bigger influence on this change than the walking buddha himself, the spiritual leader of all nose-to-tail pork-centric aficionados, Fergus Henderson.

"When Fergus Henderson opened **St. John** restaurant, and soon after published his nose-to-tail cookbook, he gave all of us who cook anywhere in the Western world permission to rediscover the truly tasty mysteries of other parts. He refocused attention on a much-maligned, and grossly underappreciated, culinary tradition."

Tony returned to St. John again and again, finding much to evangelize about. "Toasted bone marrow with toasted bread, parsley caper salad, and a little sea salt—my single favorite dish in the world. Or so I thought. This next dish takes things to a whole new level entirely: the English blood cake, treated, finally, with the respect and French technique it has always deserved. Oh, blood cake. Oh, now that is a thing of beauty. This is what black pudding should be: rich, moist, deep, dark blood cake, with two lightly fried eggs, please. Perfect."

St. John, in a rather plain but elegant dining room in the Clerkenwell neighborhood, also excels at steak-and-kidney pie, large enough for at least two hungry guests; unfussy seasonal salads; and simple, excellent desserts like warm rice pudding with stewed fruit, or ginger loaf with butterscotch sauce.

ST. JOHN: 26 St. John Street, Clerkenwell, London EC1M 4AY, Tel +44 020 7251 0848, www.stjohnrestaurant.com (50–75 pounds/ US$65–$95 per person)

. . . AND DRINKING LIKE ONE, TOO

Wherever in the world he went, Tony sought out the somewhat seedier side of a city, as expressed through its dive bars. In London's Soho neighborhood, it was a place **"variously known as Trisha's, also as the Hideout, or the New Evaristo Club. These names lead you through an unmarked, innocuous-seeming door to one of the true glories of London."**

It's a private club of sorts, but access can be had by nearly any comer upon entry, for a few pounds and a signature in a book. Originally an Italian drinking and gambling den, the space, in operation as a club for over seventy-five years, has been largely untouched by time, with new photos of valued regulars and beloved celebrities, living and dead, added to the aging wall display. The drinks are undistinguished, the closing hour (1:00 a.m.) is later than at most English bars, and the crowd represents a healthy mixture of regulars, journalists, actors, tourists, and unclassifiable weirdos. In insisting that we include it in this guide, Tony described it simply as **"fucking awesome."**

TRISHA'S/NEW EVARISTO CLUB/THE HIDEOUT: 57 Greek Street, London W1D 3DX, Tel +44 020 7437 9536 (no website) (cocktails about 6 pounds/$7.50 USD)

EDINBURGH, SCOTLAND
(PRONOUNCED "EDINBURRAH," PLEASE)

In keeping with their knack for being in the right place at an important time, Tony and the *Parts Unknown* crew happened to be in Scotland just after the 2014 referendum, in which the Scottish people decided whether or not to split from the United Kingdom.

"Edinburgh is a place I feel at home. It's a place with a criminal past, at least as far as some of its food is concerned. But a place

where things are getting better and better. It's easily one of the most beautiful cities on earth, proud of its history, its separate national identity."

ARRIVAL AND GETTING AROUND

Edinburgh Airport (EDI) is Scotland's busiest, handling flights to and from most major European cities, and a handful of North American, Middle Eastern, and Asian destinations. Visitors can reach the city center via bus, train, tram, or taxi. It's about an eight-mile drive from airport to city center, with a taxi taking about twenty minutes and costing about 20 pounds/about US$25. Tipping isn't expected, but it's good manners to round up to the nearest pound, and to give a small tip if the driver handles your luggage. In town, there are city bus lines and taxis.

Tony was fascinated by the importance of the written word in the United Kingdom, and he tended to seek out fellow writers for all his visits to the British Isles. In Edinburgh, he accompanied the crime novelist Ian Rankin to the writer's favorite pub, **the Oxford Bar**, which Rankin has used as a setting for his recurring protagonist, Inspector Rebus. Plain, brightly lit, with no pulsing music, no food on offer, just a place for people to gather, drink, and talk, the Oxford Bar was also Tony's favorite Scottish watering hole.

"I thought it was the kind of bar my guy [Rebus] would drink in," said Rankin. "Very unaffected, very unpretentious, basic, stripped back. Almost like a private club. Everybody knows everybody else. . . . The kind of Edinburgh I was writing about was this secret Edinburgh that tourists never saw, the stuff that was happening just below the surface, and I thought [Oxford Bar] a nice representation of that." In late 2018, a longtime Oxford barman, Harry Cullen, turned the place over to a relative, Kirsty Grant, who vowed, in the *Scotsman* newspaper, to make no changes to the Edinburgh institution, saying that she wished for it to remain "a proper boozer."

THE OXFORD BAR: 8 Young St, Edinburgh EH2 4JB, Tel +44 131 539 7119 (average drink about 4 pounds/US$4.50)

GLASGOW, SCOTLAND

"One of my favorite cities on earth. I was going to say one of my favorite cities in Europe, but is Glasgow Europe? I don't think so. It feels somehow older than that. To many outsiders, Glasgow is seen as a hardscrabble, even fearsome, place. A place that history has moved on from.

"In the end, 55 percent of Scots voted to stay in the union. That left almost half the population still hungry for independence. And with 73.5 percent of teenagers voting yes, England had its undies very much in a bunch over the possibility of an unraveling of the union with Scotland. It's an idea that is overwhelmingly popular in this city, above all others. Glasgow has long endured, among other things, a reputation for being the most violent area in the United Kingdom. It's a familiar cycle: Hard times, disappearing manufacturing base, unemployment, a general sense of apathy, that the government can't or won't fix what's broken. That in the corridors of power in London and Edinburgh, they just don't give a shit about Glasgow."

ARRIVAL AND GETTING AROUND

Glasgow International Airport (GLA) serves flights to and from continental Europe, North America, and the Middle East. Use an airport express bus or local bus city lines to get into Glasgow from the airport, or make use of queued taxis, which can be prearranged. It's about a ten-mile drive from the airport to city center, and a taxi will cost about 17 pounds/US$22. Glasgow has a fifteen-station subway system, running in a loop that centers on the River Clyde, that serves the west and central areas of the city.

DEEP-FRIED LATE NIGHTS

"We all have national idiosyncrasies. Scotland's is 'deep-fried just about everything.' I want to go no deeper than the bottom of a bubbling cauldron of hot grease. It's calling to me: A happy place from my past, where once I frolicked, young and carefree in the field of fry-o-lated arts."

That happy place is the **University Café**, a century-old chip shop known for its fried foods.

"Yes, they do a deep-fried Mars Bar here. And deep-fried pizza. Been there, done that. But Carlo here, and his twin brother, have been keeping the Verrecchia family tradition alive since 1918, and it ain't about no Mars Bar. I order the fish and chips, and some haggis.

"Haddock, battered and floating adrift in a sea of mysterious, life-giving oil, the accumulated flavors of many magical things as it bobs like Noah's ark, bringing life in all its infinite variety.

"Deep-fried haggis, my personal favorite: sinister sheep parts, in tube form in this case, and if you don't like chopped-up liver and lungs and all that good stuff, believe me, the curry sauce sets you right.... There is no more unfairly reviled food on earth than haggis. Its ingredients are, in fact, no more unusual, or bizarre, or unappetizing, than any hot dog you ever ate. How many anal glands are in a chicken nugget? I don't know, and I'm not suggesting that there are anal glands in a chicken nugget, but would you be surprised if there were?"

THE UNIVERSITY CAFÉ: 87 Byres Rd, Glasgow G11 5HN, Tel +44 141 339 5217 (no website) (various items from 2 to 7 pounds/ US$2.25–$7.75)

UNITED STATES OF AMERICA

LOS ANGELES, CALIFORNIA

Once hooked after an initial *No Reservations* shoot, Tony returned to LA again and again—for *The Layover*, two episodes of *Parts Unknown*, and a few seasons of the cooking competition show *The Taste*, as well as a good long run as an Emmy nominee and sometimes winner, stops on book tours, and assorted other business.

"I am a liar. I am scum. I used to talk shit about LA, 'cause that's kinda what you're expected to do as a New Yorker. I go out with a usual New York attitude, thinking, 'Ah, it sucks out here. They don't know anything. It's the end of the world. It's corrupting. It's la-la land, lotus land.'

"But I long ago agreed to suck the scabby dick of the great television saint. So, really, I ain't hardly no virgin when it comes to LA or Hollywood, or just being a big, nasty, media whore. Talk to me one day later, after driving around in a nice car with the top down. I'm thinking, 'I could live out here. Oh yeah.'

"So, I can admit it now: I love it out here. I love the palm trees, the strip malls, the Pacific Ocean, the whole quirky, straight-out-of-a-million-movies thing."

ARRIVAL AND GETTING AROUND

Los Angeles International (LAX) is the city's iconic, massive airport, with nine terminals and flights to and from all over the United States, Canada, and Mexico, and major cities in Asia, Australia, Europe, South America, and the Middle East. LAX, a hub for Alaska, American, Delta, and United Airlines, is one of the world's busiest airports, always somewhere in the top five, along with Atlanta, Beijing, Dubai, and Tokyo Haneda. It's eighteen miles southwest of downtown LA. There are a few public bus options between LAX and the city (see flylax.com for details). For those feeling more flush, take one of the many free Lax-it buses circling outside the terminals, to the enormous lot where taxis and app-hailed car sevices queue for passengers. This arrangement was devised to reduce the monstrous car traffic outside LAX terminals, and as of this writing, will be in place until 2023, when extensive LAX construction is completed. (See www.flylax.com/lax-it for more details.) Via taxi, a typical fare between LAX and, say, West Hollywood will be about $60, which includes a standard 15 percent tip.

"I like LAX because I prefer direct flights, like most sane people, but the legendary LA traffic means where you stay has a big effect on which airport you use. Los Angeles International's on the west side, **Long Beach (LGB)** is down south, and **Bob Hope Airport (BUR)** is up in Burbank."

Those with time on their hands may wish to arrive via Amtrak train into **Union Station**, built in 1939 in the architectural style known as Mission Moderne, an amalgam of Spanish colonial, mission revival, and art deco. Amtrak runs a number of routes that start and end at Union Station, which also serves local and regional train lines and is a bus depot. There are regular art installations, film screenings, and other cultural events staged at Union Station, along with a more-than-decent array of dining and drinking options, making it a place you may want to visit whether or not you'll ever board a train.

UNION STATION: 800 North Alameda Street, Los Angeles, CA 90012, www.unionstationla.com

LA is, of course, a legendary car town. **"While there are several options for public transportation, they all pretty much suck. Nobody walks in LA. Everybody drives. That's just the way it is."** This is not entirely true anymore, but Tony was fond of renting a Dodge Charger for getting around town, when not relying on drivers hired by various studios and networks.

That being said, **Metro**, the umbrella agency that handles all of Los Angeles's transportation, reports that it serves over a million riders per day on its buses and subways, so not *everyone* is driving; check schedules, routes, and fares at metro.net if you're inclined to go against the cars-only tide while in LA.

"I LOVE NO HOTEL MORE"

"I am seriously loyal to, and enthusiastic about, the few hotels in the world that I genuinely love, and I love no hotel more than Chateau Marmont. It's classic; has been since 1929, survived five major earthquakes, as well as guests like Jim Morrison, John Belushi, Hunter S. Thompson. Checking in, some checking out.

"The main hotel is like, legendary, dark, comfortable. It's informal. You feel like you're staying at a kooky uncle's place. Generally, anybody can get in here, as long as you behave according to certain undefined rules: You don't geek out on who you may or may not see here. You definitely don't take pictures, and you just don't behave like an asshole. You will be treated the same as the famous guy at the next table. Welcome to my happy place."

Even the most modest of rooms in the main hotel is generously proportioned, with substantial furnishings, closets, draperies, and old-school tile bathrooms. And then there are the bungalows, across the pool area, more discreet, great for starting or ending a torrid love affair, a novel, or a stylish vial of now-legal recreational marijuana, then raiding the well-curated minibar.

"When I first came here, I really didn't like LA that much. I didn't want to mingle. I didn't want to be out there. So, if like me, you're uncomfortable with even being here in the first place, this is the perfect hotel. You can hide here. You don't even know you're in LA. You can't see anything, 360 degrees. You've got your own little yard. And they can't see you, and that's true anywhere in the hotel. This is campus, and you could be totally forgiven for never wanting to leave campus. Just watch the drinks. They're expensive."

CHATEAU MARMONT: 8221 Sunset Boulevard, Hollywood, CA 90046, Tel 323 656 1010, www.chateaumarmont.com (rooms start at about $450 per night)

IN-N-OUT ON THE WAY IN AND OUT

"It's a ritual on the way from the airport, on the way to the airport: In-N-Out Burger. Oh, it's so good." In-N-Out, a well-loved fast food burger chain, was established in 1948 by Harry and Esther Snyder, who started with a single store in the city of Baldwin Park, California, and slowly expanded beyond greater Los Angeles and into the rest of the state; there are now over three hundred stores, including outposts in Nevada, Arizona, Utah, Texas, and Oregon.

Order a double-double animal-style burger, "cooked with mustard and grilled onions, pickles, lettuce, tomato, and extra spread, whatever that is. It is, indeed, fast food. It is, indeed, a chain. They also manage to cook every damn burger fresh to order, and they'll cook it whatever temperature you want it. The only American chain worth a damn. These things are even good cold and congealed. Take it from me. They also treat their employees like human beings, and make very good french fries and shakes. Take that, evil clown."

IN-N-OUT BURGER: locations throughout Southern California and beyond; www.in-n-out.com (burgers $2.50–$4)

LA IS A TACO TOWN

Though New York's Mexican food scene has improved and diversified in the last decade, it has yet to hold a candle to that which can be found in Los Angeles.

"Over in Atwater Village, home to generations of Mexicans and Filipinos, there's this place, **Tacos Villa Corona**. It's only a couple of miles from downtown LA, but the distance keeps most travelers away. Family-run, hole in the wall: all the marks of quality. Maria and Felicia Florez churn out tacos and burritos from a closet-size kitchen." They're known for their substantial breakfast burritos, but the tacos, too, are sublime.

TACOS VILLA CORONA: 3185 Glendale Boulevard, Los Angeles, CA 90039, Tel 323 661 3458, www.tacosvillacorona.net (breakfast burritos $3–$7; tacos $2–$3)

JUMBO-SIZE FAMILY FUN

There are strip clubs in L.A., many, many strip clubs, but there is only one that captured Tony's heart: **Jumbo's Clown Room**. "This is a last refuge for the ancient art of burlesque. The girls here take their acts very seriously, and fucking athletically. And I mean this absolutely sincerely. This is a place I'd bring a date. It's a lot of fun, attracting a great mix of types. There's something remarkably wholesome about this establishment. I mean, it's kinda charming."

Jack "Jumbo" Taylor opened the place in 1970 in the East Hollywood neighborhood of what's now known as Thai Town. It was, at first, a simple neighborhood bar, with pajama parties, pig roasts, and other fun activities for the community. Briefly a disco and then a country-and-western bar, since 1982, Jumbo's has been a strip club—or, technically a "bikini bar," in keeping with city codes. Taylor's daughter Karen has run the place since 1990, the bartending staff is largely female, and the dancers control the well-stocked jukebox, all of which contribute to a vibe that's far more fun, respectful, and celebratory than your average titty bar.

Do be aware that, despite its name, Jumbo's is not a very large place, and waits for entry and drinks can be a bit long, especially on weekends.

JUMBO'S CLOWN ROOM: 5153 Hollywood Boulevard, Los Angeles, CA 90027, Tel 323 666 1187, www.jumbos.com (average cocktail about $7; two-drink minimum, no cover charge, though tipping the dancers is highly encouraged)

"GET OFF MY LAWN"

"Musso & Frank is a perfectly preserved old-school Hollywood restaurant, where professional adult bartenders know how to mix a perfect cocktail, because it's their job, not because they have a steampunk fetish or stumbled across Dad's old moustache wax in the basement," said Tony to *Haute Living* magazine in 2016. Though he didn't film any television there, it was a favored place to entertain journalists and friends when in LA, to have a perfectly-cooked bone-in ribeye steak, creamed spinach, and sautéed mushrooms ordered from a classic menu that has barely changed since the restaurant opened in 1919.

"That's something that LA does really, really well," Tony told Katherine Spiers, a journalist, during an interview on her *Smart Mouth* podcast, in 2016. "It has great old bars, and old institutions that are still going, in a complete unironic way. There's no irony at Musso & Frank. They're just so straight-up, 'This is what we do, this is what we've always done, move it along, get off my lawn.'"

THE MUSSO AND FRANK GRILL: 6667 Hollywood Boulevard, Los Angeles, CA 90028, Tel 323 467 7788, www.mussoandfrank.com (entrées average $42)

K-TOWN

Parts Unknown dedicated an entire episode to the Korean American experience in Los Angeles, beginning with the Immigration Act of 1965, which spurred the arrival of thousands of Korean immigrants in LA. Tony addressed, with chef Roy Choi, the LA riots of 1992 and their outsize impact on what had come to be known as Koreatown, where local business owners and families were left to defend themselves against looting, arson, and personal violence, having been abandoned by local police. With the help of Choi and the artist David Choe, Tony explored present-day Koreatown, where second- and third-generation Korean Americans are continuing culinary traditions utterly unchanged to suit the Western palate, and since rebuilding after the riots, share the neighborhood with Thai, Filipino, Samoan, Mexican, Central American, and Bangladeshi restaurants.

"**Park's Bar-B-Q:** that's a place I make sure to hit every single time. I order everything: tongue, make sure to get the tongue. Some *galbi*, some short rib—whatever they send me. And I think their *banchan* [assorted side dishes and rice, mostly vegetable- and fish-based] are some of the best I've ever had," Tony said to Jeff Miller for *Thrillist*, in 2016.

Jenee Kim arrived in Los Angeles in 2000 with a degree in culinary science from Seoul Women's College, and in 2003 opened Park's, which specialized in American Wagyu beef but equally delivers on its pork, seafood, tofu, stews, and noodle dishes. As the late Jonathan Gold wrote in a special section of the *Los Angeles Times* devoted to K-Town in early 2018, "It is probably beyond argument that Jenee Kim's modernist restaurant is still the best place in Koreatown to eat Korean barbecue."

PARK'S BAR-B-Q: 955 South Vermont Avenue, Los Angeles, CA 90006, Tel 213 380 1717, www.parksbbq.com ($40–$60 per person for a full beef barbecue experience at dinner; lunch special $15)

It's not all beef, muscle cars, and classic cocktails in LA. There's a particular pleasure to be found at **Book Soup, "one of the last great independent bookstores,"** which has been in continuous operation since 1975. Its very existence chips away a bit at the stereotype of Los Angelenos as lacking any interest in culture unrelated to Hollywood. **"Their every shelf is personally curated by the well-read staff. They have an amazing and esoteric collection of unsurpassed LA-related weirdness. A great and rare pocket of wonderful and strange and beautiful. And they're a major stopover for all the heavy-hitting authors to read. Everybody loves this place."** As a bonus, there is even parking, a rare treasure in this car-mad city.

BOOK SOUP: 8818 Sunset Boulevard, West Hollywood, CA 90069, Tel 310 659 3110, www.booksoup.com (typical retail book prices)

MIAMI, FLORIDA

Tony found himself in Miami with some frequency: on family vacations, shooting TV, promoting books, and appearing at a corporate-sponsored annual bacchanal of food and wine personalities on the beach.

"Miami sneaks up on you. Or, do we change, and find ourselves sneaking up, washing up, ending up in Miami?

"It's a big place. Bigger and more multifaceted than it's given credit for. We tend, over the years, to focus on Miami's, how shall I put this? . . . *Party zone*. It's a temptation that's almost irresistible. The seductions of flash, of palm trees, balmy nights, deco architecture, the manufactured dreams of many television shows made real."

But Miami is more, much more, than the neon and flash of South Beach and Lincoln Road. Don't miss the islands, Coral Gables, newly arty Wynwood and the Design District, or downtown. "And, of course, not to be overlooked are the neighborhoods of Little Havana and Little Haiti. Miami is the most Latin American of cities, home to untold numbers of Cubans, South Americans, and also Caribbean immigrants, with all the good stuff that comes with that.

"The dreamers, the visionaries, crooks, and con men who built Miami envisioned many different kinds of paradise. A New Jerusalem in a piece of seemingly infinitely expanding real estate. Just fill in where there's water and you've got property. Or, as in Coral Gables, build a new Venice, complete with Othello Moorish Hollywood fantasy architecture and grand canals. Gondolas to ferry the new seekers to their palazzos in the sun. The dream was as expandable as the space. Where there was water, there was now, magically, terra-sort-of-firma.

"And in the 1980s, where there was decline, a vacuum, suddenly there was a new and vibrant economy. One that raised all boats, filled

Miami with new buildings, shiny cars, swanky nightclubs, floods of cash, and a new reputation for murder and criminality to go with it. Cocaine.

"Say what you will, cocaine altered the skyline of Miami forever. It made, for better or worse, Miami sexy again."

ARRIVAL, GETTING AROUND, AND A NOTE ABOUT THE RALEIGH

Miami International Airport (MIA) is the region's largest airport, a place to change planes between North and South America, handling flights to and from many parts of the United States, Central and South America, Mexico and the Caribbean, and a few dozen European and Middle Eastern cities.

Hail a metered taxi or take a SuperShuttle to get from the airport to your hotel; see www.miami-airport.com for a list of flat rates that vary by zone (i.e., distance from the airport). There's also a two-line train system called Metrorail, and a few bus options; see www.miami dade.gov for details.

Tony was a loyalist to the **Raleigh Hotel**, an art deco gem in South Beach with quirky, period-specific furnishings, a luxurious pool (and excellent poolside service), and the kind of privacy and discreet personal attention that made it hard to leave campus.

"I come here not just for the bar, or the old-school interior, or even the gorgeous pool, but because it's one of the few offbeat, grown-up, slightly dysfunctional refuges I truly and deeply love. It's a place that feels like home."

Alas, as of this writing, the hotel is out of service and in a kind of real estate limbo, with the new owner threatening to convert it to a residence unless he's given a zoning variance to build a towering hotel on an adjacent property. The most recent reports on the ground suggest that he's been given his way, so the Raleigh may well survive.

"A GLORIOUS REFUGE"

Restaurants, hotels, and festivals come and go in Miami; only the ocean and **Mac's Club Deuce** are eternal.

"There's one place I keep coming back to. It's a place where, if you look deep enough, ask the right questions, you can get a whole history of Miami from one man. This man, Mac Klein: the owner, proprietor, and regular bartender at Mac's Club Deuce turned a hundred years old this year," said Tony, in 2014; Klein died the following year, though the bar remains.

"Mac came to Miami in 1945 from New York's Lower East Side by way of the Battle of Normandy. During World War II, Miami saw a massive influx of military personnel. Hotels, which had seen a sharp drop in business, made a deal with the government to house troops at the empty resorts. By the fall of 1942, more than 78,000 troops were living in three hundred hotels in Miami and Miami Beach."

The bar was opened as the Club Deuce in 1933; Mac took over and added his name in 1964. The place has remained a perfectly preserved time capsule, a classic dive bar unchanged in over fifty years, the walls still painted black, the unassuming stucco exterior still wrapped in neon (though *Miami Vice* set dressers added interior neon in the 1980s, before shooting a scene in the bar), the crowd still a motley mix of high and low. **"It's a glorious refuge for distinguished guests from all walks of life, perfect for late afternoons or late nights. I love this place. I mean, I love it. It's my favorite bar in Miami."**

MAC'S CLUB DEUCE: 222 14th Street, Miami Beach, FL 33139, Tel 305 531 6200, www.macsclubdeuce.com (drinks are 2-for-1 from 8:00 a.m. to 7:00 p.m. daily; cash only)

ATLANTA, GEORGIA

"Atlanta: been through a few times, don't know it well, and it's been a long time since I did any serious eating there," said Tony at the start of an episode of *The Layover*. What he found was a deeply diverse food scene, with chicken-fried steak classics like the Colonnade, excellent tacos, and northern Chinese specialties standing alongside "New Southern" places making sophisticated, cliché-defying dishes.

"There is this *notion* of southern food. It's not just a misunderstanding by people who live outside the South, it is a notion propagated by people *within* the South that heavily deep-fried everything is classic southern country cooking. But if you've got somebody with a cookbook, saying 'Ya'll' on the cover a lot, chances are everything's cooked in lard, everything's breaded, everything's heavy. It wasn't always so," said Tony, meaning, the real southern cooking, worth traveling for, is full of fresh vegetables, beans, grains, pickles, carefully raised meats, and fresh Atlantic and Gulf seafood.

GETTING THERE AND AROUND

"Hartsfield-Jackson Atlanta International (ATL) is a major hub, big, sprawling, not fun at all." It's the world's busiest airport by number of flights and passengers served annually. There are direct flights to and from pretty much every major world destination, along with regional flights all over the South.

Being so massive, ATL has a handful of rail, bus, and people-mover options just to get passengers between terminals and concourses. There are also shuttle and municipal buses to get passengers to the city, along with rail service provided by the Metropolitan Atlanta Rapid Transit Authority (MARTA), in addition to the usual metered taxis and other private transport. The drive between ATL and the city is about thirteen miles, takes about thirty minutes and, in a metered taxi, costs about $35, plus tip.

And, once you're to your hotel: **"Traffic in Atlanta? Not so good. Everybody drives. Even so, you probably should, too."** Public transportation can leave you wanting, especially if your time is tight; rent a car or take taxis.

SHOP AND EAT THE WORLD ON BUFORD HIGHWAY

"Atlanta is, every year, more of a city of transplants from somewhere else. All you gotta do is go out to Buford Highway and find yourself in the delicious international zone, a long stretch of strip malls featuring every variety of good shit from foreign lands."

Take a souped-up rental out for a drive, and stop for *tacos de lengua* (beef tongue) at El Taco Veloz. "Drive right the fuck up and get yourself some authentic fucking deliciousness, *vato*. Tacos, burritos, wash it all down with an horchata, perhaps." Taco Veloz is a small Atlanta chain with about a half-dozen locations. The first, on Buford Highway, was established in 1991, and named "best tacos in Atlanta" by readers in an *Atlanta Journal-Constitution* local poll.

EL TACO VELOZ: 5084 Buford Highway, Doraville, GA 30301, Tel 770 936 9094, www.tacoveloz.com (tacos about $2, burritos about $5, entrées about $9)

"Other highlights on the Buford Highway, this veritable stairway to heaven? There's **Northern China Eatery** or Crawfish Shack Seafood.

"Northern China, or Dongbei, is wheat, not rice, country: that means dumplings, *good* dumplings, buns, noodles, with like, meat—lamb kebab seasoned with cumin and chili, or Mandarin lion's head with brown sauce, which is not lion, by the way. They're giant pork meatballs. The thing to get, my opinion, is fish in hot and spicy pot—deep-fried fish with lots and lots of chili. No frills, dirt cheap, and really, really good. Put that right at the top of your list."

NORTHERN CHINA EATERY: 5141 Buford Highway, Doraville, GA 30304, Tel 678 697 9226, www.northernchinaeatery.com (fish in hot and spicy pot $20; dumplings $8–$9)

And then, "**Down the yellow brick road to Cajun-style Asian mutation is Crawfish Shack Seafood, run by Mr. Hieu Pham, an Atlanta native of Vietnamese-Cambodian descent. Deep-fried fish, low country boils—not your typical Cajun, but oh, so good.**" The Louisiana crawfish boil is a nod to the Vietnamese immigrant communities who first settled there in the 1970s, and Pham adds lemongrass to his spice mixture, but otherwise it's a fairly straightforward, very well-executed menu of steamed or fried fish and shellfish, po'boy sandwiches, and sides.

CRAWFISH SHACK SEAFOOD: 4337 Buford Highway, Atlanta, GA 30341, Tel 404 329 1610, www.crawfishshackseafood.com (seafood platter for one, $30; whole po'boy, $10–$15)

"**The mammoth Buford Highway Farmer's Market makes no sense at all, in the best possible way. The whole world of food, it seems, is under one big roof. Asian from all over Asia, Eastern European, African, and elsewhere, all in one improbable place. . . . It just goes on and on, doesn't it? The Philippines, Thai, Chinese, Indian, the ramen section.**" As you stroll the aisles of this 100,000-square-foot international megastore, marvel over periwinkles, durian, catfish heads, live conch, and hundreds of specific cuts of meat, and snack on Korean dumplings freshly steamed in one of many on-premises food court stalls.

BUFORD HIGHWAY FARMER'S MARKET: 5600 Buford Highway, Doraville, GA 30340, Tel 770 455 0770 (no website) (prices vary)

"**Designed expressly for the chefly sensibilities of other cooks and chefs and restaurant people, Holeman & Finch Public House is now a hit with everybody. The future of American dining, the next thing, is probably happening south of the Mason-Dixon. It's been happening for a while and is only going to get bigger and better.**"

Here, you'll find "country ham, treated with the same respect as a fine Iberico *jamón* or a prosciutto; deviled eggs, three ways; and souse [pickled pork head cheese], something any chef would be proud to have on their menu, especially this good." Follow that with "Johnnycake, poached egg, bacon, duck liver, and sorghum syrup," and "lamb fries, a.k.a. sheep nuts, with spiced pecans, onion, mint, and a mustard beurre blanc."

In years past, Holeman & Finch offered two dozen "double-stack" burgers to customers on a first-come, first-served basis at 10:00 p.m. each night. Now they also have a dedicated burger operation, H&F Burger—and still make their limited two dozen available at the start of each service at Holeman & Finch.

HOLEMAN & FINCH PUBLIC HOUSE: 2277 Peachtree Road NE, Atlanta, GA 30309, Tel 404 948 1175, www.holeman-finch.com (starters average $12, entrées average $25)

"Atlanta has many wonderful things to see besides strip clubs, but they do—incongruously, one would think, for the relatively conservative South—have a lot of those. I don't like conventional strip clubs; one of the few exceptions to this rule, however, is in Atlanta.

"Georgia's the Bible Belt, isn't it? The South is supposed to be conservative, right? God-fearing, Baptist, Evangelical? So why is this the strip club capital of America? The best, the finest, the most uniquely weird and wonderful beloved Atlanta institution, is the Clermont Lounge. This place should be a national landmark. The most beloved institution in the entire city, a place of Renaissance-era beauty and erotic and sophisticated nightlife, where the shots flow out in tiny, plastic cups. It's not like other strip clubs. It's operating on a whole other level."

Tony (and his guest Alton Brown) sat for an interview with the legendary Blondie (Anita Ray Strange), at the time in her midfifties and still crushing beer cans between her breasts and dancing on the Clermont's tiny single stage. Blondie explained what makes this place, which has been in continuous operation since 1965, so special: "It's really down-to-earth, and the girls are really sweet. I mean, the youngest girl's twenty-nine, but the oldest girl is sixty-six. And this club is for the girls who are not built so great, but we all have got great personalities." Later, after Tony handed her a twenty-dollar bill, Blondie offered to do dropkicks and splits if he'd pay for her next song—there's no DJ at the Clermont, and the dancers must under write the cost of the jukebox whose songs score their performances.

"Blondie and I, it turns out, are not nearly as different as you might think. Pretty close to the same age, performing for others whom we don't know, and from the look of things, some days she might actually appreciate and like her job more than I do. If you live in Atlanta, or travel here often, and have yet to pay your respects to this woman's greatness, please do so. It is well worth the acknowledgment, and there is no better single evening's worth of entertainment in town."

The Clermont Motor Hotel, with which the lounge shares its space, was once a run-down, pay-by-the-week kind of place, closed by order of the health department in 2013 and newly reopened as a boutique hotel after a multimillion-dollar renovation. Fortunately, miraculously even, none of that has affected the charm of the lounge.

THE CLERMONT LOUNGE: 789 Ponce de Leon Avenue NE, Atlanta, GA 30306, Tel 404 874 4783, www.clermontlounge.net ($10 cover charge most evenings)

CHICAGO, ILLINOIS

Tony's genuine and unabashed love for Chicago was a consistent joy to witness. He made one episode each of *No Reservations*, *The Layover*, and *Parts Unknown* in the city, each time shining a light on the bars, hot dog and sandwich joints, sports fans, grounded chefs, aspiring performers, and grandiose architecture that define the city.

"I've done shows in LA, but LA is a fantastic sprawl. San Francisco, a great town. New Orleans, a state of mind. But Chicago: Chicago is a *city*.

"Chicago doesn't ever have to measure itself against any other city. Other places have to measure themselves against *it*. It's big, it's outgoing, it's tough, it's opinionated, and everybody's got a story.

"This is one of the truly most awesome cities in the world. They do not fuck around in Chicago. I don't know whether it's physically the biggest or most populated, but really, I don't care what the numbers are; this is, like, the greatest city in America. It's one cultural Mount Everest after another. This is the city without an inferiority complex."

And, at the end of your visit: "**Done right, you drag your ass sleepily off to the airport, chin smeared with the grease from an Italian beef sandwich, belching mustard from last night's red hot, dimly trying to remember to whom you must apologize for your previous misadventures. Oh, Chicago, you are indeed, a wonderful, wonderful town.**"

ARRIVAL AND GETTING AROUND

The city has two airports, the much larger of which is **O'Hare International Airport (ORD)**.

"**The first thing is, unfortunately, most layovers in the great city of Chicago are involuntary, because there are few airports you want to be in less. The O'Hare experience usually kinda sucks. Due to its size, its importance as a hub, and unpredictable midwestern weather, it's among the most-likely-to-be-laid-over airports in the world. It blows. No other way to put it. In its favor, you could do a hell of a lot worse than find yourself stuck in Chicago.**"

O'Hare services an extensive roster of domestic flights, and many more to Central and South America, Europe, Africa, Asia, and even Australia and New Zealand. It's located about eighteen miles northwest of downtown; a metered taxi should take about forty minutes and cost $35–$40, plus a gratuity of 15–20 percent of the fare.

There are a number of shuttle bus services, like Coach USA and Go Airport Express, making trips between O'Hare and the city, and between airports. Chicago Transit Authority's blue line train ("the El," as the metro system is called locally, a reference to its mostly elevated tracks), runs 24/7 from O'Hare to Forest Park, with many opportunities for transfer to other lines. The fare from O'Hare is $5 one way, and $2.50 when using the El to move between most other stations.

"**It should be noted that Chicago's Midway International Airport (MDW) is a smaller, more reasonable option.**" It's a hub for Southwest Airlines, and the majority of the routes served are domestic, but there are a few flights to Mexico, Jamaica, the Dominican Republic, and Canada. Midway is about twelve miles southwest of downtown Chicago, a twenty-five- to forty-five-minute ride that will, just like a trip from O'Hare, cost $35–$40, plus a gratuity of 15–20 percent of the fare.

There are also Go Airport Express shuttles between Midway and the city, and the CTA's orange line departs from the airport to Adams/Wabash, with plenty of opportunities to transfer to other lines. Unlike O'Hare, there's no premium charged for the trip from Midway; it's $2.50, the standard one-way fare on the El. Note that this line doesn't run between 1:00 and 4:00 a.m.

Once in town, Chicago is a rather walkable city, with its broad avenues and sidewalks, and there's plenty to see along the way. For longer distances, or in extreme weather, use the CTA's elevated trains and extensive bus systems, or call or hail a taxi, which abound in this city. You can, of course, rent a car; parking and traffic are about as challenging and expensive as in any major metro area, so let your tolerance for these things be your guide.

GOLD COAST LUXURY

"**I'm staying at the Four Seasons, motherfucker. It's swank as all getout, with the industry gold standard of big-ass, comfortable beds.**" The hotel occupies a privileged position in the upscale Gold Coast neighborhood, with Lake Michigan views and walkable access to fancy shopping on the so-called Magnificent Mile, plus superb service and amenities like on-call ice cream sundae and martini carts, a spa and indoor Roman pool covered by a glass ceiling—in short, it's the kind of place that Tony enjoyed retreating to after a hard day of dive bars, meaty sandwiches, and tough characters.

FOUR SEASONS CHICAGO: 120 East Delaware Place, Chicago, IL 60611, Tel 312 280 8800, www.fourseasons.com/chicago (rooms start at about $425 per night)

A DIFFERENT TYPE OF CULTURE

Another advantage of staying at the Four Seasons is its proximity to a cultural institution that catered to Tony's longtime fascination with medical maladies, oddities, and unusual, gruesome, or woefully ineffective remedies.

"I like museums. I know it might not look like that, as I seldom am seen going into museums. And of course, I do constantly advise you to avoid them, but not in Chicago. They've got good museums in Chicago, a lot of them. You've got the Art Institute, which is great, but you also have the awesome International Museum of Surgical Science off Lake Shore Drive."

Located in the château-like childhood home of Dr. Max Thorek, who founded the International College of Surgeons, the museum's exhibits of historical medical tools are fascinating means to drum up gratitude for the relative advances of modern medicine.

"I have an interest in trepanning," Tony told a museum employee, referring, of course, to the ancient practice of drilling a hole in the skull of a living human to relieve a variety of ailments. "Back in the day, if you had a bad headache or were acting weird or just felt out of sorts, a popular treatment involved popping open your skull like a beer can and letting the pressure out. Fun, huh? Sometimes, it even

worked. Don't try this at home, kids." In addition to trepanning kits and the preserved skulls of those unlucky subjects of the procedure, the museum also contains historic texts, medical-inspired artworks, and a particularly gnarly gift shop. **"I am so happy. This is a dream come true."**

INTERNATIONAL MUSEUM OF SURGICAL SCIENCE: 1524 North Lake Shore Drive, Chicago, IL 60610, Tel 312 642 6502, www.imss.org (adult admission $16, children $8)

DRINKING IN THE OLD TOWN

"On a quiet corner in the Old Town neighborhood sits one of the most storied, legendary drinking establishments in the nation, a touchstone of our country's cultural history, a Roman senate of enlightened discourse." This, of course, is **Old Town Ale House**. **"Many iconic figures of literature, comedy, the stage and screen, along with philosopher-poets for whom recognition never came, all have at one time or another rested, however briefly, their noble brows upon its bathroom walls."**

The bar has been open since 1958; it was destroyed in a fire in the 1960s, and so moved from one side of West North Avenue to the other. When owner Beatrice Klug died, in 2005, she left the bar to Tobin Mitchell and her ex-husband, **"author, world-famous painter, golf hustler, raconteur, enabler, and blogger Bruce Cameron Elliot,"** as Tony described him.

Elliot maintains a lively, profane blog, detailing the comedic (and occasionally tragic) comings and goings and drinkings and fightings of the bar's regulars, along with political discourse and personal narratives. In the bar's basement, Bruce maintains an ad hoc yet serious artist's studio, making loving portraits of the bar's regulars and esteemed visitors, and satiric and hilarious portraits of an ever-growing cast of buffoonish and/or criminal elected officials and those who aspire to be so.

"As late afternoon gives way to evening in Chicago's Old Town, it's time to drink—though, to be fair, almost anytime is time for a drink at the Old Town Ale House. The chorus assembles, to give their opinions on matters of the day, subjects of great import to this city on the lake, this city of broad shoulders, this true metropolis."

OLD TOWN ALE HOUSE: 219 West North Avenue, Chicago, IL 60610, Tel 312 944 7020, www.theoldtownalehouse.com (typical pitcher of beer $10)

ROAST BEEF TWO WAYS

Chicago has no shortage of world-class fine-dining options, but again and again, Tony was drawn to the meaty, the inexpensive, and the handheld among the city's culinary offerings.

"We're gonna need a boatload of napkins. There's no delicate way to eat this, you just hoist and go." At the invitation of the legendary Chicago musician and producer Steve Albini (see "Where I'd Take Tony, If He Were Still Here" on page 350), Tony made a run at "the particularly unholy delights of the breaded fried steak sandwich" for which Ricobene's, an old-school Chicago pizza parlor, is very well known. A skirt steak is breaded and fried, then doused in tomato sauce (somehow remaining crisp), folded around generous handfuls of shredded mozzarella and pickled peppers, and stuffed into a french bread roll that is up to the task of delivering this majesty without leakage. "It's a thing of beauty—and tasty."

RICOBENE'S: 252 West 26th Street, Chicago, IL 60616, Tel 312 225 5555, www.ricobenespizza.com (regular steak sandwich about $9)

Where I'd Take Tony,
If He Were Still Here

BY STEVE ALBINI

The proletarian eats in Chicago are fantastic. There's a hot dog stand called **Jim's Original** which is open twenty-four hours a day, and has been for decades. It sells a very short menu of hot dogs, Polish sausage, and pork chop sandwiches. And, of them, the Polish sausage is an absolute masterpiece. I can't count the number of times I've been on the highway late at night, and remembered that I could pull off and go to Jim's for a Polish, and then done it, and I've never been dissatisfied by it. There's a kind of a society that grows around Jim's, in that there are always panhandlers and people selling packages of tube socks and secondhand porno movies. It's in the neighborhood of the Maxwell Street Market, which was an open public market that operated for 150, 170 years, something like that. So that would be the first place I'd take Tony, late at night: I would take him to Jim's. And we'd get a Polish sausage with grilled onions.

There are other hot dog places in the city that are good for one reason or another. There's a place called **The Wiener's Circle**, near Wrigley Field, where the staff are famously abusive of the customers, and that's part of the experience of going there. Their hot dogs are fine, but you go there because it's such a pleasure to be insulted and abused by an expert.

For eating value, probably the best hot dog joint in the city is a place called **Superdawg** on the northwest side. They have a very large menu of hot dog styles, all of them charmingly named. The Superdawg is a classic dressed Chicago dog on a poppyseed bun. The Whoopskidawg is a chili dog. The Francheesie is a Polish sausage that's been split and stuffed with cheese and then grilled, and then it's wrapped with bacon. So, that's a real experience.

Other than hot dogs, there are several places in Chicago where you can get really fantastic cold cuts, and cured meats, and things like that. There's a placed called **Publican Quality Meats**, which is an offshoot of the Publican bar and restaurant. And that's a downtown walk-in joint, where they have an enormous array of house-made charcuterie, and it's all fantastic.

If I had to go buy meat to cook for an occasion, I would go to **Paulina Market**. It's a meat market that has classic, old-school, very well trained, talented butchers, and they make their own charcuterie and their own smoked meats; everything is exceptional. They also have supported progressive political causes in the past, so that makes me even more sympathetic to them.

Then, the other thing that the city is famous for is its barbecue culture, and there are many, many, many barbecue options in Chicago. There is one king of barbecue, and that is **Lem's Bar-B-Q**. Their barbecue is intensely, deeply smoked, and saturated with their own sauce, which is an absolutely delicious vinegar-based sauce. Their ribs are otherworldly, and that's really what they're famous for. But they also have a hot link, which is chopped-off cuts and gristle in a sausage casing. And that hot link is a masterpiece. It's the kind of sausage that tries to fight being eaten. It's quite gristly and gnarly, and full of texture and intensely flavored.

If you're in the neighborhood of Lem's, a few blocks away is a place called **Original Soul Vegetarian**. It's an all-vegan soul food restaurant. It's run by members of an odd religious sect. I try not to let that cross my mind while I'm there, because the food is fucking fantastic. It's all the soul food classics—greens, macaroni, sweet potato pie—all of the fantastic things that go in soul food, that make soul food such a unique and rich culinary tradition. And it's all vegan. And it's one of the few truly delicious vegan eating experiences you can have.

But another truly delicious vegan experience is **Amitabul**, which has traditional Korean food, but cooked without any animal component. And it's really great. Very wide menu, something for every palate. It's delicious.

For chicken, there's **Harold's Chicken Shack**, a famous institution with twenty locations in and around Chicago. For barbecue chicken, my recommendation would be a place called **Hecky's**. Hecky's is a rarity, in that it's a really great BBQ place that opened in the suburbs. Most of the great BBQ in the city is in the city, but Hecky's is in the class of great BBQ, and they're in Evanston. Smoked chicken is *their* masterpiece. It's chicken that's intensely smoked, then covered in barbecue sauce after cooking, and it's really, really great.

Tony's been to **Kuma's Corner**, and he appreciated it, both from a cultural and culinary standpoint. There are some perversities to licensing laws in Chicago. It's extremely difficult to open a tavern that's just a tavern, where you drink booze and listen to music. So almost all enterprises like that in Chicago are, for terms of licensing, restaurants, which means they have to have food service of some kind.

The guys who opened Kuma's wanted to open a heavy metal bar, because there wasn't really a heavy metal bar in Chicago—a place where metal dudes could hang out and listen to heavy metal music really loud and watch slasher films—so they wanted to make one. But they couldn't open a bar, so they opened a hamburger restaurant, and named all the hamburgers after different heavy metal bands. They could have done that without the food being exceptional, but their food is exceptional—very well thought out in the hamburgers themselves, the condiments they use, and the flavors they put together.

They also have a side menu, which is fantastic. They make pulled pork fries, kind of like poutine, made with pulled pork and BBQ sauce.

And a kind of "call your shot" macaroni and cheese, where you can add literally anything else they have in the building to it. So, you can say, 'Yeah, I'd like macaroni and cheese with bourbon-poached pears and peas and andouille sausage,' and, yup, no, problem, they'll whip it right up for you.

Hearty portions, very satisfying meals there. And they have an extensive bar, an extensive selection of bourbons; the drinking there is also great. But the food is why you'd go, if you weren't a heavy metal fan. And the metal is why you'd go, if you didn't care about food.

Every neighborhood in Chicago has a little taqueria. And probably, a typical one would be called **La Pasadita**, in Wicker Park. They're generally open either late or all night, and the food is very similar to Oaxacan food—*tacos al pastor*, *carne asada* tacos, tacos with *lengua* or *chicharrones* or *barbacoa*—because a lot of the cooks in Chicago come from Oaxaca. And it's all fantastic.

There are other Latin food places that are not Mexican, but the Mexican food is probably the most prominent Latin food in Chicago. There's a place called **Irazú**, which is all Costa Rican food, and that has a slightly more Caribbean slant to it, and it's delicious. Super fantastic.

There's a place called **Café Tola** that sells tacos and burritos like all the other taquerias; they're one of the few taquerias in town that have a very wide assortment of utterly delicious empanadas, and a specialty horchata drink, which is a kind of a hybrid coffee called the horchata latte.

And there are a bunch of Vietnamese pho places in town. I particularly like **Nhu Lan Bakery**. And, there's another place, **Ba Le**. It's been open for almost forty years. It's a fantastic Vietnamese sandwich and pho place. They bake their own bread. They're in the Uptown neighborhood, which is not a particularly ritzy neighborhood, and it's great that they maintained their pricing so that neighborhood people can afford to eat there, as well as people who have made the trip there.

Philly's got the cheesesteak, New Orleans has the po'boy, and Chicago has this: the Italian beef sandwich.

"On my way back to the dreaded O'Hare, I stop for an important station of the cross, Johnnie's Beef, where they do the all-important Chicago staple, Italian beef, right." Johnnie's, in operation since 1961 in the suburb of Elmwood Park, is no nonsense and cash only, and there is often a line for service—none of which should deter you.

"Beloved by Chicagoans, as it well should be, superbly moist, some might say, drenched and delicious, this transcendental amalgam of slowly cooked round steak, sweet, sweet peppers, hot peppers, dripping with magical, greasy beef juice. . . . Let us see this magnificent creation, a favorite son of Chicago—oh, Jesus, look at this. Holy crap."

JOHNNIE'S BEEF: 7500 West North Avenue, Elmwood Park, IL 60707, Tel 708 452 6000 (no website) (Italian beef sandwich about $5)

NEW ORLEANS, LOUISIANA

Tony was a staff writer on *Treme*, the David Simon– and Eric Overmyer–produced HBO series about life in New Orleans, post–Hurricane Katrina. It was, as he said, a high-water mark in his career as a writer, and it allowed him to play to his strength at writing kitchen scenes and dialogue, while digging deep into the city's singular culture.

"There is no other place on earth even remotely like New Orleans. Don't even try to compare it with anywhere else. Even trying to describe it is tricky, as chances are, no matter how much you love it, you

don't really know it. No last call at bars, lots and lots of great food. We know that. Locals who are, well, uniquely wonderful. There's an attitude here that defies all setbacks, all the things wrong with this fabulously, famously fucked-up city that defies logic in the very best possible ways."

ARRIVAL AND GETTING AROUND

By air, you'll land at **Louis Armstrong New Orleans International Airport (MSY)**, about eleven miles due west of the center of the city, in Kenner. It services flights to and from many major US cities and a handful of destinations in Canada, Mexico, and Europe.

From MSY, you can take a flat-rate taxi into town; it's $36 for up to two passengers, or $15 per passenger with three or more, as of this writing, plus a customary 15–20 percent tip. There are airport shuttles for $24 per person one way or $44 round trip; purchase tickets at kiosks in the baggage claim area. And, for a truly economical option (fares are $1.50–$2), there are bus routes between airport and city, administered by Jefferson Transit (JeT) and the New Orleans Regional Transit Authority; see www.jeffersontransit.org and www.norta.com for schedule and route details.

Once you're in town, Tony advised, "**Public transportation in New Orleans, like pretty much everything administered by politicians or bureaucrats here is, well, spotty at best. So, plan to walk, rent a car, or take one of the many cheap and awesome cabs in the city. Drivers here have seen it all, so they know what to do.**"

COCHON, PO'BOYS, MUFFULETTAS, DAIQUIRIS, AND CHRISTMAS: EATING AND DRINKING IN NEW ORLEANS

Chef Donald Link was a steadfast friend and on-camera sidekick, and Tony loved his restaurants, especially **Cochon**. **"Here, Link and partner Stephen Stryjewski allow guests to share their passion for roots Cajun and southern home cooking. We're not talking dough-nut burgers or deep-fried freaking stuffing. We're talking food that actual grandmothers once made, somewhat tweaked for restaurant service, of course."**

Dinners consist of typical Cochon delights like boudin sausage, breaded pork cheeks, smoked ham hock with red beans, charred radish and chicken hearts, macaroni and cheese casserole, and roasted pork with turnips, cabbage, pickled peaches, and cracklins. "*Cochon* is French for 'pig'—and there's lots of it here."

COCHON: 930 Tchoupitoulas Street, New Orleans, LA 70130, Tel 504 588 2123, www.cochonrestaurant.com (average entrée $24)

"The best po'boy in New Orleans: I ain't making that argument. I'm not starting that discussion. All I can tell you is that **R&O's** is a seriously excellent version of the roast beef po'boy, an unlikely, but near perfect, combination of bread, beef, debris-flecked gravy, mayo, lettuce, and tomato." The bread is toasted, the sandwich is messy, and the portions are enormous.

At R&O's, the service is warm but casual, the room sprawling and bright, and for antsy children (and grown-ups), there's a small arcade featuring a vintage *Galaga* game. R&O's is in an area known as Bucktown, originally a fishing camp settlement between the 17th Street Canal and Lake Pontchartrain, now home to a massive gate and pumping station meant to stave off the kind of destruction that Hurricane Katrina wrought—but also still a destination for locals and savvy visitors to enjoy fried seafood, Italian specialties, and po'boys at a handful of remaining family restaurants, like R&Os.

Tony visited R&O's in the company of the author, journalist, and New Orleans expert Lolis Eric Elie. As Tony noted that the menu didn't identify the sandwich in question as a po'boy, Elie explained, "There's a distinction between the New Orleans restaurants that are sort of gearing themselves toward tourists, that are just saying, 'OK, sir, this is where you find the things you've read about.' And I think R&O's is saying, 'Look, we're for the local people, 'cause you [tourists] come here once a year.'"

R&O's: 216 Metairie-Hammind Highway, Metairie, LA 70005, Tel 504 831 1248, www.r-opizza.com (sandwiches about $9, entrées $10–$20, pizzas about $16)

Another revered po'boy purveyor is **Domilise's Po-Boy and Bar**, which has been operated by successive generations of its namesake family since 1918, with very little changed over time. It's still in an un-assuming yellow house on the corner of Annunciation and Bellecastle

Streets; the sandwiches are still made on airy white Leidenheimer bread; and the staff tends to stick around for decades.

Ask for the off-menu special sandwich of fried shrimp, Swiss cheese, and roast beef gravy. **"You really gotta get messy for this."**

DOMILISE'S PO-BOY AND BAR: 5240 Annunciation Street, New Orleans, LA 70115, Tel 504 899 9126, www.domilisespoboys.com (sandwiches $5.50–$18)

From the comfort of your hotel room, call in a delivery order to the venerable **Verti Marte**, a liquor and convenience store that also offers an impressive variety of hot foods and sandwiches, and is open twenty-four hours a day, every day. Go for the "Mighty Muffuletta," the sandwich with roots in New Orleans's Sicilian community, built on a puffy round seeded bread of the same name and filled with Genoa salami, ham, swiss and provolone cheeses, and an olive salad made with greek and kalamata olives, roasted red peppers, olive oil, and romano cheese. It's a massive thing—Tony suggested eating half the sandwich right away, and pressing the remaining half under a book overnight, to better saturate the bread with the oil and olive juices.

VERTI MARTE: 1201 Royal Street, New Orleans, LA 70116, Tel 504 525 4767 (sandwiches $2.25–$10)

"I am a pretty loyal guy. When I fall in love, I fall hard. And even if we part, years later, there's still, chances are, love in my heart. And my love for this place, dimly but fondly remembered from years ago, will last forever. It's a national treasure."

Nowhere but a dive bar could inspire such a heartfelt monologue—in this case, **Snake & Jake's Christmas Club Lounge**, an Uptown bar owned, since 1992, by Dave Clements, a New Orleans native. The building is ramshackle, drinks are cheap, cocktails nonexistent, and the lighting is quite dark, punctuated dimly by Christmas tree lights, an homage to a previous owner, named Sam Christmas. There was once a mean house cat who would drink your whiskey and bite you; now there's a friendly dog, Peeve, for whom you can buy "shots" of dog treats, the proceeds from which are donated to animal shelters. The bar is open from 7:00 p.m. to 7:00 a.m.; all are welcome.

SNAKE & JAKE'S CHRISTMAS CLUB LOUNGE: 7612 Oak Street, New Orleans, LA 70118, Tel 504 861 2802, www.snakeandjakes.com (drinks about $3)

PROVINCETOWN, MASSACHUSETTS

Provincetown, Massachusetts, figures heavily in Tony's origin story, as any reader of *Kitchen Confidential* will know. He returned with the *Parts Unknown* crew after decades away to see what remained of that formative summer haven.

"**There's nothing like the North Atlantic. It's majestic. I love the beach. Pretty much had my first everything on a beach. You name**

it, first time I did it, beach. I was miserable in love, happy in love, alternately, as only a seventeen-year-old could be. This is where I lived a very happy summer in the early 1970s. It's an amazing spot if you think about it, a bunch of knuckleheads working as dishwashers and waiters and pizza servers; we could live on a beach like this. Happier, stupider times.

It was here, all the way out at the tip of Cape Cod: Provincetown, Massachusetts, where the pilgrims first landed. And it was where I first landed, 1972, washed into town with a head full of orange sunshine [LSD] and a few friends. Provincetown, a wonderland of tolerance, longtime tradition of accepting artists, writers, the badly behaved, the gay, the different. It was paradise. The joy that can come only with an absolute certainty that you're invincible, that none of the choices that you make will have any repercussions or any effect on your later life. Because we didn't think about any of those things."

ARRIVAL AND GETTING AROUND

Provincetown has a small municipal airport (**PVC**), a ten-minute drive from the town center, that services flights from Boston and, in the summer season, New York. Once on the ground, there are airport car rentals, a handful of independent taxi services (it's about $7 per person to get to town), and a $2 shuttle bus between PVC and the town center. There are also a number of seasonal ferry operators between Boston and Provincetown. The fast ferry is a ninety-minute journey, for about $100 round trip; the traditional ferry takes three hours and costs about $60 round trip.

Simply driving to Cape Cod from Boston or elsewhere is, of course, another option, but in the summer season, vacation traffic may make it a slower and less-pleasant option than plane or boat.

P-TOWN EATS

"**Many of the old places in P-Town are gone, but the Lobster Pot is still going strong, all these years later, and still has what I want, and need: the essentials.**" The Lobster Pot showcases the Azorean Portuguese flavors and ingredients that have been a longtime staple of Provincetown cuisine. The rather extensive menu of cold and steamed seafood cocktails, soups, stews, lobster, and fish preparations now includes outward-facing options like Thai chicken satay, tuna sashimi, and gluten-free items.

Order the "**P-town version of caldo verde, just what I remembered: kale, fiery red chorizo, linguiça, kidney beans, potatoes. That was precisely what I loved about the food here—the Portuguese thing.**" Also delicious: "**stuffed cod crusted with ground Portuguese sausage and breadcrumbs, stuffed with scallop and crab, finished with some sherry, some red sauce.**"

THE LOBSTER POT: 321 Commercial Street, Provincetown, MA 02657, Tel 508 487 0842, www.ptownlobsterpot.com (appetizers $11–$16, entrées $23–$40)

Spiritus Pizza is the amazing true story of a Provincetown business that's held on with the same owner, John "Jingles" Yingling, since 1971, slinging pies and coffee and ice cream, and making its walls available for the work of local artists.

"This town is everything to me," Yingling told the *Parts Unknown* audience. "Provincetown is a really special place, where people can be themselves. We all did drugs, acted young and crazy, and Tony . . . he was probably a little wilder than some, and not as wild as others. But he was always a guy who I always liked."

"And you let me sleep on top of the walk-in!" Tony recalled. "I cannot tell you how frequently I dream about Spiritus Pizza. I'm walking down Commercial Street and I'm sort of dimly aware that Spiritus has moved, and there's this sense of dislocation and loss as I stumble around this Provincetown dreamscape of forty years ago. Well, we're still here. And living in hope."

SPIRITUS PIZZA: 190 Commercial Street, Provincetown, MA 02657, Tel 508 487 2808, www.spirituspizza.com (pizzas about $25 each; slices about $3 each; cash only)

Every good fishing port/party town needs an old-man bar, and Provincetown once had a handful. **"Back when I worked in town, for fishermen, there was the Fo'c'sle, Cookie's Taproom, and this place: The Old Colony. Of the three, it's the only one left. This place had been here forever when I rolled into town. I think this is the only place in town that's unchanged."** It's been in the Enos family since 1954, and appears virtually untouched by time. There are paintings and photographs of regular (and long-deceased) customers on the wood-planked walls, sports pennants, nautical bric-a-brac, Christmas lights behind the bar, tables carved with generations of initials—in short, it's a classic seaside dive.

OLD COLONY TAP: 323 Commercial Street, Provincetown, MA 02657, Tel 508 487 2361, www.old-colony-tap.business.site (drinks about $5)

DETROIT, MICHIGAN

Tony was long intrigued by Detroit. He visited in 2009, as part of a *No Reservations* episode called "Rust Belt" that also included Buffalo and Baltimore, and he returned in 2013 for an episode of *Parts Unknown*. He made sure that his lecture and book tours stopped there, and he helped produce a documentary film about the city, inspired by journalist and author David Maraniss's book *Once in a Great City: A Detroit Story*.

"It's where nearly everything American and great came from. The things the whole world wanted, made here. The heart, the soul, the beat of an industrial-cultural superpower. A magnet for everyone with a dream of a better future, from eastern Europe to the Deep South. American dream? You came here."

"It is one of the most beautiful cities in America. It speaks of those industrial age dreams of an endlessly glorious future. People who built these structures, they were thinking big.

"You wanna take pictures here. The place, like so much of Detroit, invites it. Urban exploring, as they call it, sifting through the remains of Detroit's great American ongoing tragedy. Photographing them, posing in front of them, is something of an irresistible impulse. Detroiters hate it. All the visitors—like us, I should point out—wallowing in ruin porn.

"It's hard to look away from the ruin. To not find beauty in the decay. Comparisons to Angkor Wat, Machu Picchu, ancient Rome are inevitable. Magnificent structures representing the boundless dreams of the dead left to rot. Yet unlike Angkor, and Leptis Magna, people still live here. We forget that."

ARRIVAL AND GETTING AROUND

Detroit Metro Airport (**DTW**) is a major Midwest hub that handles domestic and international flights on a wide range of large and small carriers. A taxi from DTW to downtown Detroit will take about thirty minutes and cost about $55 plus tip. The Regional Transit Authority of Southeast Michigan system (RTA) offers a bus route between DTW and downtown Detroit that takes about forty-five minutes and costs $2; see smartbus.org for details.

Amtrak has a downtown Detroit station, and arriving by train makes sense if you're coming from Chicago. It's a journey of about five and a half hours, on the Wolverine line; see www.amtrak.com for details.

In town, if you don't have your own car and are not inclined to walk, there are plenty of taxi services, but you'll most likely need to make a call to get one, as it's rare to see a taxi cruising for fares. There's also an extensive bus system, administered by the Detroit Department of Transportation, and downtown Detroit has a mono-rail, the People Mover, that runs clockwise around the area, making several stops at local attractions. See www.detroitmi.gov for schedules, routes, and fares.

CONEYS, EASTERN BLOC COMFORTS, AND MUSSELS

"You tell people you're going to Detroit, and chances are, somebody from the home team is gonna say, 'Be sure to get a Coney.' I never really understood that. I mean, I live like thirty minutes from a place called Coney Island, where, presumably, they know something about freakin' hot dogs, right?"

Duly's Place, an old-school diner, in business for nearly a century, is the perfect place to give in to curiosity. Alongside a classic menu of eggs, burgers, wings, sandwiches, and pie, you'll also find an excellent version of the aforementioned hot dog.

"I can't tell you how deep this creation runs here. Deep dish in Chicago, cheesesteak in Philadelphia—you'll find some ambivalence. Not here. It seems like a simple thing: hot dog, chili, raw onion, mustard, steamed bun. But the delicate interplay between these ingredients, when done right, is symphonic." You may find yourself ordering a second dog to chase the first, as Tony did. Duly's is cash only.

DULY'S PLACE: 5458 West Vernor Highway, Detroit, MI 48209, Tel 313 554 3076 (no website) (hot dog about $2)

For unreconstructed Polish food, visit **Polonia**, in the two-square-mile hamlet of Hamtramck, a small city within the city of Detroit that was once home to Polish immigrants seeking good jobs in the auto industry. It still retains a core of Polish culture, though the jobs and many of the people have moved on. Polonia has served hearty, earthy fare for nearly fifty years, in a room full of Polish folk art and enlivened with Polish folk music, heavy on the accordion.

The restaurant's legendary bacon spread arrives with bread and pickles to cut the fat. "A promising beginning when a meal starts with pork fat and crispy pork bits. Then, fresh sausage, stuffed cabbage, potato dumplings, a nice goulash option, roast duck with applesauce, a big latke thing stuffed with mushrooms, and a mysterious and delightful 'city chicken,' which is actually veal on a stick," cubed, breaded, fried, braised.

"Now, I've heard of people substituting chicken for other more expensive meats, but the Rust Belt classic, the so-called city chicken, is a rare example of things being the other way around. Apparently it emerged in the 1930s—back then, beef, pork, and veal weren't as expensive as the relatively luxurious chicken." There is also, naturally, a selection of a half-dozen vodkas and other spirits.

POLONIA, 2934 Yemans Street, Hamtramck, MI 48212, Tel 313 873 8432, www.polonia-restaurant.net (entrées about $10)

"Smell the blood, sweat, and tears of mortal combat: the arcane and brutal subterranean world of feather bowling. Welcome to the **Cadieux Café**. On the outside, it looks normal enough, but, like one of those anonymous warehouses in Thailand from a Jean-Claude Van Damme film, inside, it's a different story. The only place in the world where traditional feather bowling is played every day and night as well."

Feather bowling is a Belgian sport, somewhat akin to bocce, pétanque, or horseshoes, in which pucks shaped like whole cheeses are strategically hurled toward an upright feather at the end of a lane. Flemish immigrants to Michigan brought the game with them in the 1930s. After decades as a closed, league-only thing, the proprietors of Cadieux Café made the wise decision in the 1980s to open it up to public play. Savor the juxtaposition of an arcane drinking sport and a classic plate of mussels and fries, washed down with a Belgian ale.

"I mean, it makes no sense, in the most wonderful way. It's a business model that if you went to pitch to a banker—'You know, I'm thinking of opening a Belgian-themed place with feather bowling and mussels.'" Most evenings, Cadieux hosts live music or karaoke, and the leagues rule the lanes on Tuesdays and Thursdays, but at other times, the lanes are available for public play, with advance reservations strongly suggested.

CADIEUX CAFÉ: 4300 Cadieux Road, Detroit, MI 48224, Tel 313 882 8560, www.cadieuxcafe.com (mussel dinners $19.95; feather bowling $25/hour on weekdays, $50/hour on weekends)

LIVINGSTON, MONTANA

"Some people must live in great spaces, where the sky goes on forever. Where everyone must bend to the land. Where to hunt, to fish, to sleep under that big sky, aren't activities, but a way of life.

"Next time you turn off a news cycle filled with shouting bobbleheads, convinced that America is devolving into a moronic inferno, questioning the greatness of your nation: maybe you should come here. Here are your purple mountains majesty. This is the landscape that generations of dreamers, despots, adventurers, explorers, crackpots, and heroes fought and died for. It's one of the most beautiful places on earth. There is no place like it: Montana.

"Many have come to claim their piece over the years, but before the prospectors and explorers, there were the Plains Indians. The Absaroka have been master horsemen since they adopted Spanish-

introduced mustangs in the eighteenth century. Better known as the Crow, they were once part of the larger Hidatsa tribe. Centuries ago, they split off on their own and wandered, or were pushed by conflict with the Blackfeet, Cheyenne, and Dakota, until settling here in the Yellowstone River valley."

GETTING THERE AND AROUND

Montana is a vast state, the fourth-largest in the nation (but number 42 out of 50 in terms of population). Tony's travels centered on Livingston and the surrounding area; the closest airport is **Bozeman Yellowstone International Airport (BZN)**, which serves about twenty nonstop flights to US cities, concentrated in the West, on all the major US carriers. BZN is about a thirty-five-minute drive from Livingston, via rental car or commercial shuttle, of which there are a handful of options.

If you don't have your own rented vehicle, or plans with a tour operator, there are a few private taxi services in town, plenty of bike rental outfitters, and a free bus service, called Windrider, that runs a fixed route around town on weekdays from 6:30 a.m. to 6:30 p.m.

LIVING IT UP IN LIVINGSTON

"Livingston, Montana, is unique, but strangely typical for small-town America, where old guard and new mutants live together, form alliances, get along, and become indistinguishable in their weirdness. I like this place."

Beginning in the 1960s, a handful of artists and writers began to arrive and make their homes and their art in Livingston, among them the author and screenwriter Tom McGuane, the actors Margot Kidder and Jeff Bridges, the painter Russell Chatham, and the poet and author Jim Harrison.

In more recent times, the superwealthy have arrived, flush with cash to buy up parcels of ailing cattle ranches, and looking for a bucolic escape. Everyone's interests and needs intersect at the **Murray Hotel**.

"Descendants of the original cowboys, homesteaders, and railroad workers, they've all got history, at one time or another, with the Murray Hotel. Once I find in my travels a fine, eccentric old hotel, I stay loyal. I go back whenever I can. I like a hotel with a past, and the Murray Hotel has plenty of that. For over a century it's been host to a slew of the famous and the infamous—Calamity Jane and Buffalo Bill were regulars, but what I find cool is that Sam Peckinpah, director of *The Wild Bunch* and *Ride the High Country*, chose this place to hole up for some of his last, craziest months. Paranoid from prodigious amounts of cocaine and drinking like a wild man, he would occasionally shoot holes in the walls, doors, and ceilings. He was, nonetheless, a popular guy around town."

Built in 1904 and renovated in the early 1990s, the Murray is a four-story hotel with twenty-five the furnishings and interior reflective of the plac was originally called the Elite Hotel, sengers on the Northern Pacif James E. Murray, who served f construction, and assumed ov the original operator went h home base for visitors to Ye away.

"It's a great hotel, and said Tony, who logged ma

bar. Its neon entrance signs are intact, its walls lined with photo portraits of all the legendary local fly fishing experts, its seats comfortably full of regulars and visitors, and there is often live music.

The hotel's fine-dining restaurant, Second Street Bistro, opened in 2004 under chef Brian Menges, who continues to run, expand, and perfect the food service at the hotel.

"He is, without question, the best chef around," said Tony in 2009, **"and he has specifically been cultivating relationships with area farmers and producers, all in an effort to create a truly local and yet also truly excellent menu of top-flight preparations reflecting what Montana is great at. In a small kitchen, minimally staffed, out there alone on what's pretty much the cutting edge for these parts, Brian works long and hard and he does a tremendous job with relatively little. It's hard being an ambitious local chef out there on the edge, almost alone. But I guess there's a tradition of doing just that kind of thing around here since it all started."**

Menges has been known to go off-book with dishes like buffalo, elk, and chicken galantine; crisp-fried local pork rillettes; and a paupiette of braised whitefish with smoked trout and whitefish caviar, all worth trying if the opportunity arises. More in line with the restaurant's daily offerings are the lavender-crusted rack of lamb and braised beef short ribs with locally foraged morels. **"It absolutely is as good as anything anywhere on the planet."**

MURRAY HOTEL: 201 West Park Street, Livingston, MT 59047, Tel 406 222 1350, www.murrayhotel.com (rooms start at about $240 er night)

NEW JERSEY

Tony grew up in the bedroom community of Leonia, New Jersey, in a nuclear family that valued arts, culture, education, and good table manners—just the thing for him to chafe against as a rebellious youth with a taste for the more-venal pleasures of New York City, though he always retained a nostalgic soft spot for the Garden State.

"Oh, enchanted land of my childhood! A cultural petri dish from which regularly issues forth greatness.

"New Jersey, in case you didn't know it, has got beaches, beautiful beaches, and they're not all crawling 'roid-raging trolls with reality shows. I grew up summering on those beaches, and they are awesome.

"Jersey's got farmland. Beautiful bedroom communities where that woman from *Real Housewives* who looks like Doctor Zaius does not live, nor anyone like her. Even the refineries. The endless cloverleaves of turnpikes and expressways twisting in unknowable patterns over the wetlands are, to me, somehow, beautiful. To know Jersey is to love her."

ARRIVAL AND GETTING AROUND

New Jersey's only major airport is **Newark Liberty International Airport (EWR)**, located southwest of New York City, in Newark; it's connected to Manhattan by New Jersey Transit trains and buses. Amtrak trains also stop at Newark Liberty, Newark Penn Station, and a handful of other stations throughout the state. New Jersey Transit has a fairly comprehensive network of buses and trains throughout the state, but really, when you're in Jersey, you're in the heart of car culture.

HOT DOGS BY THE BRIDGE, AND SUBS DOWN THE SHORE

"Fort Lee: you may have heard of it. Some of [former] governor Chris Christie's minions allegedly conspired to jam up traffic for a few days here. It's a town with a jokey history of corruption. It's also where my beloved Hiram's is. Open since 1932 and pretty much unchanged ever since, my dad started bringing me and my younger brother, Chris, here in the 1950s, and they still honor tradition. It is a great point of pride and personal satisfaction that I've convinced my daughter that these are the finest hot dogs in the land. She gets very excited to come out here, which makes me very happy."

At Hiram's, the hot dogs are Thumann's brand, with natural casings, and are deep-fried to wonderfully snappy effect, especially when left to tear open lengthwise under the pressure of an extra-long fry time; this specialty is known as the Ripper.

"Remarkably, the great gastronomes of history have ignored both the french fry and the essentially french fried hot dog, known

as 'the Ripper,' in their writings. Their loss. Named for its characteristic lengthwise tearing, 'the Ripper' is considered by its devotees to be the very apex of the fry-o-lated arts." The compact menu also includes burgers, fries, onion rings, draft beer, and the iconic chocolate beverage known as Yoo-hoo.

HIRAM'S ROADSTAND: 1345 Palisade Avenue, Fort Lee, NJ 07024, Tel 201 592 9602, www.restaurantsnapshot.com /HiramsRoadstand (hot dogs about $4 each)

"As I always like to say, good is good forever: great music, great songs, and a classic Jersey sandwich." Nothing fits the bill better than an Italian submarine sandwich done properly, as at **Frank's Deli** In Asbury Park.

"At Frank's they honor that Jersey tradition of assertive layers of sliced ham, salami, pepperoni, provolone, with some tomato, onions, shredded lettuce. You got your roasted peppers in there and most important your oil and vinegar, which soaks into that soft, fresh-baked bread and marries it all together into a soggy, glorious delivery vehicle for deliciousness."

Note that Asbury Park is a beach boomtown between Memorial Day and Labor Day, and that Frank's is small, well established, and quite popular, so be prepared to wait, and try not to linger.

FRANK'S DELI & RESTAURANT: 1406 Main Street, Asbury Park, NJ 07712, Tel 732 775 6682, www.franksdelinj.com (sandwiches under $10)

Revisiting New Jersey with Tony

BY CHRISTOPHER BOURDAIN

In 2015, Tony told me he'd be filming a *Parts Unknown* episode focused on New Jersey, and it would include stops at some of our old childhood haunts. He asked if I'd like to join for parts of it, and before he'd even finished asking, I said yes.

On the appointed day, I met Tony in Manhattan for the drive to Long Beach Island. Tony drove, in his car. That was actually a notable thing to me, because Tony had never owned a car until about that time. I don't even think he ever got a driver license until well into his forties (although, like most of us, he learned how to drive in his late teens). This was the first time in my life that Tony was driving me around our home turf.

Tony's playlist was fully reflective of his eclectic music tastes. Somewhere on the Garden State Parkway, one song leapt out at me: "L'Amour Avec Toi," a ballad by Michel Polnareff, a French pop singer, big in the 1960s. When Tony and I traveled with our parents to France in 1966, most of the songs that we'd hear playing on jukeboxes were American: "Whiter Shade of Pale" by Procol Harum; "Strangers in the Night" by Frank Sinatra; and "These Boots Were Made for Walkin'," by Sinatra's one-hit-wonder daughter, Nancy. But we also heard "L'Amour Avec Toi." I was surprised Tony had it on his Jersey road trip playlist. I mean, our *mom* liked that song!

Arriving in Barnegat Light, the plan was for us to have lunch at one of our old summer haunts, or at least something reminiscent of that.

Now, it's possible we might have found one of our old haunts open if we'd been there in summer, but it was February. Most places were closed for the season, but Kubel's was open. It's a classic Jersey Shore place, located on the more-sheltered bay side of Barnegat Light. I vaguely remembered a restaurant being there, but couldn't promise you that Tony and I ever went there as kids. Still, it fit the bill, perfectly: a cozy local hangout with fried calamari, beer, fish and chips, burgers—that sort of thing. And it's been pleasing people for generations, which was the common thread linking most of the places featured on the New Jersey episode.

Our family rented a few different places in Barnegat Light in the 1960s and 1970s, typically one-floor units in two-unit houses on the ocean side, usually for two weeks, sometimes four. We weren't wealthy: it was just a more affordable place back then. Our dad had only two weeks of vacation each year, so in years we had a place for a month, he would stay two weeks, and then take the bus down from New York the other two weekends.

Things we loved: the old-fashioned Surf City five-and-dime store, with its colorful cacophony (and unforgettable smell) of sand toys and inflatable plastic beach balls and floating mattresses, tubes, and rafts. Miniature golf. The outdoor trampoline play center called Tumble Town (a near impossibility to contemplate in today's age of hyperprotective parents and aggressive litigators). Barbecuing on the deck in the ocean air. Daily access to soft ice cream cones.

And: Hanging out in the dark, on the beach, at night. This was just cool, and sometimes spooky, with shadowy figures always drifting around in the darkness. Packs of us kids would just be out there, sometimes for hours. And somebody always managed to have sparklers (which were legal) and firecrackers and bottle rockets (which were illegal, but procured by somebody, somehow, in Manhattan's Chinatown or one of the Carolinas). To this day, I still love setting off fireworks on the beach at night.

Barnegat Light has numbered streets, and we usually rented in the 20 blocks. So there we were in 2015, with a camera operator and a sound setup in Tony's car, driving around to see if we could find some of the places we remembered.

But things around Barnegat Light had changed—a lot—with small cottages and modest houses replaced by bigger, more showy houses. This was driven, no doubt, by the rising tide of wealthier visitors, and high-spending packs of young adult renters. Add in the swath of destruction created by "superstorm" Sandy in 2012 and the attendant reconstruction, and the place was barely recognizable.

We moved on to Atlantic City.

Our parents took us to Atlantic City for a couple of brief visits as kids. I have only a few spotty, photo-like memories of those times. I liked the vast boardwalk, the arcades, the amusement rides on the pier, and the arena-size landmark Captain Starn's seafood restaurant. On one visit, we stayed at the historic Marlborough-Blenheim Hotel. It was the first hotel I'd seen with an indoor pool, which I thought was awesome. Built before 1910, with exaggerated Spanish and Moorish design elements, it was at one time the largest reinforced concrete building ever built, and in its heyday, it drew prominent politicians, Hollywood stars, etc. Like most of its cohorts, however, it was demolished, in 1978.

I had a great time with my brother, but the tail end, in Atlantic City, was depressing to me. This was once a world-famous seaside mecca, but it had been sliding into decay for decades.

The hope, peddled in the 1970s, of new wealth and jobs for locals from legalized casinos fell far short of what was promised, even in the brightest of the early years. Casino developers built a Berlin Wall–like battery of monolithic, windowless buildings that basically cut off the Atlantic from its namesake city. Most of them did OK, for a time, but later went bust. By the time of our 2015 visit, most of the boardwalk casinos were closed and empty, with a former Trump casino standing out as one of the most garish, hulking failures. Instead of the promised rebirth, Atlantic City looked to be facing a re-death.

Sadly, I was traveling for business the day they filmed at the New Jersey venue most personally sacred to me: Hiram's Roadstand in Fort Lee, a lifelong happy place.

Tony and I enjoyed countless visits to Hiram's as kids in the adjacent town of Leonia. When our mom didn't feel like cooking, Hiram's was on the short list of places we would go for dinner.

In business since 1932, Hiram's is one of many classic roadside food establishments that arrived on the heels of the 1931 opening of the George Washington Bridge, an event that uncorked the first generation of car-driving vacationers and day-trippers from New York. In the case of Hiram's, its convenient location, near the already-decades-old Palisades Amusement Park (which inspired Freddy Cannon's catchy 1962 radio hit "Palisades Park"), was a key part of its success.

Many other roadside attractions in the region, including Callahan's, a long-standing next-door rival of Hiram's, and Red Apple Rest on Route 17, halfway to the Catskills, are long gone, displaced by change or real estate markets or by the interstate highway system that cast many of them into irrelevance. Palisades Amusement Park itself, which drew hordes of visitors to Fort Lee for decades, closed in 1971, to be replaced by a set of large apartment buildings.

But Hiram's is still there. Bless them. They have resisted fads for generations. It's all about wonderful basic hamburgers and their famous (and fabulous) crackly-skinned deep-fried hot dogs. And fries, or onion rings, or both. Everything comes on paper plates, in a little foldable cardboard serving box.

As far as I can tell, Hiram's has never tested new menu items like Cajun buffalo wings or bacon salsa burgers or pricey yogurt smoothies. No kale or acai berries here. The menu is basic, and eternal.

The building is pretty much the way it's always been, too: enclosed sidewalk counter in front, small dive bar–ish (but family friendly!) dining room to the side. And the kitchen, where God's work goes on in front of you. Hiram's had an open kitchen long before it was cool!

And last: that scary gas station–style rest room, which is to say, outside, around the back. Why mess up a little piece of 1930s perfection?

NEW YORK CITY

How to narrow down the best of New York City, a place where Tony lived and worked his entire adult life? He visited Chinatown with his family as a child; worked as a Manhattan bike messenger as a teen; picked up cooking shifts in the city as culinary student; and settled in to New York for the next four decades to play out a boom-bust-boom career of cooking, writing, and making TV, leaving with increasing frequency and duration in the last fifteen or so years, but always returning home to one side of Manhattan or another.

In all, Tony and his Zero Point Zero colleagues made eight dedicated New York episodes. What follow are the places he loved returning to, with and without cameras. You'll notice a slight emphasis on what he called "Dinosaural New York": beloved institutions that provided a through line between the old days and the new—and a few newer places that felt, to him, like instant classics.

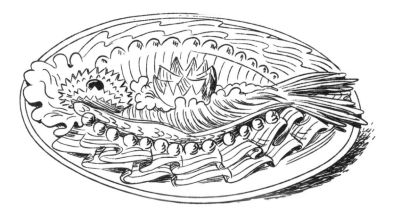

"Even in the ruins of late 1960s and early 1970s New York, there was plenty of evidence of an earlier, somehow nobler culture; places that remained windows into days gone by, that were worth holding on to, even though they were surely anachronisms. What they serve is in no way fashionable, in some cases to the point of craziness, but they're worth cherishing just the same."

ARRIVAL, DEPARTURE, AND GETTING AROUND

New York has three major airports: the massive, busy **John F. Kennedy International Airport (JFK)**, in the southeastern section of the borough of Queens; the smaller, scrappier **La Guardia Airport (LGA)**, also in Queens, on Flushing and Bowery Bays; and **Newark Liberty International Airport (EWR)**, southwest of New York City, in Newark, New Jersey. JFK and Newark are connected to the city via air train links, and there are public and private bus options to get passengers between the city and each of the three airports, in addition to the usual array of taxis and car services. See www.mta.info for JFK AirTrain info, and www.njtransit.com for Newark info.

"They all pretty much suck, and it's a pain in the ass compared with a lot of other cities getting to and from them on anything resembling mass transportation. The smartest way to go, my opinion, especially if you have luggage, is to look for signs for ground transportation, get on the taxi line, and take a yellow cab."

Traffic, of course, is always the limiting factor, and it's wise to be aware of projected travel times, ongoing construction, and other obstacles between you and your flight.

New York also has two major train stations: the magnificent Beaux Arts **Grand Central Terminal**, on Manhattan's east side, which serves as the southern terminus for Metro -North, a commuter rail line that reaches into the metro areas of southern New York State and Connecticut; and, on the west side, the decidedly unlovely **Pennsylvania Station**, which serves as the New York hub for Amtrak, the Long Island Railroad, and New Jersey Transit, in addition to several subway lines. It is also the home of the sporting and entertainment arena **Madison Square Garden.** Those arriving and departing New York City by bus may do so via the legendarily grim (but really not so terrible) **Port Authority Bus Terminal**, which serves riders on Greyhound, New Jersey Transit, and several regional carriers.

Though he seldom used it, even in his leaner days as a working chef, Tony was, in theory, a fan of the New York City subway system, run by the Metropolitan Transportation Authority (MTA). **"It runs on a pretty easy-to-navigate grid system, like our streets, and it's cheap. One fare will get you just about anywhere in the five boroughs, plus a free transfer is included in the fare."** The same applies to most city buses, though there are a few select express lines that require the purchase of a separate ticket, from a kiosk located at the bus stop.

LOWER MANHATTAN

"The Lower East Side was, in many ways, the cradle of New York— where new arrivals first settled, built communities, and later, moved on, only to be replaced by others. In the New York City of the 1970s, nearly bankrupt, riddled with corruption, the Lower East Side, particularly Alphabet City, was left to fend for itself. Huge swaths of it were abandoned, ruined, or simply empty. Much of it became an open-air supermarket for drugs. Whole blocks taken over by organized drug gangs. Rents were cheap, and the neighborhood started to attract a newer, highly energized, and creative group of people

who wanted to make things: music, poetry, movies, and art. It seemed, at the time, everybody was a star, and for a while at least, that it was a golden time. But it was dangerous: you live down here, you have to be tough, and talented, and often very quick. Now, things are different. Very different.

"From the beginning and straight through since, **Russ & Daughters** is a shop specializing in smoked and cured fish, a direct descendant of the pushcarts, a type of appetizing store—a tradition that grew up alongside delicatessens in the 1800s, but which never really caught on outside New York. These guys are like the last buffalo. Mark Russ's grandfather started the business, catering to the oldest and most humble of Old World tastes. There's still the same personal service you had back in the day, when it was still a neighborhood. You get a taste on paper. Hopefully, you buy. Scratch that, once you taste, you definitely buy."

Note: "One hundred years ago, the surrounding neighborhood was mostly Jewish, and almost entirely poor. Like so much of what's good, what we used to have to eat 'cause it was cheap is now upwards of forty bucks a pound."

In 2014, a century after the business began, Russ & Daughters opened a café on Orchard Street, a few blocks from the storefront, so that patrons could sit and linger over a platter of smoked fish or caviar, with a salad or soup and a glass of wine or a cocktail.

RUSS & DAUGHTERS: 179 East Houston Street, New York, NY 10002, Tel 212 475 4880, www.russanddaughters.com (prices vary)

"**Katz's Delicatessen,** that most quintessential of New York establishments, remains defiantly the same. The price of admission is only that you love New York, and that you like pastrami.

"New Yorkers tend to roll their eyes a little when outsiders gush about the place, but you need only to walk over to the counter, take a long, lingering look at that heap of steaming pastrami, corned beef, and brisket, take a deep breath, and you remember again what it means to be alive, to be proud, to be a New Yorker."

Tony's go-to order? "Pastrami on rye. Hand-sliced pastrami—it's so tender, a machine would turn it to mush—[in] thick slices; a mix of fat and lean. It must be put on rye bread, warm, fresh, and with a generous schmear of brown mustard. And of course, you gotta have some sour pickles and a cream soda."

KATZ'S DELICATESSEN: 205 East Houston Street, New York, NY 10002, Tel 212 254 2246, www.katzdelicatessen.com (pastrami sandwich $23)

Undeniably low key from the outside, yet something of a sleeper haven for popular musicians and actors, **Emilio's Ballato** is a classic Italian American restaurant that's operated unassumingly since 1956 on East Houston Street. Current owner and chef Emilio Vitolo has been the man in charge, often set up at a table by the door, since 1992. Sensitive Yelpers and their ilk have complained about the clubby vibe, but why not enter with confidence and take your chances? Plenty of downtown Italian relics still serve the likes of unreconstructed *cacio e pepe* or veal parmesan with a side of spaghetti, but Emilio's does it particularly well.

EMILIO'S BALLATO: 55 East Houston Street, New York, NY 10012, Tel 212 274 8881 (no website) (typical meal about $50/person)

"For a kid growing up in New Jersey, my family's regular trips into Chinatown were thrilling adventures. It was an exotic wonderland full of dragons, fortune-telling chickens, and Skee-Ball. And yet, the food of that time is falling increasingly out of favor. People slowly became aware that there are, in fact, various regions within China and that just maybe this isn't what real Cantonese food is like after all. We grew more sophisticated and discovered more authentic dishes, but I think maybe we lost something. And I miss that old stuff—places like **Hop Kee** still feature the never-ending teapot, the egg rolls, and certain other classics of that day." Tony's go-to order, imprinted during childhood, included wonton soup, egg rolls, barbecued spare ribs, pork fried rice, and sweet and sour pork.

"My family might, at first, not have known that there were worlds, delicious worlds beyond what we knew. It seems silly and postironic now to look back fondly, but those were happy times, when all this was bright and new."

HOP KEE: 21 Mott Street, New York, NY 10013, Tel 212 964 8365, www.hop-kee-nyc.com (typical meal about $25/person)

MIDTOWN MANHATTAN

"Thank God for **Esposito's Pork Store**. One of the last of the really great butcher shops, as far as I'm concerned. And, you know, when I lived upstairs a few doors down, this for me was a perfect breakfast: calf's foot, honeycomb tripe, the nice smoked pig's tails right in the window." Officially known as Esposito Meat Market, the retailer was established in 1932 and now, in its original location, is under the stewardship of Teddy Esposito, representing the third generation of family butchers.

ESPOSITO MEAT MARKET: 500 Ninth Avenue, New York, NY 10018, Tel 212 279 3298, www.espositomeatmarket.com (prices vary)

It hardly seems in danger of extinction, but **Keens Steakhouse** is one of the last of its kind thriving in Manhattan, serving the kinds of simple old pleasures that have been around for decades.

"It seems nowadays that every celeb chef, restaurant group, hot-shot operator, or TGI McGrilly's is trying to get in on the steak house act—but they can't do this, not really. If you want the real New York–style steak house, it helps to actually do it in New York. And you really can't do any better or more authentic than Keens, a place that goes right back to the old-school, all-male world of beefsteak parties, of political power built around beef and bloody aprons and smoke-filled rooms. At Keens, it's all about the meat and a few other untouchable, unimprovable elements: jumbo shrimp cocktail—and they'd better be jumbo, big boy, and with horseradish cocktail sauce, too; I don't want no wasabi mayo. Meat, of course, either lamb or mutton chops, steak, or a mammoth slab of bleeding roast beef, to be accompanied only, but only, by creamed spinach, and maybe some hash browns." The service is convivial and professional, the bar long on whisky and red wine, and the key lime pie an excellent way to end the night.

KEENS STEAKHOUSE: 72 West 36th Street, New York, NY 10018, Tel 212 947 3636, www.keens.com (typical meal about $100/person)

Often cheaper, and certainly more sanitary and delicious than a "dirty water" tube steak from a Manhattan street cart, is a hot dog from **Gray's Papaya**. "This is *the* New York institution for late-night chefs and local wanderers alike. It's my second home. The classic New Yorker's poor-man meal: meat, starch, and veg, all in a few mouthfuls. That particularly New York smell of hot dogs seared on tin foil, sauerkraut, and the foamy deliciousness of a nutritious papaya drink. Man, when I start missing New York, this is what I miss." In recent years, branches of Gray's and similarly named hot dog shops have fallen victim to rising Manhattan rents, but there are still thriving locations on the Upper West Side and in Times Square close to Port Authority. Both locations are open twenty-four hours.

GRAY'S PAPAYA: 2090 Broadway, New York, NY 10023, Tel 212 799 0243, and 612 8th Avenue, New York, NY 10018, Tel 212 302 0462, www.grayspapaya.nyc (loaded hot dog and drink about $7)

"It's a remnant of another era," Tony told *Food & Wine* magazine, about **The Distinguished Wakamba Cocktail Lounge**, whose name is a bit of a bait and switch. "There's no mixologist behind the bar. If you were to order a drink with more than two components, you'd get the dirty look." You can't help but love the unreconstructed tiki decor, or the "ultracheese kitsch with an element of danger. I believe people have died there."

THE DISTINGUISHED WAKAMBA COCKAIL LOUNGE:
543 Eighth Avenue, New York, NY 10018, Tel 212 564 2042 (beer $4–$5, cocktails $8–$10)

UPTOWN MANHATTAN

"A black hole in the universe, a portal to another dimension." This is the preserved-in-amber, oldest of the old-school French fine-dining dinosaurs, **Le Veau d'Or**. "Hiding behind a modest facade and some temporary scaffolding, it's a time warp back to France. But not just France: France of the 1930s and 1940s. Inside, the paintings, the woodwork, the waiters in tuxedoes, it's sixty years ago. It defies fashion, time, logic, and reason gloriously. The menu is a journey through the past. Through dishes that were old even when I was a kid."

Tony was making loving, nostalgic reference to such French classics as celery remoulade, *saucisson chaud en croute*, *pâté du chef*, *poussin en cocotte*, and peach melba. "I'm so happy. It's fantastic. Life is good again. Order has been restored to the universe."

In 2019, veteran chef-operators Riad Nasr and Lee Hanson announced that they had purchased and would revamp Le Veau d'Or, promising to maintain the essential DNA of the classic menu (including frogs' legs, snails, and tripe) and service while making necessary upgrades to the physical space. As of this writing, renovations are underway.

LE VEAU D'OR: 129 East 60th Street, New York, NY 10022, Tel 212 838 8133 (moderate to expensive; prices in the renovated restaurant yet to be determined)

Tony never took a TV crew into **Pastrami Queen**, an Upper East Side kosher deli in the vein of Katz's, but he loved it just the same, and mentioned it whenever possible to local press outlets looking to find out what he liked to eat when he wasn't on the road. Early one morning in April 2016, Tony had just returned from a long overseas shoot, somewhere far from the likes of New York deli fare; he emailed me the following:

"**Can you please arrange a delivery order from PASTRAMI QUEEN to my apt.? For delivery any time before 1:00 pm? Thanks!**

1 pastrami on rye
1 lb sliced turkey
2 lbs chopped liver
1 sliced rye bread loaf
2 potato pancakes
½ lb sliced tongue
½ lb potato salad."

PASTRAMI QUEEN: 1125 Lexington Avenue, New York, NY 10075, Tel 212 734 1500, www.pastramiqueen.com (hot pastrami sandwich $20)

"Whenever I want to treat myself to the best breakfast in New York—in fact, the best breakfast in the *universe*—I go to a place in my neighborhood, well, famed for just that: the legendary **Barney Greengrass, the Sturgeon King.**" The dining room isn't particularly distinguished or comfortable, the service is best described as gruff, but for many New Yorkers, there is no finer purveyor of the quint-essential breakfast foods. If an editor did a particularly great job in stitching together footage to make an episode of *No Reservations* or *Parts Unknown*, Tony would show his appreciation by having a Barney Greengrass gift basket sent to his or her home.

"**It's been a New York institution since 1908, when over a million Jews from Eastern Europe made New York City their home. It's a problem ordering here because there's a lot of good stuff on the menu. Sturgeon is the absolute king of smoked fish. It's flaky, but firm, with a delicate, almost buttery flavor. So of course, I order the sturgeon platter.**" He was also a fan of the nova lox cooked with caramelized onions and eggs, and would often leave with a container of chopped liver, rich with schmaltz, more caramelized onions, and chopped hard-boiled eggs. Not known for his religious piety, a visit to Barney Greengrass actually moved Tony to declare, "**If God made anything better, he kept it for himself.**"

BARNEY GREENGRASS: 541 Amsterdam Avenue, New York, NY 10024, Tel 212 724 4707, www.barneygreengrass.com (eggs and lox about $20)

Though they came from very different worlds, and worked in very different parts of the culinary canon, Tony and Daniel Boulud had a long-standing friendship, collaborating or just enjoying each other's company with some great food and wine as often as their schedules allowed. For the "Food Porn" episode of *No Reservations*, much of which was shot in New York, Tony and Daniel got intimate with the charcuterie menu, developed and executed with the guidance of master charcutier Gilles Virot, at **Bar Boulud.**

"The old masters, the chefs of yore, of France in the eighteenth and nineteenth centuries, they knew. They knew what to do with the slivers and bits of many wild beasts; that's where good charcuterie comes from. Layered and shaped and garnished and chilled, wrapped in delicate pastries, studded with truffles and garnished with diamonds of clearest aspic, this is food for the gods. At this level, a near-forgotten art.

"For me, the culmination of the charcutier's art, the single most outrageously anachronistic blast from a past that few alive even remember, is *tourte de gibier.* It's a supremely over-the-top version of *pâté en croute*, a layering of distinct-tasting pheasant, wild boar, wood pigeon, elk, and foie gras, nestled inside a perfect pastry crust, and separated and protected from the cruel forces of the outside world by a thin layer of golden natural aspic.

"A house specialty here is the obscenely good boudin noir, one of the very best things on earth. A dish so ancient and primeval you can taste the whole history of pleasure in every bite. Deep, dark, and gorgeous. Soft, yet slightly resilient at first, you cut and it gushes across your plate. Blood and onion and spice, sublime yet somehow ever-so-slightly evil.

"Finally, *fromage de tete*, or head cheese: bits of cheek, tongue, ear, a mélange of flavors and textures so bright and alive."

Reflecting on that lunch and his memories of Tony, Boulud elaborated: "So, the *fromage de tête*—what's beautiful is the complexity you get out of one part of the pig, which is really the head: the nose, the ears, the cheeks, the tongue, and all the gelatinous meat of the sides of the cheeks. It's cooked on the bone, directly on the skull; that's the beauty and the delicious part of it, to me. And for Tony, I think, anything we could cook on the skull, it was a good thing."

BAR BOULUD: 1900 Broadway, New York, NY 10023, Tel 212 595 0303, www.barboulud.com (appetizers about $21, entrées about $33)

"You know what's good? Books. I'm not ashamed to say it. I read. And not only do I read, I kinda collect books, on matters to do with food and cooking. Big surprise there, right? On the Upper East Side of Manhattan, we happen to have a particularly wonderful bookstore called **Kitchen Arts & Letters.** And they have one of the best, if not the best, selections of rare and hard-to-get books on all things food." Visitors should note that the store also carries the best current releases and periodicals, and is presided over by a small and supremely passionate staff, headed by managing partner Matt Sartwell.

KITCHEN ARTS AND LETTERS: 1435 Lexington Avenue, New York, NY 10128, Tel 212 876 5550, www.kitchenartsandletters.com (prices vary)

THE OUTER BOROUGHS

"I've lived, I think, a pretty full and rich life. I never denied myself anything. I've seen the world, done a lot of things. But my own city, it appears, my home that I claim to be so proud of, it remains, if I'm going to be perfectly honest, a mystery. I know nothing. It's kind of ironic that I've been all over the world and that I probably know Singapore, for instance, better than I know the outer boroughs of my own city. I'm talking about the boroughs of Queens, the Bronx, Staten Island, and Brooklyn, for God's sake. I know them not.

"It becomes clearer every day that on the subject of my own town, of New York freakin' City, the culinary capital of America, I've missed the boat, train done gone, parades gone by, the bus has left without me. Too late now. But, at least I can take a few desultory apologetic bites, stick a knife right into the wound, remind myself what I've been missing, what could've been. Hopefully, it's not too late for you."

QUEENS

"Making a Queens joke these days says more about the teller than the subject. Because it's Queens—if you're looking for sheer volume, the big mix—where the real action is.

"Masterfully hand-pulled noodles, lamb meat, all swimming in a milky broth which is complimented by fragrant vegetables and herbs such as cilantro, lily buds, Chinese wolf berries, and black tree fungus. A little spice brings all these ingredients together." The original location of **Xi'an Famous Foods**, a two-hundred-square-foot

basement stall in Flushing, Queens's Golden Shopping Mall, has since closed, but there is a new, larger location a block away, in addition to several outposts in Manhattan, Queens, and Brooklyn. Jason Wang, whose father, David Shi, started the business after working the East Coast Chinese restaurant circuit for a decade, went into business with his father shortly after graduating from college, having, as he did, a vision for scaling up a business that was rapidly gaining traction after Tony's visit.

Wang noted, for this book, "As for the signature dishes: they are inspired by Xi'an or Shaanxi Province's cuisine, but it's our family's take on it. The food is definitely not supposed to be exactly what you'd find right off the streets in Xi'an. We've added our interpretation of the food, based on our own preferences. For example, our spicy cumin lamb noodles, and the spicy cumin lamb burgers that Tony made famous, aren't commonly found in Xi'an at all. Cumin lamb dish is common, but it's not served on noodles, or in the burger bun. Our food will either remind someone (like a Chinese immigrant from northern China) of an authentic taste of home in a foreign land. Or, it will introduce someone not from China, or even familiar with this specific cuisine at all, to a new taste profile that will break their knowledge of Chinese food."

XI'AN FAMOUS FOODS: 41-10 Main Street, Flushing, NY 11355, Tel 212 786 2068, www.xianfoods.com (noodle dishes $7–$8)

BRONX

"**This is exactly the kind of thing I thought we'd lost in New York, that one after the other faded away in the neighborhoods I lived in. And all along, all along it was there, right underfoot: a gusher of porky goodness.**" This is **188 Cuchifritos**, where you'll find "old-school **New York Puerto Rican good stuff"**: dishes like *morcilla* (blood sausage), *mofongo* (fried green plantains with garlic and pork rinds), *plátanos* (fried ripe plantains) and, of course, *cuchifritos*, deep-fried off-cuts like ears, tongue, and snout. **"What's not to like about that? This is as much the center of the pork universe as I've ever seen it in New York."**

188 CUCHIFRITOS: 158 East 188th Street, Bronx, NY 10468, Tel 718 367 4500 (no website) (typical plate about $7)

BROOKLYN

The final episode of *No Reservations* saw Tony exploring Brooklyn, **"a place right next door, a place I've never really gotten to know."** It's a sprawling, endlessly diverse borough, recent gentrification notwith-standing, and Tony ranged from one end to the other, making a stop near the sea, in Sheepshead Bay, at **"a cornerstone of red sauce Italian, Randazzo's Clam Bar."**

Born of a decades-old family business that began as a seafood market and evolved into a lively and thriving family restaurant, Randazzo's is known for the long-simmered, oregano-intensive red sauce that adorns a range of seafood and pasta preparations. **"The menu dates back to the day that you may be at a clam bar, but you have to have chicken parmesan, broiled salmon, *lobster fra diavolo* . . . You don't see that on Manhattan menus much anymore, an Italo-American mutation that's basically lobster, shrimp, mussels, clams, and a spicy marinara tossed with pasta that doesn't even remember what al dente means, served in portions that could once have fed an entire block on the Lower East Side. If you can't find it in your heart to enjoy Randazzo's, you're a lost soul."**

RANDAZZO'S CLAM BAR: 2017 Emmons Avenue, Brooklyn, NY 11235, Tel 718 615 0010, www.randazzosclambar.nyc (pastas about $20, entrées about $25)

STATEN ISLAND

"Affectionately known as 'the rock,' the borough of Staten Island has always been a mystery to me. I knew [American mob boss] Paul Castellano lived there, that's about it. Stuck out there somewhere between Brooklyn, Manhattan, and Jersey, Staten Island just never had an identity as strong as its neighbors."

They're still small in number relative to the many robust immigrant groups in New York, but the core of the city's Sri Lankan population is on Staten Island; accordingly, this is where the best Sri Lankan food is to be found.

"**New Asha** is a little slice of home for many of the island's Buddhists, Muslims, and Hindus as well as anybody who likes spicy Sri Lankan food. The main attraction being black curry goat, which is similar, I guess, to Indian curry, but made spicier and richer by pan-roasting the spices." You can also enjoy egg hoppers (bowl-shaped crepes made with a fermented rice flour batter, with a sunny-side-up egg cooked into the center), and an assortment of the highly seasoned pulses, vegetables, and coconut-based condiments at which Sri Lankan cooks excel. New Asha is a small, unassuming place, with just a few tables and casual counter-style service.

NEW ASHA: 322 Victory Boulevard, Staten Island, NY 10301, Tel 718 420 0649 (curries about $5; hoppers, $4)

"For a drink, it's only appropriate that we head over to the magnificent **Jade Island**, an absolutely untouched-by-time, unsullied-by-irony temple of tiki." Jade Island also purveys the kind of old-school Cantonese food—egg rolls, wonton soup, sweet and sour pork—that Tony grew up eating in Manhattan's Chinatown.

"I hit that Head Hunter hard—a mixed-fruit-and-rum concoction. Who cares, really, as long as it's got an umbrella in it and it's served in a head? I feel belligerent already. You know, I love this place. I'd be a better man, and a better human being, if I had this in my neighborhood."

JADE ISLAND: 2845 Richmond Avenue, Staten Island, NY 10314, Tel 718 761 8080, www.jadeislandstaten.com (typical meal about $14)

PORTLAND, OREGON

Tony was drawn to the pioneering spirit of the Pacific Northwest— the way that geographic isolation, a history of technological, artistic, and musical innovation, the gloomy weirdness of the weather, and the abundance of great seafood, produce, wines, and (legalized) weed combined to make something far greater than the sum of its parts.

"Portland: kind of a libertarian government here. Lovely city, only 650,000 people, most of whom seem to be cooks or foodies. But it's not all artisanal cheese, really good organic products raised by hippies. Oh no, my friends, there is a dark side to Portland."

ARRIVAL AND GETTING AROUND

Portland International Airport (PDX) serves flights from around the United States, along with flights to and from Canada, Mexico, Western Europe, and Japan. As befits the city's reputation for indie quirk, the airport is home to a microcinema that showcases the work of local filmmakers, a place to get your bike repaired, and a retail tasting room, the first of its kind in a US airport, for House Spirits Distillery, which makes whisky and other hard stuff.

To get from PDX to the city proper, you can take the light rail, called MAX Red Line, which costs $2.50 per ride and takes about forty minutes. (See www.trimet.org for complete information about the city's light rail, bus, and commuter rail systems.) Taxis are also available, for about $35 plus tip; the ride takes twenty to forty minutes, depending on traffic and destination.

Three Amtrak trains—the Cascades and Coast Starlight, which run north–south, and the Empire Builder, running east–west between Chicago and the Northwest, make stops in Portland, at Union Station. (See www.amtrak.com for details.) Located in the city's downtown area, close to the western bank of the Wiliamette River, Union Station was built in 1896 and is distinguished by a neon sign inviting passersby to "Go By Train."

Portland is a bike-friendly city, with lots of dedicated lanes, paths, and trails, and an independent, reasonably priced bike share system called Biketown—see www.biketownpdx.com for details.

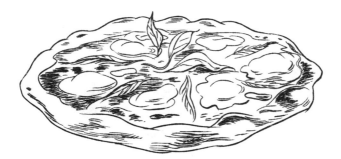

SLEEP AT THE HAUNTED HEATHMAN

"At first glance, the **Heathman Hotel** is a stylish yet warm, comfortingly luxurious lodging. Lush teakwood, crystal chandeliers, art by Andy Warhol—but closer inspection reveals a grisly and violent backstory, an evil history of tragedy, death, and possible haunting." According to local lore, a guest leapt from the hotel's eighth floor sometime in the 1930s, supposedly haunting every room he passed during his rapid descent, which is to say, those that end in "03." There have been reports of furniture and belongings being rearranged with no clear explanation, or glasses of water disappearing, and prescription drugs going missing.

Supernatural rumors (or disgruntled staff) aside, the Heathman is a grand hotel, built in 1927, with generous proportions in its guest rooms and public spaces, excellent service, and great on-site restaurant, Headwaters, helmed by chef Vitaly Paley and his wife, Kimberly. The Heathman is located within walking distance of the Portland Art Museum and next door to Arlene Schnitzer Concert Hall.

HEATHMAN HOTEL, 1001 SW Broadway, Portland, OR 97205, Tel 503 241 4100, www.heathmanhotel.com (rooms start at about $150 per night)

"Obsession can be a strange and sometimes beautiful thing. Some people collect glass eggs, others gather nail clippings and dead skin so they can build a dream woman in their cellar. Others make pizza.

"Welcome to Portland's **Apizza Scholls**. In a community that is already a showcase for artisanal foods, this place demonstrates a particular ferocious dedication to getting it right. And owner Brian Spangler is the reason why." Spangler's deep dedication to understanding and perfecting the art of fermentation, along with his rules that limit the number of toppings on any given pizza, and the excellent quality of his product, won him Tony's respect and admiration.

Spangler explained the "no more than three toppings" rule to Tony during his 2008 visit for *No Reservations*.

"Pizza's about the balance," he said, "crust with sauce, and the cheese, and keeping that in balance is the mark of someone who really knows their craft. We make our dough one hundred percent by hand—there is no mixer—in order to get the texture: not only some pull, but also some crackle. There's something so simple yet so elusive about it."

Upon tasting the end product, Tony said, **"The moment of truth . . . Oh yeah! This is New York pizza. This is really, really good, high-end New York pizza. I mean, that's what he wanted to do; that's what he's doing obsessively, though I don't know *anyone* in New York who mixes their dough by hand. I mean, that's nuts, that's obsessive, that's crazy good."**

APIZZA SCHOLLS, 4741 SE Hawthorne Boulevard, Portland, OR 97215, Tel 503 233 1286, www.apizzascholls.com (antipasti and salads, $11–$14; 18-inch pizzas about $25 each)

"**The exotic delights of Voodoo Doughnut. Cap'n Crunch with Crunchberries? Wait a minute, and those are Froot Loops! Is that bacon on top of that? It's a doughnut and bacon. Together!**

"**Kenneth 'Cat Daddy' Pogson and partner Richard 'Tres' Shannon have joined a perversely anarchistic world view with one of America's favorite snack foods! Arise, ye nonconformist doughnuts!**" What was, during Tony's 2008 visit, a single-store operation, Voodoo Doughnut has now expanded into eight locations (and counting) in Oregon, California, Colorado, Texas, and Florida. The weirdo ethos of the original store remains intact, with the Portland, Colorado, and Texas locations open 24/7, and such signature items as the

Old Dirty Bastard (a raised yeast doughnut with chocolate frosting, Oreo cookies, and peanut butter) and Tangfastic (a vanilla-frosted cake doughnut dusted with Tang drink mix and studded with marsh-mallows) attracting long lines of hungry customers at every location.

VOODOO DOUGHNUT, 22 SW 3rd Avenue, Portland, OR 97204, Tel 503 241 4704, www.voodoodoughnut.com (doughnuts $0.95 and up, depending on size and toppings)

PHILADELPHIA, PENNSYLVANIA

It wasn't until the second season of *The Layover*, in 2012, that Tony, after more than a decade of making travel TV, found his way to Philadelphia with a camera crew, an omission that hadn't gone unnoticed.

"So, Philadelphia, the 'City of Brotherly Love': We're going to try to avoid all of that bullshit. There will be no cheesesteaks. Philadelphia has long since moved past that, too. Nothing against the cheesesteak, mind you, I like 'em fine, but things have changed a lot.

"My relationship with Philadelphia has always been . . . let's call it complex. For a while, it was getting to the point that when I passed through on book tour people would say, 'Hey, you should come to Philly and do a show,' which quickly became, 'How come you haven't done a show in Philly?' which just as quickly became, 'Fuck you. We don't need you anyway.' It's like that here. And oddly enough, I find that attitude kinda charming."

ARRIVAL AND GETTING AROUND

Philadelphia International Airport (**PHL**) is roughly seven miles south of the city center, and is serviced by all the major carriers. To get to the city, you can take the municipal SEPTA train (see www.septa.org), which takes about twenty-five minutes and costs $8, or a metered taxicab, which will take twenty to thirty minutes and cost about $30, plus tip.

Once you're in town, Tony advised, "**Philadelphia is pretty walkable, so you don't really need a car. In fact, parking is painful around here, so don't rent a car if you can avoid it. Public transport is pretty decent.**"

As for accommodations, Philadelphia can be an expensive hotel stay, on par with New York or DC, though there are some bargain chain options in and around Center City. Having only a few days in town, and the corporate dollar in his pocket, Tony, ever the luxury hotel fan, suggested:

"**The Rittenhouse Hotel at Rittenhouse Square is an old-school grand hotel—luxury, at luxury prices.**" The pet-friendly hotel has an on-site pool and spa, complimentary shoe shine service, on-call

drivers who will ferry you around town in a Jaguar, twenty-four-hour room service and concierge, four restaurants, a hair salon, and a florist.

RITTENHOUSE HOTEL, 210 West Rittenhouse Square, Philadelphia, PA 19103, Tel 215 732 3364, www.rittenhousehotel.com (rooms start at about $400 per night)

Note that the **Four Seasons** in Logan Square, where Tony stayed for *The Layover* (**"I'm staying at the Four Seasons, because that's the way I roll, and the service here is impeccable"**) closed in 2015; as of this writing, its replacement, at the Comcast Center, has just opened, and is, by all accounts, up to the brand's usual standard, with prices to match.

CHEESE, SANDWICHES, MEGACOLONS

"Italian immigrants started setting up in South Philadelphia as far back as 1884, and today, the neighborhood is still considered the beating heart of Italian American Philadelphia. This place, Di Bruno Brothers cheese shop, on Ninth Street, is a family-owned storefront that's been around since 1939. The owner, Emilio Mignucci, grew up on this street.

"I know what you're thinking: I'm going to open the door and see mozzarella, some prosciutto, some hanging provolone, and a deli counter, right? And they got that, big time. But holy crap, they have so much more—amazing soft, smelly, runny, wonderful cheeses from all over the world."

Di Bruno Brothers now has five retail locations, plus a robust online business and a wine and cheese bar, but the original Ninth Street location, tightly packed with imported specialties and flanked in the Italian market district by open-air produce vendors, butchers, fishmongers, bakeries, and more, is where it all started, and it's staffed by friendly people who really know their business.

DI BRUNO BROTHERS CHEESE SHOP: 930 South Ninth Street, Philadelphia, PA 19147, Tel 215 922 2876, www.dibruno.com (prices vary)

Next stop: a serious sandwich at **Paesano's**, crafted by owner Peter McAndrews. **"Yeah, OK, he isn't Italian, but he serves a mean sandwich here, most of them as batshit crazy as he is. The Liveracce sandwich doesn't sound good—crispy fried chicken liver, salami, gorgonzola, orange marmalade, lettuce—you know, I like all of these things, but together, I was dubious. Somehow, it works. Magnificently."**

Arrive with a healthy appetite and a few friends, and sample the Arista (roast pork, broccoli rabe, Italian peppers, and provolone), the Paesano (beef brisket with provolone, pepperoncini, and a fried egg), and the Gustaio (lamb sausage, cherry mostarda, gorgonzola, and roasted tomatoes). You're on your own to find antacids and a safe place to nap.

PAESANO'S, 148 West Girard Avenue, Philadelphia, PA 19123, Tel 267 886 9556 (sandwiches average $10)

"History: there's a lot of it here. I mean, they signed the Declaration of Independence here, the Constitution, it's home of the first White House—but I like history when there's lots of boning and killing and venereal diseases and merkins.

"Philadelphia has good museums, no doubt about it; my favorite is the Mütter Museum in West Philly, a teaching museum housing an awesome collection of medical oddities, anatomical and pathological specimens, wax models, and antique medical instruments. Good times."

To the game museum employee who accompanied him on his tour, Tony remarked, "I'm looking particularly for curiosities related to the lower intestines and bowels. . . . Oh geez, is that a butt crack? Ah, that's just awful. Syphilitic necrosis. So this is what happens to your skull, you know, when the syphilis gets really bad; it actually eats holes in your skull. Where's the fistulas, Dad? Where's the fistulas? Oh geez. Human horn. Ew, that's gotta hurt. Oh, *Herpes zoster.* Look at that! You'll never go to the Jersey shore again."

Finally, the holy grail: "The magnificent megacolon. 'At sixteen, he would go as long as a month without a movement of the bowels. His colon, at death, weighed about forty pounds.' You know, I guess the message here is food always wins in the end."

MÜTTER MUSEUM: 19 South Twenty-Second Street, Philadelphia, PA 19103, Tel 215 560 8564, www.muttermuseum.org (admission $20 for adults, $18 for seniors, $15 for children, five and under free)

PITTSBURGH, PENNSYLVANIA

"Pittsburgh is a city of neighborhoods, each with its own rites and rituals; a patchwork of cultures that took shape over a century ago. Back then, the city was a beacon of hope and possibility for people all over the world, offering the promise of work, prosperity, a new life. Pittsburgh could have been another company town gone to beautiful ruin, but something happened. The city started to pop up on lists of the most livable places in America. It became attractive to a new wave of people from elsewhere looking to reinvent themselves and make a new world."

Of course, economic transition and new ways to generate income benefit some more than others. The Hill district, once a thriving African American neighborhood, was largely leveled in the name of "re-vitalization," and is now home to a hockey arena.

"And so, we find ourselves asking the same questions we ask in other cities in transition: Are the new arrivals, new money, new ideas saving the city, or cannibalizing it? Who will live in the Pittsburgh of the future? And will there be room for the people that stayed true, stuck with it their whole lives?"

ARRIVAL AND GETTING AROUND

Pittsburgh International Airport (PIT) is serviced all by the major US carriers, and a few regional ones as well. The majority of flights are to and from US cities, but there are a few nonstops to England, Caribbean resort areas, and Canadian cities. From the airport, it's about an eighteen-mile drive to the city center, which will cost about $40 plus tip in a metered taxi, $27 by airport shuttle (see www.supershuttle .com), or $2.75 by municipal bus (see www.portauthority.org).

In town, Pittsburgh's bus and light rail systems will help you get around, though much of the compact downtown is walkable. Taxis are queued in front of the major hotels and at taxi stands around town.

OLD WORLD/NEW WORLD DINING

"Alexander Bodnar fled Hungary during the Soviet Union's crushing suppression of their revolution in 1956." Now he's in Pittsburgh, running what is essentially **"a house party with food"**: a reservations-only, BYOB supper club called **Jozsa Corner**. There's Hungarian *chicken paprikash*, *langos* (leavened, deep-fried potato bread) and kielbasa, served family style. Between the singing, dancing, and storytelling, you're likely to be friends with strangers by the end of the evening.

JOZSA CORNER: 4800 Second Avenue, Pittsburgh, PA 15207, Tel 412 422 1886, www.jozsacorner.com (multicourse family-style meal is about $28 per person, cash only)

A month out from its 2017 opening, Tony sat down in the dining room of **Superior Motors** in Braddock, Pennsylvania, an eastern Pittsburgh suburb, with then-mayor John Fetterman who, with his six-foot-eight football player's frame, shaved head, goatee, tattoos, and casual clothes, **does not look like your typical mayor; and he isn't. He came to Braddock in 2001 to help at-risk youth get their GEDs, and ran for office here in one of the most depressed towns in the state four years later."** His wife, Gisele Fetterman, runs a nonprofit that provides food and essential supplies to over one thousand local families every month.

Superior Motors is now up and running, so to speak, with chef-owner, Kevin Sousa, serving dishes like walleye pike from nearby Lake Erie, and short ribs with blanched milkweed and sunchoke chips, a dish that Tony declared **"fucking awesome."** Superior Motors was the first restaurant of any type to operate in Braddock since the local hospital's café closed in 2010; chef Kevin Sousa offers a deep discount to local residents, and has plans to develop a cooking school for the community.

SUPERIOR MOTORS: 1211 Braddock Avenue, Braddock, PA 15104, Tel 412 271 1022, www.superiormotors.com (average entrée $27)

And, finally, some good old-fashioned fun: the **New Alexandria Lions Club Crash-a-Rama.** "**If you head east thirty miles from Pittsburgh, you will find yourself here, in New Alexandria. It's a whole other world, no tech incubators here, or fears of gentrification, just good, heartland fun on a Friday night. Family, fried dough, and demolition.**"

Organized by the local Lions Club chapter, this demolition derby raises funds for local charities. "**The winner gets $900. All over western Pennsylvania, from small towns like this, to the largest city—Pittsburgh—people face the same struggles as beleaguered, deindustrialized areas across the country: How do you move into the future and hold on to what you love about the past? There are probably no easy answers. Things will change; they are changing. But for now, let's just wreck some cars.**"

NEW ALEXANDRIA LIONS CLUB CRASH-A-RAMA: 1874 Lions Club Road, New Alexandria, PA 15670, www.newalexandrialions .com/demolition-derbies.html

CHARLESTON, SOUTH CAROLINA

"The South is not a monolith. There are pockets of weirdness, awesomesness, and then there's Charleston, where, for some time now, important things have been happening with food, a lot of them having to do with this guy." Meaning chef Sean Brock, who may be, if not the unofficial mayor of Charleston, at least one of its biggest ambassadors, with an impressive collection of restaurants under his command and a national platform from which to shine a light on the forgotten and disappearing foods of the American South.

"It took me a little time to discover the ferocious intellect, the inquiring nature, the uniquely focused and purposeful talent of the man—without a doubt, one of America's most important chefs. A guy who is redefining not just what southern cooking is, was, and can be, but American cooking as a whole."

ARRIVAL AND GETTING AROUND

Charleston International Airport (CHS) is the state's busiest airport, offering flights to major cities east of the Mississippi, a few Texas and Colorado locations, and a seasonal London flight. The airport is about twelve miles from downtown Charleston; taxis are metered, with a $15 base rate, and a typical ride takes about twenty minutes and will cost about $30, with tip. The Charleston Downtown shuttle is another option, costing $15, arranged via an information desk near the baggage claim area. Cheaper still is the CARTA bus, which is $2 for the ride from the airport to various downtown stops, with express and local options (www.ridecarta.com).

Once in town, use CARTA's thirteen-line bus system to get around, local taxi services, or light out on foot—it's a good-looking, friendly, walkable city.

EATING IN THE LOW COUNTRY

"What is 'down home southern cooking'? Where did it come from? Who's responsible? Well, it's always useful when asking those kinds of questions, wherever you are, to ask first, 'Who did the cooking back then, in the beginning? Where did they come from?'

"Fact of the matter is, in the old South, the dishes, flavors, and ingredients of southern cooking—which is to say American cooking, as opposed to European—chances are that food was grown, gathered, produced, and prepared by African slaves."

Mosquito Beach, on James Island, was once a welcoming place for outdoor recreation for African American families in the segregated Jim Crow South, and remains a center of culture for the Gullah Geechee people—the descendants of enslaved Africans who live in the coastal and island areas of South Carolina and Georgia. They are united by a common language, Gullah, an African creole dialect with roots in both European and African languages.

"The flavors and textures and foodways of West Africa are all over southern cooking, and there are few better places to see how short the line is between there and here than Gullah culture." At Mosquito Beach, cooks are likely to prepare meals like "soft-shell crabs and conch in a decidedly West African–inflected peanut stew, with Carolina rice, sautéed squash, and zucchini."

Mosquito Beach had once been the site of a plantation; it was parceled and sold to the families of freed slaves during Reconstruction.

"When you meet people here, you know that you're seeing a direct descendant of a slave that was here after the slaves were freed," said Ashley Greene, whose mother's family has owned land on Mosquito Beach for generations. Gullah cuisine is characterized by the use of fresh seafood, rice, local vegetables, and fruits, and African imports like yams, sesame or benne seeds, okra, peanuts, and sorghum. "I think what happens is, you change the location of the people, but you do not change who the people were," said Greene. "You did not change the information that they came with, with their traditions."

Joining Tony and Ashley was chef B. J. Dennis, who, as Tony noted, **"has made it a personal mission to celebrate and protect the culinary traditions his ancestors passed down to him."** In planning this book, Tony wanted to find some places in or near Charleston where the general public could experience Gullah cooking, and Dennis recommended two restaurants.

"I appreciate **Buckshot's** because they don't take shortcuts," Dennis said. "They keep true to the local flavors, and they use fresh local seafood. They do crab rice, an okra rice, and an okra soup, which is a classic Low Country dish. In season you'll get local turnips, greens, zucchini, squash—they do a good job in that sense."

Dennis also likes **Hannibal's Kitchen**, in downtown Charleston, for its Low Country breakfast, popular with port workers. "You know, that hearty breakfast, that classic worker breakfast that gets you through the day, that's your main meal. Grits with fried shark—the small shark that come up into the brackish water—sautéed shrimp and crab with grits, that's a very Gullah thing."

BUCKSHOT'S RESTAURANT: 9498 North Highway 17, McClellanville, SC 29458, Tel 843 887 3358 (sandwiches about $6)

HANNIBAL'S KITCHEN: 16 Blake Street, Charleston, SC 29403, Tel 843 722 2256, www.hannibalkitchen.com (sandwiches about $6, entrées $6–$9)

"Way out in the weeds, off the main road, and good freakin' luck if you can find it, is one of the most respected barbecue joints in the US of A, run by one of the most respected old-school pit masters. Ask a chef. Ask anybody who knows good barbecue, and they will

tell you where to go: here—a run-down-looking takeout, about two hours' drive out of Charleston, in Hemingway, South Carolina."

This is the original location of **Scott's Whole Hog BBQ**, an extension of Rodney Scott's family's general store that's been in operation since the 1970s.

"**Rodney Scott is a man sought after all over the world for some of the finest whole-hog barbecue there is. Rodney and his family have been doing it like this and only like this for forty-three years. Burn barrel, fresh coals, slow, slow, slow cooked all night in the pit. There are no shortcuts. This ain't a craft, this is a calling.**"

Since Tony's visit in 2015, Scott's son Dominic has assumed control of operations in Hemingway, and Rodney has opened two new locations, in Charleston proper, and Birmingham, Alabama, in partnership with restaurateur Nick Pihakis. In 2018, the James Beard Foundation named Rodney Scott best chef in the Southeast.

SCOTT'S BAR-B-QUE: 2734 Hemingway Highway, Hemingway, SC 29554, Tel 843 558 0134, www.rodneyscottsbbq.com (pork sandwich and two sides about $10.50)

WAFFLE HOUSE

"Is the **Waffle House** universally awesome? It is indeed, marvelous, an irony-free zone where everything is beautiful and nothing hurts; where everybody, regardless of race, creed, color, or degree of inebriation, is welcomed—its warm yellow glow a beacon of hope and salvation, inviting the hungry, the lost, the seriously hammered all across the South to come inside. A place of safety and nourishment. It never closes, it is always faithful, always there for you."

Sean Brock led Tony through what he called the "Waffle House tasting menu," consisting of a pecan waffle, a burger, a T-bone steak, hash browns, a patty melt, sunny-side-up eggs, and a green salad with thousand island dressing. After, Tony professed a desire to **"clamber up on the counter and start reciting Walt Whitman, the *Star-Spangled Banner*, 'Oh say can you see?' And you know what? I doubt I'd be the first."**

WAFFLE HOUSE: nearly two thousand locations throughout the southern, midwestern, and the southwestern United States, www.wafflehouse.com (waffles $3–$4, steak and eggs about $10)

AUSTIN, TEXAS

During the final season of *No Reservations*, shot in 2012, Tony and the crew touched down in Austin, for the annual South by Southwest festival.

"For a short period each year, a midsize Texas city, its strangely un-Texan capital, becomes something else: a hipster apocalypse. There's nothing to do but surrender. For six days in March, crowds descend to see more than two thousand bands play ninety-plus venues for—I don't know, you do the math—but a hell of a lot of performances."

Over the course of a week, Tony met with, fed, and attended the performances of a handful of such bands, with the notion that touring musicians don't often get to eat well.

ARRIVAL AND GETTING AROUND

Austin-Bergstrom International Airport (AUS) is the state's third-largest airport after Houston and Dallas. The majority of its flights are domestic, with a handful of flights to and from Canada, Mexico, and a few western European cities. AUS is about five miles from downtown Austin; metered taxis have a $14 minimum fare from the airport; a typical fare to a downtown hotel will be about $40, including a 15 percent tip.

Austin's Capital MetroRail line runs from the airport to downtown Austin and on into the northern suburbs; the fare is $1.25 one way, and tickets can be purchased on the platform. In town, Capitol Metro runs an extensive bus system. (See www.capmetro.org for route and fare info for rail and buses.)

Tony's preferred home base in Austin was the **Hotel Saint Cecilia**, a boutique property composed of a handful of studios, suites, and bungalows, whose restaurant is open only to guests, which gives it a sense of privacy and seclusion in the heart of the city. The main property is a Victorian mansion built in 1888 that was once home to a direct descendant of Davy Crockett. The decor, unique to each room, falls somewhere between high design, well-curated antique shop, and rich hippie with a colorful backstory. Guests may borrow guitars and bicycles; each room is outfitted with a stereo turntable, and the hotel has an LP and book lending library.

HOTEL ST. CECILIA: 112 Academy Drive, Austin, TX 78704, Tel 512 852 2400, www.hotelsaintcecilia.com (studios start at about $350/ night in low season)

"A RELIGIOUS EXPERIENCE OF BARBECUE"

"South by Southwest is a spectacle in its own right, but there's another reason to come to Austin; reason enough to slit your best friend's throat, steal a car, drive cross-country, and then wait on line outside a dreary-looking shed for upward of two hours: Franklin Barbecue. Aaron Franklin is the obsessed and obsessive legendarily perfectionist master of slow-smoked meats. What Aaron Franklin is doing at the head of this line is truly worth waiting for."

Franklin smokes his meats—beef brisket, pork ribs, pulled pork, turkey, and homemade sausages studded with beef hearts—for eighteen hours in an oak-fired smoker, seasoning everything with just salt and pepper. His service style is highly democratic, and rewards patience: customers line up in the morning, well before Franklin's opens, and are served in order. An employee is there to manage the crowd, letting people know approximately how long they should expect to wait, and whether their position in line is far back enough that they're at risk of missing out, because once the meat is sold through, that's it for the day. In addition to the meats, Franklin offers a short roster of side dishes, pies, and beer and wine.

Based in part on their experience together in Austin, Tony commissioned a travel book, *The Prophets of Smoked Meats*, from Daniel Vaughn, about the best barbecue outlets in Texas; it was the first title he published under his eponymous imprint. While they waited for their meat, Vaughn taught Tony a few key barbecue terms:

SUGAR COOKIE: the blackened edge of the meat, where fat, salt, and meat combine to create a crisp-tender area with the texture of a sugar cookie.

SMOKE RING: a visibly pink ring in the flesh that results from a chemical reaction; the temperature must be low enough, and the moisture high enough, to form the ring that indicates tender, well-cooked barbecue.

BARK: the crusty end of a rib that resembles tree bark.

"You know, the turkey and the sausage are both great," said Tony, **"but they pale in comparison to the indefinable awesomeness of the beef. The fatty end is so insanely moist and delicious. Far and away the best that I've ever had. It is a religious experience of barbecue."**

FRANKLIN BARBECUE: 900 East 11th Street, Austin, TX 78702, Tel 512 653 1187, www.franklinbbq.com (sandwiches about $10 each; meats about $22 per pound)

SEATTLE, WASHINGTON

"Seattle, a city with a collective identity, constantly in flux, always changing. But what it's always been, and continues to be, is a magnet for creators to come experiment and to make it their own. Seattle has always been a place where you can go to reinvent yourself. It's a place that, on the surface, seemed to require commitment.

"Famously gray, rainy, not particularly friendly, and all the way up there, in the far corner of the country. A place you could get work in the aircraft industry, or make music, or rather notoriously, become a serial killer. Whether outfitting prospectors during the Alaskan gold rush or looking for some kind of cred from the music scene, it's always boom or bust. Now it's a new kind of boom: Microsoft, Expedia, and Amazon are the big dogs in town. A flood of them; tech industry workers, mostly male, derisively referred to as 'tech boys' or 'tech bros' are rapidly changing the DNA of the city."

ARRIVAL AND GETTING AROUND

Seattle-Tacoma International Airport (SEA), also known as SeaTac, serves a large number of domestic and international flights; it's the main West Coast hub for Delta's trans-Pacific flights and for Alaska Airlines.

SeaTac is located in a city of the same name; it's about fourteen miles from downtown Seattle, and a taxi will cost $45–$50 plus tip, with the ride taking anywhere from twenty to sixty minutes, depending on traffic. Currently, Seattle Yellow Cab has exclusive rights to airport pickups, but in town, there are a handful of competing taxi companies.

You may also use Link light rail to get from SEA to various points in Seattle. Trains arrive every six to fifteen minutes, depending on time of day. It's a forty-minute, $3 ride from the airport to downtown; see www.soundtransit.org for complete schedule, fare, and route information.

Train enthusiasts can get to Seattle via the Amtrak Cascades train, which runs between Vancouver, British Columbia, and Eugene, Oregon, or via the Empire Builder, a northwest route that is book-ended by Chicago and Seattle. (See www.amtrak.com for details.) King Street Station, near Pioneer Square, serves Amtrak as well as various commuter train lines. A handsome and functional station with a striking clock tower, it was built in 1906 and restored in 2013.

For getting around Seattle by public transport, the smartest move is to buy an ORCA card, which will give you access to the various systems of buses, ferries, light rail, and commuter trains that connect the region. See www.orcacard.com.

EATING IN THE EMERALD CITY

Tony explored Seattle at a semifrantic pace for an episode of *The Layover* in 2012, seeking out the best of breakfast, lunch, dinner, and drinks for forty-eight hours.

"**Breakfast first, right? Seatown is one of chef Tom Douglas's empire of really good restaurants, a particularly good one, exactly the one I need right now.**" Situated on the edge of famous Pike Place Market, Seatown offers a compact menu of raw and cooked seafood, chowders, sandwiches, plates, and drinks. Tony went for the "**famous crab and egg sandwich: a fried egg sandwich with Dungeness crab,**" paired with a well-mixed Bloody Mary, the breakfast cocktail that restarts the day.

SEATOWN MARKET DINER: 2010 Western Avenue, Seattle, WA 98121, Tel 206 436 0390, www.seatownrestaurant.com (crab and egg sandwich, $20; entrées $15–$31; oysters, $40/dozen)

For his 2017 visit to Seattle for *Parts Unknown*, Tony enjoyed incisive conversation over a remarkable lunch at **Revel**. "**The chef is Rachel Yang, and the food is Korean. To eat: cilantro noodles, *yu choy*, and thinly sliced flatiron steak. Kimchi pancakes with braised pork belly and bean sprouts. Marinated short rib rice bowl with house *sambal*, daikon, kimchi, and egg. And short rib dumplings topped with pickled shallot and scallion salad.**"

REVEL: 513 Westlake Avenue North, Seattle, WA 98109, Tel 206 547 2040, www.revelseattle.com (dishes $12–$22; cocktails $10–$12)

On Washington's coast, given the interplay between the Pacific Ocean and the deep, sprawling Puget Sound, **"You have a ton of cold water that turns out some of the best freshwater fish anywhere. One of the very best places to explore the stunning variety of Pacific Northwest seafood is The Walrus and the Carpenter, an oyster bar and casual restaurant helmed by Renee Erickson."** Named for the 1872 Lewis Carroll poem, Erickson's restaurant has for over a decade been serving local oysters and surprising, skillful takes on standards, like a kale salad with albacore tuna and a mussel tartine with nori butter and pickled fennel.

"Seattle made people want stuff they didn't know they needed, and of course, we all needed. You may not know you need it, but you do.

"Tonight, I'm having steamed clams with bacon, garlic, and cannellini beans. That's perfect happiness for me. That's just delicious."

THE WALRUS AND THE CARPENTER: 4743 Ballard Avenue NW, Seattle, WA 98107, Tel 206 395 9227, www.thewalrusbar.com (plates $13–$22; typical meal about $50/person)

"Taylor Shellfish Oyster Bar in Pioneer Square is old school, too. The Taylor family has been farming more than twelve thousand acres of tidelands in Puget Sound, Willapa Bay, and the Hood Canal for over five generations, since 1890." In 2017, Tony made a visit for *Parts Unknown* and found, naturally, that **"they know what they're doing."** He was especially taken with the **"whole local smelt, flash-fried and served with pepperoncini sambal aioli; local Dungeness crab, cooked and chilled with pickled ginger sauce; and oysters, lots of oysters."**

TAYLOR SHELLFISH OYSTER BAR (Pioneer Square location): 410 Occidental Avenue South, Seattle, WA 98104, Tel 206 501 4060, www.taylorshellfishfarms.com (oysters $2.50–$3.25 each; raw and cooked dishes, soups and sandwiches, $5.50–$19)

Tony spent a few of his *Layover* hours at the fine-dining restaurant **"Canlis, a stunningly beautiful example of nonironic retro glamour. A kitchen with sixty-some years of tradition that knows how to do a proper hunk of bleeding meat. It's one of the few jackets-required dining rooms in usually dressed-down Seattle. It is swinging."** Canlis has operated in the Queen Anne neighborhood since 1950, in a stunning custom-built modern home with views of city, lake, and mountains. Brothers Brian and Mark Canlis are third-generation owners of the restaurant, whose origin story weaves in the likes of their grandfather working for Teddy Roosevelt in Egypt, helping in the aftermath of the attack on Pearl Harbor, and smuggling fresh seafood between Hawaii and the mainland. (See the restaurant's website for the entire tale.)

Chef Brady Williams presides over the kitchen, which, during Tony's visit, turned out **"artichoke tortellini, steak tartare, and Dungeness crab cake to start,"** followed by **"Muscovy duck, dry-aged for fourteen days, roasted whole, dressed with orange chutney, fennel, and cipollini onion; a Gleason Ranch monster rib eye, medium-rare; and an Iberico pork cheek with strawberry and fennel."** Current menu items include mackerel cured in kombu, huckleberry-glazed carrots with chorizo and clams, and black cod with corn velouté.

CANLIS: 2576 Aurora Avenue North, Seattle, WA 98109, Tel 206 283 3313, www.canlis.com (four-course tasting menu, $135 per person plus automatic 20 percent service charge)

WESTERN WEED

"Weed, smoke, ganja, reefer; call it what you will, it's marijuana. Oh, I can go on all day. Long story short, Washington State legalized weed in 2012. And I plan to make the most of it while scrupulously adhering to the letter of the law, like I always do. The options available in places like this, **Emerald Haze,** are mind-boggling." Tony visited Emerald Haze in 2017, to get his hands on some Blueberry Kush, Alaskan Thunderfuck, and Dutch Treat from **Hollingsworth Cannabis Company**, a true mom-and-pop operation:

"While corporate suits are rushing to cash in on the new crop, the Hollingsworth Cannabis Company is doing it a slower, but more personal way: solar-powered greenhouses, hand-trimmed buds, hand-packed bags ensuring only the finest and freshest high-quality chronic up in your ass. They're keeping it all in the family: Raft runs the manufacturing and growing, Joy does the processing and sales, Auntie came out of retirement to assist with the oil cartridges, Dad puts labels on the packaging, and Mom fills the ready-rolls and assists in quality control. As I will, and have, and will again."

EMERALD HAZE CANNABIS EMPORIUM: 4033 NE Sunset Boulevard #5, Renton, WA 98056, Tel 425 793 4293, www.emeraldhazece.com (prices vary)

HOLLINGSWORTH CANNABIS COMPANY: See www.hollingsworthcannabis.com for a list of Washington State retailers carrying their products (prices vary)

WEST VIRGINIA

A year after the election of Donald Trump to the office of president, Tony and the *Parts Unknown* crew visited West Virginia, seeking to better understand, without prejudice, what life was like in a fiercely Red state in 2017.

"It's easy to think, having lived in New York City all my life, that this is what America looks like, thinks like, that the things that are important to me are important to everybody. That every place else is . . . 'out there.' Unthinkable, maybe even unknowable.

"Six hundred miles away from Midtown Manhattan is McDowell County, West Virginia: another America." Nestled along the southern border of the state, it was once a prosperous area, powered by coal mining.

"The town of Welch, known in its glory days as 'little New York.' The rest of the country took a lot of money out of these hills over the decades. Billions and billions of dollars. And when it became cheaper or more convenient to pull the coal we needed to power our electrical grids and to make our steel elsewhere, this is what was left behind." Blocks of empty storefronts, a dwindling population, a rural town being reclaimed at the edges by nature, it's an hour's drive to the nearest Walmart.

"But do not pity the people here, who, despite what you may think, are not unrealistic about a return to the glory days of coal and better times.

"In the minds of many of my fellow New Yorkers, it's the heart of God, guns, and Trump country; the existential enemy. To think about, much less empathize with, somebody who comes from five generations of coal miners, in a place that looks like this is, to our enduring shame, unthinkable. Well, I went to West Virginia, and you know what? Here in the heart of every belief system I've ever mocked or fought against, I was welcomed with open arms by everyone. I found a place both heartbreaking and beautiful. A place that symbolizes—*contains*—everything wrong, and everything wonderful, and hopeful, about America."

ARRIVAL, GETTING AROUND, AND WHERE TO STAY

McDowell County, West Virginia, doesn't really have a local airport. The closest you'll get by commercial flight will be **Yeager Airport**

(**CRW**) in Charleston, West Virginia, a two-and-a-half-hour drive from McDowell County); **Piedmont Triad International Airport (GSO)** in Greensboro, North Carolina, a three-and-a-half-hour drive; **Charlotte Douglas International Airport (CLT)** in Charlotte, North Carolina, a four-hour drive, or **Pittsburgh International Airport (PIT)**, a five-hour drive. The nearest Amtrak train station is in Prince, West Virginia, a ninety-minute drive from Welch.

There are a handful of regional taxi services, but none in Welch, and while the app-based ride companies show some action in the area, cell service is unreliable at best. In short, you will need your own vehicle.

While in Welch, Tony stayed at the spare but clean and comfortable **Count Gilu Motel**, rare for being family-owned and operated in a region of soulless chain options. There is a garden area behind the property, a coffee maker, microwave, and refrigerator in each room, and the sounds of a nearby babbling brook to remind you, as Tony said about southern West Virginia, in an interview with the *Welch News*, **"There aren't a lot of places this beautiful left in the world, and that's something of incredible value."**

COUNT GILU MOTEL: 201 Vocational School Road, Welch, WV 24801, Tel 304 436 3041 (no website) (rooms from $80/night)

EATING THE PAST AND FUTURE IN APPALACHIA

"Appalachia has a rich and deep culinary culture that's increasingly fetishized, riffed on, and appropriated for the genteel tastes of the hipster elite willing to pay big bucks for what used to be, and still is in many cases, the food of poverty."

Through their work restoring a long-dormant family farm, proprietors Amy Dawson, a law school graduate, and chef Mike Costello, who has a degree in journalism, "are looking to keep that culture alive and appreciated, and paying off locally, for the region it originated in. They run a traveling kitchen [Lost Creek Farm] that brings local ingredients, Appalachian recipes, and the stories behind them around the state."

Dawson and Costello hope to raise enough money, and awareness, in their regional travels, to eventually open a permanent kitchen and education center on the farm. For now, they do catering, private events, workshops, and pop-ups.

An outdoor meal at their farm will feature ingredients grown, raised, and foraged hyper-locally, such as pawpaws spun into ice cream, rabbit, venison, and true heirloom vegetables grown from seeds carefully saved for generations.

"This is what heirloom looks like outside of Holy Foods: Bloody Butcher corn, Fat Horse beans, Candy Roaster squash, and Homer Fikes yellow ox heart tomatoes. These ingredients define a near-lost time and flavor."

LOST CREEK FARM: 104 Sunrise Road, Lost Creek, WV 26385 (see www.lostcreekfarmwv.com for a calendar of events and regional pop-ups)

URUGUAY

"Enticing hints of an alternate family history in Uruguay. Who are we, really?" Tony asked, as he and his brother visited the country together in the hopes of tracking down their ancestry, in 2008, for *No Reservations*; the results were mixed (see Christopher Bourdain's essay "Uruguay Dreamin'," on page 428). Tony returned several years later with *Parts Unknown*.

Uruguay was, from the 1500s till the early 1800s, a colony of Spain, with occasional incursions by the Portuguese. Much like the United States, Uruguay benefited economically from World War II, and it experienced a surge of social and political activism, centered on student movements, in the 1960s and 1970s, and this attracted some unwanted attention from those in power.

"One could say that the prospect of socialist (or, God forbid, *Communist*) movements in Latin America in the 1960s was an area of great concern for the United States and its more authoritarian-leaning allies in the region, so the emergence of the radical National Liberation Movement, known as the Tupamaros, was cause for alarm at the CIA.

"With covert and overt support by our country, a state of emergency was declared, and a right-wing dictatorship grabbed hold of the instruments of power, launching a period of repression that lasted from 1973 until 1985. Supported and often guided by CIA officers, trained in what we call, these days, 'enhanced interrogation methods,' some of the most brutal bastards in the ugliest military juntas on earth crushed minds and bodies in cells across Latin America. In the mid-1980s, the people of Uruguay had had enough. Massive demonstrations and strikes finally forced the government to hold elections, and the military was swept from power."

Of current-day Uruguay, Tony said, "It's really one of my favorite countries. Things to know about Uruguay: It's progressive. Weed is legal. Abortions are easily accessible. Gay marriage, universal health care, free education—including college. And, democracy is no joke here. Ninety-six percent of eligible Uruguayans voted in the last election."

GETTING THERE

Carrasco International Airport (MVD) Is the gateway to Montevideo and the rest of Uruguay. As of this writing, the only flights from the United States originate in Miami. There are also a few flights from Madrid and from a handful of South and Central American cities. The airport is about fifteen miles from the center of the city, a thirty- to forty-minute drive. To get to your hotel, you can book a private car service in advance, online, for about 1,500 Uruguayan pesos (US$40), or take a metered taxi, which requires less advance planning but tends to be a less comfortable though no less expensive experience. There is also bus service between the airport and the city center, but the buses tend to be crowded, and not all have storage for luggage.

Travelers already in Argentina may also choose to cross the River Plate, actually an estuary, on a ferry from Buenos Aires to Montevideo, a journey of two to just over four hours that costs between 1,900 and 5,600 pesos/US$50 to $150 each way, depending on time of day and whether your journey is boat only, or includes a bus transfer. Bear in mind that as this is an international crossing, you will pass through security, passport control, and customs, just as if you were flying in. The two major carriers are Buquebus (www.buquebus.com) and Colonia Express (www.argentina.coloniaexpress.com).

MONTEVIDEO

"Founded by the Spanish in the early 1700s, Montevideo exudes a crumbling cool, a peeling grandeur in its older sections. It's not just what this city is, but it's what it's not. It's not crowded. There's not too much police presence, no pictures of the benevolent President-for-Life, or anything like that. Uruguay is relatively tiny, and Montevideo is, dare I say, charming. Montevideo is the country's only major city and it contains half the country's population, which is still not a whole hell of a lot.

"In 1868, Montevideo's **Mercado del Puerto**, the Market of the Port, was erected of girder and glass. The smell, that lovely smell, hits you a block away. It buckles the knees with its siren song: hardwood smoke and sizzling meats of every imaginable manifestation.

"Today's Mercado, while still the same magnificent structure, has been virtually taken over by that most impressive of cooking devices, the *parrilla*. Prometheus himself could not have envisioned such a masterful harnessing of coal and flame. Enormous, constantly replenished pillars of flavorful hardwood are reduced down to glowing embers. The coals are raked underneath the bars of a massive grill. More wood is thrown on. The coals heat, and are fed by, the sizzling and sputtering fat of a thousand cuts of meat and tasty entrails. Pork loin, chops, hunks of lamb, small birds, steaks, flanks, filets, whole joints, a mosaic of sausages, all hissing and spitting, the smell wafting over everything: a glorious, joyous miasma of meatness."

For a true carnivorous feast, visit **Estancia del Puerto**; look for any purveyor with a long line of locals, and if you like drinks that go down easy, be sure to seek out a *siete y tres*, a local specialty that's seven parts red wine, three parts cola.

MERCADO DEL PUERTO: Rambla 25 de Agosto de 1825, 228, 11000 Montevideo, www.mercadodelpuerto.com (prices vary)

"**Bar Arocena**, in Montevideo's Carrasco neighborhood, specializes in Uruguay's unofficial national sandwich, the legendary *chivito*, twenty-four hours a day, seven days a week, since 1923. A prince, a king, a Gargantua among sandwiches—this terror-inspiring heap of protein is built out of steak, ham, bacon, cheese, hard-boiled egg, mayo, and garnishes."

BAR AROCENA: Avenida Alfredo Arocena, 11500 Montevideo (*chivito* about 425 pesos/US$10)

GARZÓN

"I MOVED HERE TO START AGAIN WITH SILENCE"
"The sleepy village of Garzón is about twenty miles inland from the coast. Population: two hundred. But one of that number is an extraordinary chef who has abandoned the restaurateur's gold rush in nearby José Ignacio for these quiet, ghost-town-like streets.

"Francis Mallmann was born and raised in Argentina, but he's happiest now in the country of his mother. What is he seeking? Quiet he certainly found in abundance, but with a successful trajectory such as his, one that covers three continents, there must be something further, something perhaps to do with the distant sound of crackling flames and searing flesh.

"The food arrives on simple wooden boards. No bullshit. Pork roast, pumpkin cooked in ash, vegetables roasted over hot stones. Elemental, fundamental, and delicious. Seasonings are minimal. Citrus for acid, sea salt, pepper, olive oil. Why would one need more? Mallmann's methods diverge barely at all from the cave, yet are executed with somewhat more precision." The food at **Restaurante Garzon** is profoundly simple, but, owing perhaps to the remote location, it is very expensive, with appetizers for around 1,700 pesos/US$40, entrees priced at about 2,900 pesos/US$70, and local table wines for about 4,200 pesos/US$100 per bottle. There is a five-room hotel attached, with rooms for close to 38,000 pesos/US$900 per night.

RESTAURANTE GARZON: Costa José Ignacio, 20401 Garzón, Departamento de Maldonado, Tel +598 4410 2811, www.restaurantegarzon.com (see above for prices)

Uruguay Dreamin'

BY CHRISTOPHER BOURDAIN

"A chest of old photographs, crumbling documents found thirty-five years ago in France. As kids, my brother and I used to pore over them and wonder who these people were. Aurelien Bourdain, our great-grandfather: like most in the part of France where we vacationed as children, an oysterman. At the time, that's pretty much all we knew of the Bourdain family tree. But inside that old chest were clues to an unexplained transatlantic crossing to a remote South American capital.

"When our aunt Jeanne died in 1972, Chris and I helped clear out her house. Curious about this treasure trove of faded photographs and documents suggestive of all kinds of South American adventure and intermarriage, we became, for a summer, amateur genealogists. My brother never stopped."

That was Tony's voice-over intro for the *No Reservations* Uruguay program I joined him on in 2008. He exaggerated a bit to add some drama, but the gist was right: The backstory we had heard from our dad as young kids was that his mother and father came, separately, from France around the end of World War I, and met and married in New York. We were, therefore, French. And France was where we went on our first big overseas family trips, in 1966 and 1967. On both trips, we spent some time visiting our father's aunt Jeanne at her home in La Teste in southwest France.

But later, as teenagers in 1972, after Tante Jeanne died, we went to La Teste one more time, mostly to help clean out her house and get it ready for sale. This was when we found the old documents. And in these, we learned of at least two ancestors named Jean (John), living for a time in southern Brazil and Uruguay in the mid-1800s before ultimately returning to France after 1860.

Oh, and the Uruguayan great-great-grandmother.

So we were Latinos! The whole story fascinated us. How many family members had lived in Uruguay? How were they making their living: Fishing? Selling escargots from a cart, or French apparel, or perfume? The even more exciting notion that they may have been gunrunners came years later, when I learned that the entire area of South America in question had been a hotbed of contention among local and interfering European powers in the mid-1800s.

And what did we, or anyone, know about Uruguay anyway? In US schools in the 1960s and 1970s, you perhaps learned a bit about Incas and Mayas and Aztecs, and a bit about the early European explorers, but nobody taught about Latin America after Europeans arrived and decimated the old cultures there. I don't think that situation is so different now.

And the *World Book Encyclopedia*—our childhood's printed version of Google—didn't offer much help. Uruguay was more or less a footnote. They raised cattle there. Kind of like Argentina.

Having no particular sense of Uruguay added to the mystery of what the Bourdain family might have been doing there.

Tony asked in late 2007 if I'd like to join him filming an episode of *No Reservations* in Uruguay. I'd had huge fun on my previous TV jaunt with Tony to France in 2001, and I'd always hoped I'd get to travel with him again. Honestly, I would happily have joined him anywhere. Congo, the Louisiana bayou, the Gobi Desert? Yes, yes, yes.

The ostensible reason I was invited along on this particular show was for genealogical research, but really, it was all about Tony exploring the food scene in Uruguay. I did go on my own for a fifteen-minute off-camera side visit to the French embassy in an unsuccessful attempt to get some historical info, but that was the extent of any actual family research.

Happily, the shoot was scheduled for February, which in Uruguay is summertime. (And the living is easy.) When the day arrived, I left straight from my comfortable but not terribly exciting NYC office job, and was soon winging my way to Montevideo with my itinerant brother and his production company entourage: producers Max Landes and Diane Schutz, and cameramen Zach Zamboni and Todd Liebler.

I tried not to let on that, for me, this was an insanely fun vacation, taking me completely out of my usual place, because this was work for everybody else.

I'm generally pretty adventurous when traveling, and my core concept whenever I get to a new place far from home is "This may be the last time I'll ever be here." I like to take a long walk to scope the place out, even if it's the middle of the night, or raining. So on our arrival in Montevideo, I wanted to go exploring more or less right away.

Zach and Max were game to join me, and we were all interested in lunch, so we set out together. Our goal was the Mercado del Puerto, Montevideo's famous central food market, but we wandered a bit through the old part of the city to get there.

I've always had a special affection for places that exude faded glory, whose heyday has come and gone: crumbling once grand train stations; early Industrial Age canal systems; defunct century-old factories; faded mansions of long-ago forgotten VIPs. The old parts of Montevideo, with a hulking empty train station and a neighborhood of majestic but somewhat-haunted-feeling colonial homes in pastel hues, out of use and long boarded up, fit this profile perfectly. I liked it. Like Salvador, Havana, and Buenos Aires, this was once a huge hub of eighteenth- and nineteenth-century transatlantic trade with Spain and Portugal and other countries, but by the twentieth century, these former hubs had shrunk in importance and prosperity.

Max, Zach, and I eventually arrived at the Mercado del Puerto, a fantastic nineteenth-century paradise of meat and drink purveyors operating individual stalls under a high, smoke-stained roof in what amounts to a massive shed. A few old guys wandered around the place with guitars, singing old-style songs, for which others paid them with cash or drinks. We hung out with some of the locals at one of the bars, and drank *medio y medio*, a very easy-to-guzzle mix of still and sparkling white wines. These first couple of hours on the ground set the tone for a very fun trip.

During this first visit and when I returned with Tony, I noticed the specifically Uruguayan way to grill meat: It's all about keeping the metal grill surface on a diagonal slant, immediately next to—but not directly above—a wood fire. The grill tender periodically sweeps a shallow layer of hot embers from the fire under the grill. This technique makes for some of the best, most flavorful meats in the world. I will swear by it for the rest of my life.

In one of our first on-camera scenes, Tony picked me up in a 1951 Chevy Bel Air (supposedly the same car used in the 2006 *Miami Vice* movie, whose Havana scenes were shot in Montevideo), the premise being that we were taking in the sights, driving around the old parts of the city.

What viewers didn't see were Max and the local fixer, Sofia, crammed down on the back-seat floor for the entire weaving, bumpy ride. Had they been only two or three feet shorter, their forced embrace might have been peculiarly romantic, but I think the reality was more painful.

Zach, meanwhile, rode facing backward on a small motorcycle just ahead of us, filming our brotherly joyride at great risk to personal health and safety, without a clue as to which way his driver would be banking the next second. Somehow, he lived through the shoot.

In subsequent days, we went to the Los Mortados cattle ranch in the interior state of Lavalleja—site of a wonderful outdoor banquet, which was one of my favorite parts of the trip (despite a somewhat emotional scene involving dispatching an armadillo). It was a long, solitary drive to get there: in Uruguay, once you're about twenty miles inland from the coast, there are very few people, just pastureland with cows and other animals. Twenty to thirty minutes would elapse between sightings of a building, though there was no shortage of fences.

We made a stop for lunch in a small saloon-like place in a zero-horse town straight from a Sergio Leone western. I half expected Lee Van Cleef to walk in wearing a gunbelt, with the Ennio Morricone score from *The Good, the Bad and the Ugly* playing in the background.

Our next stop was Cabo Polonio, a point of land at the angle of two long and unspoiled strips of beautiful wide beach on the Atlantic coast. It's miles from anything else—closer to Brazil than to any of the major towns in Uruguay. And it's a place where somehow, a 1960s-style hippie commune survived into the twenty-first century, a bit like the Christiania enclave in Copenhagen, but on the beach and off the grid.

Some of the denizens clearly had taken Timothy Leary's "turn on, tune in, drop out" suggestion to heart. Sort of interesting, I suppose, but to me, the whole place had a kind of "Island of the Misfit Toys" feeling. Not my scene, honestly. But I guess I'd rather see it stay that way than turn into just another millionaires' enclave.

A later stop on the route down the eastern coast was certainly one of the more vivid and memorable parts of our trip: the Argentine chef Francis Mallmann had arranged for an entire cow to be butterflied(!), laid on a troublingly crucifix-like structure outside on a square near his restaurant, and cooked slowly for days above an open fire. This is not something we do in the suburbs of New York City. It was astonishing in every respect, amazingly delicious, and I was delighted to learn that Mallmann had the endless pounds of leftovers carved up and basically handed out around the entire small town. Brilliant and generous.

Our last stop, at the famous resort strip of Punta del Este, included the small city of the same name, and a string of other communities along the coast. Some parts are like Rodeo Drive, drawing a super-glam caste of wealthy Argentine and Uruguayan visitors and second-home owners. The town of José Ignacio is more low key, with unpretentious sun-bleached wood buildings—much more Fire Island than Hamptons. My type of place.

Our visit to the restaurant La Huella, right on the beach, was probably my favorite part the whole trip. The weather was great, and I was happy and relaxed. I'd just spent several days traveling around with Tony and his fun gang of cohorts, seeing interesting things and enjoying some awesome meals. (And not being at work!) At La Huella, I had a welcome and delicious mojito (well, more than one), and all sorts of great food kept showing up at the table, with the sound and sight of the waves constant in the background.

It was relaxed and unpretentious, just like Uruguay itself. I love travel, and I've been lucky enough to do a lot of it. I've noted that some countries seem to care about reminding us that they are good at this or that, or had some sort of empire once, or are important now because . . . whatever.

Uruguay is delightful because it's so *not* pretentious. No palaces or pyramids or naval museums there. What it offers is lots of space, a beautiful coastline, and an unstressed lifestyle. Good food and drink are abundant and affordable. And people there seem to take pleasure in the small enjoyments of life, including the unique national habit of carrying around and constantly sipping from a decorative thermos of maté. It's sort of "teatime all day." I'm hoping to make it back some day, to meet up with some of the people I met while filming the 2008 show, and raise a glass to Tony.

VIETNAM

"Do you smell that? Motor bike exhaust, fish sauce, incense, the far-away smell of . . . something. Is that pork grilling over charcoal?

"Vietnam: It grabs you and doesn't let you go. Once you love it, you love it forever. I've been coming here since 2000, the first time I'd been in this part of the world, and it's held a special place in my heart and my imagination since. I keep coming back; I have to."

CENTRAL VIETNAM: HOI AN AND HUE

Often overlooked when Western travelers plan their first visit to Vietnam, Hoi An and Hue offer relatively quieter experiences than Hanoi or Saigon, though each is a vital city in its own right, with regional food specialties and plenty of cultural and historical interest.

ARRIVAL

Neither city has an airport; the region's largest city, Da Nang, is home to **Da Nang International Airport (DAD)**, just over a mile from the city center, about twenty miles from Hoi An, and sixty miles from Hue. There are taxis available outside the arrivals hall, and a limited number of rental cars are available in the terminal. A taxi or prear-ranged car service from DAD to Hoi An will take thirty to forty minutes and cost 345,000–700,000 Vietnamese dong, or US$15–$30;

the same service to Hue will take about two hours and cost between 1.150 and 1.610 million dong/US$50–$70. Taxis drivers appreciate but do not expect tips.

You can take the northbound Reunification Express train, operated by Vietnam Railways, between Da Nang and Hue, which is about a two-and-a-half-hour journey (see www.vietnam-railway.com for schedules and fares, and to buy tickets). The train doesn't stop in Hoi An, so a taxi is your best bet for the relatively short distance.

HOI AN: PEACEFULLY INTACT

"Hội An, in Vietnam's central region, managed to mostly escape destruction during the war, surviving much as it was before the dawn of the twentieth century. Picturesque streets and ancient shop houses date back to when it was a shipping and commercial capital for wealthy Chinese and Japanese traders. There is a peacefulness here that is really specific to the central region. This is the real thing. There is no 'improvement district' here, there is no effort; this is it, and that's the beauty of it."

Tony's favorite banh mi sandwich in all of Vietnam can be found at a place called **Bánh Mì Phuong**. "In the heart of the old town, in the central market, a passerby whispered to me that this banh mi was the best in town and I could well believe it. Certain banh mi are very light; this one is loaded with everything. That's a banh mi deluxe. That's the banh mi platter with everything in it. Liver pâté, cucumbers, this kind of ham, fish paste, mayonnaise. The baguette alone is something of a miracle. How do they stay so crunchy, crispy, and fresh on the outside? So airy, so perfect on the inside?"

BÁNH MÌ PHUONG: 2b Phan Chu Trinh, Cam Chau, Hoi An, Quang Nam 560000, Tel +84 905743773, www.tiembanhmiphuong .blogspot.com (about 29,000 dong/US$1.25)

HUE: A CITY OF GHOSTS

In and around the city of Hue, you'll find "vast palaces, pagodas, and tombs," arguably "the center for the intellectual, artistic, culinary, and religious life of the country.

"Hue is located on the north and south banks of the Perfume River in central Vietnam—mountains behind, sea ahead, an arrangement determined by criteria both military and spiritual. For 143 years, Hue was the seat of power for the Nguyen dynasty, which ruled the entire country until the late 1800s, when the French started taking power and land under their control. The French allowed the imperial throne to rule nominally until the end of World War II, in 1945."

Students of the Vietnam War, or those old enough to have been around during or just after it, may have heard the phrase "Tet Offensive," a coordinated action that devastated much of Hue. "Hue's place in history changed forever during the Vietnam War. In 1968, Hue became the site of some of the most bitter fighting of the war. During the Lunar New Year, the Tet holidays, when usually there was a cessation of hostilities, over a hundred cities all over South Vietnam were attacked the North Vietnamese and Viet Cong. Hue quickly fell."

BUN BO HUE

In the center of Hue's lively **Dong Ba Market**, you may find the soup of your dreams. "**In the hierarchy of delicious, slurpy stuff in a bowl, *bún bò Hue* is at the very top. Here, Kim Chau creates an elaborate broth of mixed bones scented with lemongrass, spice, and fermented shrimp paste. At the bottom, rice noodles, garnished—nay, heaped—with tender slow-cooked beef shank, crabmeat dumplings, pigs' foot, and *huyết*—blood cake. Garnished with lime wedge, cilantro, green onions, chili sauce, shredded banana blossoms, and mung bean sprouts, it's a wonder of flavor and texture. The greatest soup in the world. It's just—I mean, this is as sophisticated and complex a bowl of food as any French restaurant. It really is just the top of the mountain."

DONG BA MARKET: BÚN BÒ HUE KIM CHAU: 2 Tran Hung Dao, Phu Hoa, Hue, Tel +84 234 3524663, www.chodongba.com.vn (50,000 dong/about US$2)

HANOI

Tony's 2016 visit to Hanoi, punctuated by a casual *bun cha* meal with then-president Barack Obama, was the last in a series of rapturous Vietnam episodes, each a variation on the theme of his deep, abiding love for the place.

ARRIVAL

Noi Ba International (HAN) is Hanoi's airport, located about twenty-eight miles from the city center. Terminal 2, built in 2014, serves international flights on airlines including Cathay Pacific, Korean Air, ANA, Vietnam Airlines, Thai Airways, and Air Asia.

There are taxis for hire outside the arrivals hall; settle on a fixed rate with your driver before driving off. It should be about 420,000 dong/US$18, and though tips aren't expected, they are appreciated. To avoid a well-known scam in which the driver takes you to a different hotel, insisting the one where you've booked has been closed or moved, you may wish to arrange in advance for your hotel to send a cab.

METROPOLE MEMORIES

True to form, Tony's preferred stay in Hanoi was the gloriously re-stored **Sofitel Legend Metropole Hanoi** (originally, Hotel Metropole), in the city's French Quarter, across from the Hanoi Opera House. **"It's where writers, spies, and the infamous have stayed for decades."** The vast, inviting swimming pool and access to the bomb shelter, a relic of the United States' war with Vietnam, were also points of intrigue.

Built by the French and opened in 1901, the hotel was, in the period following independence from the French, called Thong Nhat, or Reunification Hotel. Charlie Chaplin and Paulette Goddard honeymooned at the Metropole in 1936; Graham Greene spent time there in 1951 while writing *The Quiet American*; and it was Jane Fonda's home base during her infamous 1972 visit to the city.

SOFITEL LEGEND METROPOLE HANOI: 15 Ngo Quyen Street, Hoan Kiem District, Hanoi, Tel +84 24 38266919, www. sofitel -legend-metropole-hanoi.com (rooms start at about 5.8 million dong/US$250 per night)

START WITH SNAILS

"*Bún ốc:* First meal in Hanoi, and it's something they do here better than anywhere else. A spicy, wonderful broth with tomatoes and herb and noodles and fresh snails. Okay. I'm officially in Hanoi now. Mmm. Magic." The broth gets a meatiness from pork or chicken bones and piquancy from lemongrass; the noodles that partially soak it up are rice vermicelli. In addition to the snails, the bowl is often rounded out with fried tofu, shrimp, or fish cakes, and lime wedges and *rau răm*, the minty, peppery herb also known as Vietnamese coriander, are served alongside.

BÚN ỐC PHO CO: 36 Luong Ngoc Quyen, Hong Buom, Hoan Kiem District, Hanoi, Tel +84 125 4733723 (35,000–45,000 dong/US$1.50–$2)

THANKS, OBAMA

Everyone, it seems, knows about pho, the beef noodle soup that's often a gateway drug for those yet to be initiated into the wonder of Vietnamese food. After Tony's televised sit-down with President Barack Obama in 2016, many more people became aware of *bun cha*, a mixture of grilled pork belly and pork patties served with herbs, chilis, rice vermicelli, and a spicy, sour, fishy, sweet broth for dipping.

During his first Hanoi visit, he observed a bit of organic marketing: **"Deceptively simple. A makeshift hibachi right on the sidewalk. A dark, soot-crusted storefront open to the street. The *bun cha* master fans the coals red, to just the right temperature for grilling the outside of the pork without drying the inside. Fat drips from the marinated pork, sizzling into smoke, which penetrates the meat with its own flavor. With the aid of a trusty fan, the rest of the smoke is free advertising, luring passersby with its alluring scent.**

"There is no better place to entertain the leader of the free world, in my opinion, than one of these classic, funky, family-run noodle shops you find all over Hanoi. Dinner and a beer costs about six dollars. I'm guessing the president doesn't get a lot of state dinners like this. And *bun cha* is about as typical and uniquely a Hanoi dish as there is."

BUN CHA HUONG LIEN: 29 Le Van Huu, Pham Dinh Ho, Hoi Ba Trung, Hanoi, Tel +84 439 434106 (typical meal about 140,000 dong/US$6)

SAIGON/HO CHI MINH CITY

"From the very first minute that I came to this country, I knew my life had changed. My old life was suddenly never gonna be good enough. I needed a new one, where I could keep coming back here. The streets, the stop, start, stop of negotiating the never-ending traffic. The seemingly impenetrable patterns. The mental preparedness necessary for simply crossing the street. A sensory overload, a caffeine-like rush of heightened perception, one that always leads to good things.

"When I came here first [in 2000], you could still see the Saigon of Graham Greene's novel *The Quiet American*. It was still a city of bicycles, motorbikes, and cyclos. There was the smell of burning joss from the pagodas, charcoal from storefront eateries, diesel fuel, jasmine. Women in their graceful *áo dài*s and peaked hats would pedal past. And the landmarks, like the Majestic Hotel, the opera house, the Caravelle, from whose rooftop you could once watch the war.

"Today, what was once a dream of one day owning a Honda seems to have come true for almost everybody. Bicycles have been replaced by scooters and motorcycles. Traditional peaked hats, by helmets. The old is still here, but around and in between the old French colonial architecture, everywhere there's modern construction. A building boom. The shock of the new."

GETTING THERE

Tan Son Nhat International Airport (SGN), the largest airport in the country, is served by numerous major airlines, including Cathay Pacific, United, Emirates, Korean Air, ANA, Singapore. and Air France, along with regional carriers.

You may arrange a prepaid taxi service from inside the airport, or join a taxi queue. The cost of a one-way transfer from the airport, which is about four miles from the city center, is 185,000–462,000 dong/US$8–$20. Tipping drivers is not expected but always appreciated. There are also air-conditioned yellow shuttle buses that take passengers from the airport to the city for 23,000–46,000 dong/US$1–$2; follow the signs in English upon departing the terminal.

LIVING HISTORY AT THE CONTINENTAL

The **Hotel Continental Saigon** was Tony's preferred home in the city. Finished in 1880 in the French colonial style, it was Vietnam's first hotel, built for French colonists and named after the Continental in Paris. Graham Greene was a longtime guest; the hotel is a vital location in *The Quiet American*, and it was the home base of journalists, contractors, and others during the war with the United States. The first-floor bar, open to the street, was nicknamed "the Continental shelf" by wartime journalists in the 1970s; the frangipane trees first planted in the courtyard over a century ago still remain within its white walls. The victorious North Vietnamese government took ownership of the hotel in 1975, and retains control via Saigon Tourist, the state-owned tourism enterprise. Today, though it lacks the touches of opulence found in other colonial relics, the Continental is a cool, semiluxurious respite from Saigon's bustle, noise, and heat.

HOTEL CONTINENTAL SAIGON: 132–134 Dong Khoi Street, District 1, Ho Chi Ming City, Tel +84 2838 299 201, www.continentalsaigon.com (rooms start at about 2 million dong/US$90 per night)

DRINKS AT THE REX

Once a garage and auto dealership for French colonial businessmen, the **Rex** was converted into a hotel in the late 1950s, and was the site of daily military briefings, cynically dubbed "the Five O'Clock Follies," during the war with the United States. Like the Continental, the Rex Hotel Saigon became property of the state after the fall of the city. Tony loved its rooftop bar, from which one can observe street life below. Having a drink or two there, he said, was **"a must."**

REX HOTEL SAIGON: 141 Nguyen Hue, Ben Nghe, District 1, Ho Chi Minh City, Tel +84 28 3829 2185, www.rexhotelsaigon.com (rooms start at about 3.5 million dong/US$150 per night)

LUNCH LADY

"Nguyen Thi Thanh is known as 'the **Lunch Lady**.' She's something of a maverick, because she does a different soup every day, which she makes from scratch, in a sort of a cyclic menu throughout the week."

One such offering is *bún bò Hue:* "**Hue-style beef, and I think there's pork blood involved. Stock of pork bones, beef bones, then sliced beef, sliced pork, pork leg, pig feet. Coagulated pig's blood, onion, ginger, rice noodles. A host of special spices, nasty bits, and jealously guarded trade secrets. The magic of a soup among soups.**" Expect to pay 46,000–69,000 dong/US$2–$3. And caveat emptor: if a server brings spring rolls to your table and you eat them, they'll be added to your tab, unrequested.

Since her appearance on TV with Tony, Nguyen Thi Thanh has risen from a local legend into a hot international commodity. Years after her initial brush with mass media, she's still feeding hordes of locals and visitors.

QUAN AN LUNCH LADY: Phuong Da Kao (just off Hoang Sa), District 1, Ho Chi Minh City (no phone, no website) (46,000–69,000 dong/US$2–$3)

BENH THANH MARKET

Ben Thanh Market is really two things: a daytime marketplace for textiles, shoes, souvenirs, electronics, home goods, produce, seafood, live birds, and prepared foods; and a night market, jammed with even more food and drink purveyors, a lively place to graze through some of the city's best offerings.

"The smell of a lot of live poultry and a lot of food cooking makes a rather heady mix." There are many offerings to be sampled at Benh Thanh: **"In every case, it's spectacularly fresh, and smells good. Time and time again you're struck by how proud each vendor is. They all want you to try their food."**

BENH THANH MARKET: Le Loi, Ben Thanh, District 1, Ho Chi Minh City, Tel +84 283829 9274, www.chobenthanh.org.vn (prices vary)

APPENDIX: FILM REFERENCES

BUENOS AIRES, ARGENTINA: Though set in Hong Kong, not Buenos Aires, Tony and the crew used Wong Kar-wai's *In the Mood for Love* (2000), its evocation of longing and loneliness, intercut with fleeting moments of happiness, as inspiration for the Buenos Aires episode of *Parts Unknown*.

VIENNA, AUSTRIA: Tony makes direct reference to the anxiety-provoking Ferris wheel scene in *The Third Man* (1949), directed by Carol Reed, in the Vienna episode of *No Reservations*.

BORNEO, CAMBODIA, VIETNAM: Over many years of making TV, Tony and the crew drew moody inspiration again and again from the classic Vietnam war film *Apocalypse Now* (1979), directed by Francis Ford Coppola, which was based on Joseph Conrad's 1902 novella *Heart of Darkness*, written about a Congo River journey and loosely adapted by Coppola and John Milius.

QUEBEC, CANADA: Michael Steed, directing the Quebec episode of *Parts Unknown* amid quiet expanses of northern snow and ice, found inspiration in *Fargo* (1996), directed by Joel and Ethan Coen, and *The Sweet Hereafter* (1997), directed by Atom Egoyan.

HONG KONG: Director Wong Kar-wai's use of Hong Kong's distinctive neon signage, abundant escalators, dense vertical development, and the dramatic harbor, as seen in his films *Chungking Express* (1994), *Fallen Angels* (1995), and *In the Mood for Love* (2000), provided visual inspiration for episodes of *No Reservations*, *The Layover*, and *Parts Unknown* made there.

HELSINKI, FINLAND: *Night on Earth* (1991), directed by Jim Jarmusch, and *The Match Factory Girl* (1990), directed by Aki Kaurismäki, influenced the dark drollery of the Finland episode of *No Reservations*.

MARSEILLE, FRANCE: Director Toby Oppenheimer looked to the lighter films of French New Wave director Éric Rohmer, such as *Le Genou de Claire* (1970) and *Pauline à la Plage* (1983) when planning the episode of *Parts Unknown* shot in Marseille.

PUNJAB, INDIA: Certain shots in the train transit scene of the Punjab episode of *Parts Unknown* were heavily influenced by *The Darjeeling Limited* (2007), directed by Wes Anderson.

ROME, ITALY: For episodes of *No Reservations*, *The Layover*, and *Parts Unknown*, Tony and the crew drew on the films *La Dolce Vita* (1960), directed by Federico Fellini; *Mamma Roma* (1962), directed by Pier Paolo Pasolini; and *Via Veneto* (1964), directed by Giuseppe Lipartiti.

SARDINIA, ITALY: Tony looked to the nonviolent, noncriminal aspects of *The Godfather* (1972), directed by Francis Ford Coppola, in planning the extended family scenes in this episode of *No Reservations*, which featured the family of his wife, Ottavia. He mused, "**I imagine myself, of course, keeling over among the tomato vines in the backyard somewhere chasing a grandchild around with a slice of orange in my mouth,**" which was a direct reference to the gentle passing of Marlon Brando's Don Corleone character.

TOKYO, JAPAN: Director Nick Brigden emulated the hyperkinetic editing and close-up intensity of *Tokyo Fist* (1995), directed by Shin'ya Tsukamoto, in the Tokyo episode of *Parts Unknown*.

LAGOS, NIGERIA: *Music Is the Weapon* (1982), directed by Jean-Jacques Flori and Stephane Tchal-Gadjieff, provided narrative context and musical history for this episode of *Parts Unknown*, according to the director, Morgan Fallon.

LOS ANGELES, CALIFORNIA: *Collateral* (2004), directed by Michael Mann, showcases a noirish underbelly of the city that is reflected in the episodes of *No Reservations*, *The Layover*, and *Parts Unknown* filmed there.

MIAMI, FLORIDA: Tony and the *Parts Unknown* crew staged a party scene at a Miami hotel that was an homage to the birthday party scene in the Italian film *La Grande Bellezza* (2013), directed by Paolo Sorrentino. Tony, naturally, was cast in the role of the protagonist, Jep Gambardella, whom Roger Ebert described, in his review of the film as "a simultaneously overstimulated and underwhelmed taste-making intellectual. . . . People come and go in Jep's life. They all make him a little wiser, even if they don't realize it."

NEW YORK, NEW YORK: Director Michael Steed looked to *Wild Style* (1982), directed by Charlie Ahearn, and the nonnarrative films of Stan Brakhage to set the tone for the episode of *Parts Unknown* set on the Lower East Side of Manhattan.

WEST VIRGINIA: *American Honey* (2016), directed by Andrea Arnold, looks at the beauty, the contradictions, the small joys of everyday life, in a way that inspired director Morgan Fallon for the West Virginia episode of *Parts Unknown*.

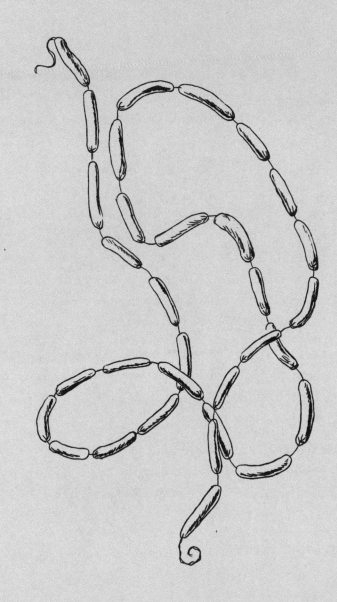

ACKNOWLEDGMENTS

I owe an enormous debt of gratitude to Tony, whose charisma, curiosity, intelligence, wit, and generosity of spirit are the reason for this book. His belief in me meant everything.

Big thanks those at Ecco—Sara Birmingham, Sonya Cheuse, Meghan Deans, Gabriella Doob, Ashlyn Edwards, Dan Halpern, Doug Johnson, David Koral, Renata De Oliveira, Miriam Parker, Allison Saltzman, Rachel Sargent, Michael Siebert, and Rima Weinberg—whose creative talents and formidable skills have turned this idea into a concrete thing.

Thank you to Kimberly Witherspoon and Jessica Mileo at Inkwell Management, for creative guidance, muscle, and keeping the wolf from the door.

Thanks to Wesley Allsbrook for her perfect illustrations, which Tony Bourdain surely would have loved.

Thank you to those who generously contributed their memories and insights to this text, namely Jen Agg, Steve Albini, Vidya Balachander, Christopher Bourdain, Bill Buford, BJ Dennis, Nari Kye, Claude Tayag, Daniel Vaughn, and Matt Walsh.

Big thanks to Chris Collins and Lydia Tenaglia at Zero Point Zero Production, Inc., for making brilliant TV with Tony and a dream team of directors, producers, shooters, and editors, including Jeff Allen, Jared Andrukanis, Nick Brigden, Helen Cho, Morgan Fallon, Josh Ferrell, Sally Freeman, Nari Kye (again!), Todd Liebler, Alex Lowry, Toby Oppenheimer, Lorca Shepperd, Michael Steed, Tom Vitale, and Sandy Zweig, all of whom willingly answered my many, many questions.

Thanks as well to all of the following, who answered more questions; offered advice, travel companionship, and/or hospitality; and otherwise helped to shape this book: Seema Ahmed, Hashim Badani, Jonathan Bakalarz, Raphael Bianchini, Daniel Boulud, Jessica Bradford, Kee Byung-kuen, Jessica Delisle, Lolis Elie, Paula Froelich, Jonathan Hayes, Fergus Henderson, Kate Kunath, Akiko Kurematsu, Matt Lee, Ted Lee, Esther Liberman, Yusra and Mohamed Ali Makim, David Mau, Claudia McKenna-Lieto, Dave McMillan, Max Monesson, Antonio Mora, Fred Morin, Inky Nakpil, Aik Wye Ng, Esther Ng, Cory Pagett, Sara Pampaloni, Matt Sartwell, KF Seetoh, Crispy Soloperto, Katherine Spiers, Gabriele Stabile, James Syhabout, Yoshi Tezuka, Nathan Thornburgh, Chris Thornton, Alicia Tobin, Alison Tozzi Liu, Jason Wang, Maisie Wilhelm, and Amos and Emily Zeeberg.

CITED QUOTES

INTRODUCTION

Page 5: All quotes from *Parts Unknown*, episode 1201, "Kenya."

ARGENTINA

Pages 7–10: All quotes from *Parts Unknown*, episode 708, "Buenos Aires."

AUSTRALIA

Pages 13–21: All quotes from *No Reservations*, season 5, episode 11, "Australia."

AUSTRIA

Pages 23–27: All quotes from *No Reservations*, season 7, episode 4, "Vienna."

BHUTAN

Pages 29–33: All quotes from *Parts Unknown*, episode 1108, "Bhutan."

BRAZIL

Pages 35–37: All quotes from *Parts Unknown*, episode 308, "Bahia, Brazil."

CAMBODIA

Pages 39–43: All quotes from *No Reservations*, season 7, episode 2, "Cambodia."

CANADA

Page 45: "I will confess my partisanship up front . . . a major, major reason to come here." **Pages 48–49:** "Once every few decades, maybe every century . . . The tradition of the *cabane à sucre* . . . Let the madness begin: . . . and maple bacon omelet." From *Parts Unknown*, episode 104, "Québec"

Pages 45–46: "Montreal is close . . . about twenty miles from the city center." **Page 46:** "The Montréal metro system . . . detail as well, okay? . . . I don't really know . . . very dangerous place." **Page 47:** "A pub, a Canadian pub . . . served with boiled potatoes . . . Montréal is a chef town . . . And it changes daily." **Page 48:** "Smoked meat . . . knock you on your ass . . . clean conscience now." From *The Layover* season 1 episode 4 "Montreal."

Pages 50–57: All quotes from *The Layover*, season 1, episode 8, "Toronto."

Pages 58–61: All quotes from *No Reservations*, season 4, episode 3, "Vancouver."

CHINA

Page 63: "China, but not China, a thing all its own. . . . no hope for you." **Page 64:** ". . . the front porch to mainland China and the rest of Asia . . . a major stopover, a frequent layover." **Pages 64–65:** "The way they talk about their subway system around here . . . over sixty destinations easily and comfortably." **Page 65:** "I'm constantly asked . . . if you say Hong Kong. Yeah, I like pork . . . is actually goose." From *The Layover*, season 1, episode 3, "Hong Kong."

Page 66–67: "At first, Hong Kong is an utterly foreign world, a shock to the system. . . . It's an instinctive move." **Page 67:** "It is awesomeness itself, . . . and busy for a reason. . . . Lau Sum Kee is run by the third generation of a family who still prepare their wontons from scratch . . . results in the perfect noodle." From *No Reservations*, season 3, episode 13, "Hong Kong."

Page 63: "All of us . . . the baggage we carry." **Pages 63–64:** "Years ago, when I first watched . . . I would be denied. I was wrong." **Page 66:** "The love of money and shiny new things . . . fire up the wok. . . . hacked-up birds . . . make me strong." **Page 68:** "Chef-owner May Chow . . . all of it truly, stunningly delicious." [May Chow] "How do I be modern, . . . make it cool again." From *Parts Unknown* , episode 1105, "Hong Kong."

Page 69: "If you live in Manhattan, as I do . . . greediest, most bourgeois of capitalist imperialists." **Page 72:** "What *is* classic Shanghainese food? . . . It's the best of both worlds: great sauces, great ingredients. . . . *Xiao long bao*: literally, 'small steaming basket buns' . . . These things alone are worth the trip." **Page 73:** "Maybe the number one thing . cumin ribs. It takes two cooks working at once . . . the flavor of the wok itself." From *Parts Unknown, episode* 401, "Shanghai."

Page 68: "Shanghai: an exploding economic superpower . . . capital of the world. **Page 73:** "How is it done?. . . . Dangerous, impossible, and unspeakably delicious." From *No Reservations* , season 3, episode 4, "Shanghai."

Pages 73–77: All quotes from *Parts Unknown*, episode 803, "Sichuan, China."

CROATIA

Pages 79–83: All quotes from *No Reservations*, season 8, episode 3, "Croatia."

CUBA

Page 85: "This is the Cuba I grew up with . . . two nations in a never-ending state of war." **Page 86:** "However you feel about the government . . . the gears of the whole system, are still largely stuck in time. . . . I've been to a lot of places . . . Look at it, because it's beautiful, and it's still here." **Page 89:** "[Once], a meal at a paladar would have been rice and beans. Now, sushi; a certain sign of impending apocalypse." From *Parts Unknown*, episode 601, "Cuba."

Page 90: "The last shot of the Cuba show [was] very deeply satisfying to me . . . without having me have to tell you how to feel about it." From *Prime Cuts*, season 6.

Page 88: "[Elizabeth is] the kind of tough, resolute, hardworking operator . . . A lot depends on who you know. . . . Today, it's pork. . . . us and them." **Pages 90–91:** "It's been a dream of mine to see a Cuban baseball game . . . gets in the way of the game . . . are given an official license to assemble publicly . . . sacrifice bunt for a political row." From *No Reservations*, season 7, episode 9, "Cuba."

FINLAND

Pages 93–95: All quotes from *No Reservations*, season 8 episode 6, "Finland."

FRANCE

Pages 97–100: All quotes from *Parts Unknown*, episode 1002, "French Alps."

Pages 100–103, 106–7: All quotes from *Parts Unknown*, episode 303, "Lyon."

Pages 108–10: All quotes from *Parts Unknown*, episode 602, "Marseille."

Pages 110–11: "Paris and the French . . . snooty waiters and haute cuisine. . . . People are actually nicer . . . woolly mammoth . . . Paris remains one of the greatest . . . Just avoid the obvious. The absolute worst thing . . . Most of us are lucky . . . See? It's easy." **Page 112:** "Even for my lazy . . . get around." **Page 113:** Now, here's the thing . . . Witch's Rock Passage." **Pages 118–19:** "If there's two things . . . through this thing." From *The Layover*, season 2, episode 1, "Paris."

Pages 112–13: "Ah, Paris . . . pace of life. . . . It's no accident . . . we take trips here. . . . Me, I always stay . . . bender that ended badly." **Page 114:**

"In the English-speaking world . . . joyous occasion." **Page 114:** "Dark street, no big sign . . . with a little *sel gris*." From *No Reservations*, season 1, episode 1, "Paris."

Page 115: "One of the great meals in memory . . . clearly love the old."

Pages 115–18: "The hardest reservation in Paris . . . grab and smear."

Page 119: "There were some places . . . very best in Paris." From *No Reservations*, season 6, episode 21, "Paris."

GHANA

Pages 121–23: All quotes from *No Reservations*, season 3, episode 2, "Ghana."

INDIA

Pages 125–27: All quotes from *No Reservations*, season 2, episode 10, "Kolkata–Mumbai."

Pages 128–31: All quotes from *Parts Unknown*, episode 301, "Punjab."

Pages 132–33: All quotes from *No Reservations*, season 2, episode 9, "Rajasthan."

IRELAND

Page 137: "Ireland: I don't know of another . . . as a birthright. Most of these stories . . . just yesterday." **Page 139:** "is what some used to call a gastropub . . . ever eaten in Dublin." From *No Reservations*, season 3, episode 1, "Ireland."

Page 138: "It's a little more . . . loving this city. . . . What do they do here . . . celestial trombones. . . . Known locally as Gravediggers . . . coddle, a hearty stew . . . but believe me, you do." From *The Layover*, season 2, episode 3, "Dublin."

ISRAEL

Pages 141–43: All quotes from *Parts Unknown*, episode 201, "Jerusalem."

ITALY

Pages 145–48: All quotes from *No Reservations*, season 7 episode 11: "Naples."

Page 149: "As so many have found throughout history . . . Rome that many Romans still live in today." From *Parts Unknown*, episode 808, "Rome."

Page 149: "No matter whose Rome it is . . . awesomeness of every little damn thing." **Page 153:** "Welcome to Roscioli, . . . Jesus, Lord, this is good." **Page 154:** "Betto e Mary is an unassuming, typically Roman, . . . Nice, nice, nice." **Pages 155–56:** "Pizzarium, [Gabriele] Bonci's place, a departure from the classics. . . . It was really, really good." From *No Reservations*, season 6, episode 20, "Rome."

Page 149: "about twenty miles from the center of Italy's capital city, but it might as well be another planet." **Page 150:** "Fiumicino Airport has the usual assortment of transportation options. . . . Take a cab, especially if you have luggage. . . . the massive transportation hub of Rome . . . none at all." **Pages 151–52:** "I suggest the Centro Storico . . . But again, it's expensive." **Page 156:** "What's a Roman specialty you might have . . . a pitcher of ice-cold Italian beer." **Page 156:** "I'm at Freni e Frizoni, . . . and many incidents, dimly, if at all, remembered." From *The Layover*, season 1, episode 7, "Rome."

Pages 157–61: All quotes from *No Reservations*, season 5, episode 20, "Sardinia."

JAPAN

Pages 163–67: All quotes from *No Reservations*, season 1, episode 11, "Japan."

Page 168: "What do you need to know about Tokyo? . . . What do I do now?'." **Page 170:** "Maybe the most important thing . . . a little frightened." **Page 172:** "The Yakuza . . . ancillary services. . . . This is where the subterranean life . . . It was the greatest show in the history of entertainment." **Pages 172–73:** "This is long my favorite place . . . a hole in the wall." From *Parts Unknown*, episode 207, "Tokyo."